LET FREEDOM RING

A Da Capo Press Reprint Series

CIVIL LIBERTIES IN AMERICAN HISTORY

GENERAL EDITOR: LEONARD W. LEVY

Claremont Graduate School

LET FREEDOM RING

By Arthur Garfield Hays

DA CAPO PRESS • NEW YORK • 1972

Library of Congress Cataloging in Publication Data

Hays, Arthur Garfield, 1881-1954.
  Let freedom ring.

  (Civil liberties in American history)
  1. Civil rights—U.S. 2. Trials—U.S. I. Title.
II. Series.
KF4749.H37   1972   342'.73'0850269   71-166329
ISBN 0-306-70227-4

This Da Capo Press edition of *Let Freedom Ring* is an unabridged
republication of the new and revised edition published in New
York in 1937. It is reprinted by special arrangement with Liveright Publishing Corporation and reproduced by permission from
a copy of that edition in the collection of the Library of Pennsylvania State University.

Published by Da Capo Press, Inc.
A Subsidiary of Plenum Publishing Corporation
227 West 17th Street, New York, N.Y. 10011

LET FREEDOM RING

LET FREEDOM RING

By

ARTHUR GARFIELD HAYS

New York
LIVERIGHT PUBLISHING CORPORATION
☆ 1937 ☆

CONTENTS

CONTENTS

vii

ILLUSTRATIONS

FOREWORD TO THE
REVISED EDITION

IT is rare that a lawyer in successful business practice makes the sacrifices of time and money which Mr. Hays has so consistently put into the defense of civil liberties over the last fifteen years. He does it solely because of a passionate loyalty to the cause of democracy and an instant sympathy with victims of oppression, whatever their beliefs. As his accounts of the dramatic trials in which he has participated show, he is wholly free of any commitment to a political or economic "ism." Those he has defended, either as counsel for the American Civil Liberties Union or on his own responsibility, cover the entire range of repression under a wide variety of charges.

His loyalty to the principle of democratic rights, regardless of his attitude toward whom they benefit, was never better illustrated than when he went into court in New Jersey, with the attorney for the Friends of New Germany, a Nazi organization, to seek an injunction against a police commissioner who had closed all halls to Nazi meetings. Mr. Hays is, of course, intensely anti-Nazi, but he defended the rights of Nazis, as of all others, on the ground that nobody's rights are safe if anybody's rights are denied.

It is commonly charged against the defenders of civil liberties that they have an ulterior motive in protecting

3

those with a program for illegally changing our system of government. The easy characterization of "Communist" is leveled against them by the self-appointed defenders of the status quo. It will seem so strange to them as to appear deliberate, that not a single major trial in this book involves a Communist. In the last chapter only does Mr. Hays report a Communist case, his successful contest of a deportation order against the distinguished British author, John Strachey, who by the way is not, in a legal sense, a Communist. The fact makes plain that the issues of civil liberty far transcend the defense of a minority political party which, though incessantly attacked, has furnished no major case of such significance as those of Sacco and Vanzetti, Tom Mooney, the Scottsboro boys, and the Tennessee evolution trial.

If any general conclusion can be drawn from Mr. Hays' accounts of the sources of intolerance and repression it is that not Communism, but any challenge to established property rights or the traditional moral code, arouses persecution. It has always been so. One need not be a partisan to see that only heretics and rebels—the innovators, the prophets, the spokesmen of the dispossessed—need defense of rights presumably guaranteed to all in a democracy. The guardians of things-as-they-are need no defenders. They stand at the gates of progress, armed with the weapons of public and private violence, commanding the organs of education and opinion, determined that the innovators and rebels shall not pass. Always the gates of progress have been forced, and multitudes have followed the vanguard. But the price of deliverance has been high in bloodshed, exile and prison.

Democracy alone offers progress a peaceful advance. At its heart lie the guarantees of civil liberty—the right to speak, print, meet, to impartial trial. In a world where democracy is increasingly on the defensive, where men visualize the struggle of the future in terms of extremes already visible, Fascism or Communism, the central issue of its survival is its fighting power. Can the forces for change by democratic methods muster enough aggression to avoid civil war, or the armed reaction of Fascism? That is, in spirit, the philosophy behind Mr. Hays' portrayal of his own militant defense of democratic rights. For he is no well-meaning liberal without a program of action, but a libertarian rooted in the conviction that freedom to agitate, to change, to grow, is at the heart of any tolerable society.

It is almost ten years since the earlier portions of this book appeared. What Mr. Hays wrote at that time, in his introduction, of the tendencies in American life are as true today as then. For ten years does not change the pattern of a repression inherent in a society divided into warring classes, where conflict has been intensified by the rise of the working-class, by the greater struggles of oppressed minorities, by the menace of movements against democracy in Europe, reflected in our own fears and actions. But in these years democracy has gained in the United States. When Mr. Hays wrote in his introduction that the prohibition amendment was unfortunate because "un-

changeable," he discounted democratic powers of
change. But the significant gains have been in the
recognition in law of the rights of labor, and in less degree, of the rights of Communists. A general loosen-
ing of repression has marked the transition from the
economics of rugged individualism to state-regulated
business. Greater tolerance of dissenters and innovators has accompanied the attempt to make the economic system work better, by distributing more widely
its benefits. Repressive and intolerant statutes which
could, if strictly enforced, send every alien Red out of
the country and every native Red to jail, remain on
the books practically unused. The Communist and left
press is freely published and distributed despite laws
which could, if enforced, put them out of business.

But no sense of encouragement from these gains for
democratic rights should blind us to the incessant conflicts which still produce in our courts case after case
of the character Mr. Hays describes. Capital versus
labor, the white South versus the Negro, the professional moralists versus the innovators, the self-
appointed patriots versus the Reds, American-born
versus the alien, colonial administrators versus the
native peoples, school boards and administrators versus teachers' freedom,—all these mark the patterns of
conflict expressed in propaganda, censorship, law,
prosecutions and violence. So entrenched are the defenders of the status quo in all these conflicts that
popular opinion is corrupted in their interest. Most
of the cases are "lost causes." These are not success
stories. But they are stories of defeats with elements

of that success that go into the salvation of democracy.
For they all tended to discredit the prosecutions
among reasonable folks, to make repetition more difficult, to win wide audiences and sympathetic support,
and to build up the forces of resistance to repression.

Some of the cases may appear trivial or remote, affecting some insignificant figure, some crank, or some
far-off issue like the political struggle in Puerto Rico.
But it is the essence of the doctrine of civil liberty that
no case, no issue, is trivial or remote. Liberty is in-
divisible. What affects the rights of one affects in the
long run the rights of all. For the same intolerance
that denies justice to one may be used against many.
Any honest defense of liberty must be blind to the per-
sonalities of those defended.

Though Mr. Hays presents a lawyer's view of a great
struggle, he steps far outside the role commonly played
by lawyers. He is interpreter and defender of a principle, a philosophy, in the tradition of the great defenders of human rights. He knows that law, as such,
the words written on paper, plays a minor part. He
knows that these battles, unlike ordinary law cases, are
shot through with men's passions, prejudices, beliefs
and fears. He knows the courtroom is but the focus
for the moment of the vast forces that are making
for the salvation or destruction of the whole democratic process.

And I suspect he knows, though he does not say
so, what history is now teaching us all, that civil liberty
can be saved, as democracy itself can be saved, only
by the organized political and economic power of those

with a stake in progress to industrial democracy. Chesterton once expressed amazement that Americans so naively expect political democracy to work in the face of industrial autocracy. And as industrial autocrats in other lands have thrown democracy overboard in favor of Fascism to preserve their privileges, so too they will here unless a powerful resistance confronts and defeats them. The unity of the "people's fronts" in European lands holds out hope for so buttressing political democracy that industrial democracy may be won without civil war. Such unity and power in American life, of which signs are clearly emerging, are the surest guarantee that civil liberties will live, and that the indefensible prosecutions Mr. Hays so valiantly contests will become only a memory.

ROGER BALDWIN.

INTRODUCTION

THERE are indications to-day that we are developing religion through ignorance, morality through law, government through acquiescence and hypocrisy through convention. I wonder. I ponder. Are these really tendencies pointing toward the future: are they characteristics of an age gone mad with materialism, intolerance and false standards, or are they survivals? Time was when we harried witches. Perhaps we don't to-day merely because we don't believe in witches. Greater intelligence, not more tolerance, may be the explanation. Chattel slavery no longer exists, but this does not necessarily mean greater democracy or deeper faith in liberty. There were compelling economic and political reasons for abolition. We remember the Alien and Sedition Laws; the arrest and incarceration of Matthew Lyon and others for exercising rights of free speech in colonial times; we remember that William Lloyd Garrison was dragged through the streets of Boston during the Abolition agitation, and these reminders suggest that suppression of fundamental rights is not wholly modern. The Sunday closing and other obsolete laws still on the statute books derive from a time when they were actually enforced. Laws once existed requiring Sabbath attendance at church, and there were prohibitions against sleeping in church which, as Clarence Darrow said, took all the pleasure out of religion. In Lancaster, Ohio, in 1828, permission was asked of a school board for the use of a

9

schoolhouse for a debate on the subject of whether
or not railroads were practicable. The school trustees
reported that the schoolhouse might be used for any
proper purpose, but that if God had intended his creatures to travel at the frightful rate of fifteen miles an
hour, He would have said so in the Gospels.

Strangely enough, all this keeps one from becoming
unduly pessimistic, for if we are making some progress,
the future is brighter, and the intolerance, repression
and stupidity of to-day less significant. A survival is
less unwholesome than a tendency.

Yet, I dare say, optimism is not justified. The aspi-
rations of the "Founding Fathers" were formed on high
ideals—and one may well question whether this idealism
is now existent. Has it not become "the bunk"? Order
has become the fetish; prosperity is its handmaiden;
respectability its emblem. Conformity is the watch-
word. Production, possessions, material success, the
end. Those who believe in liberty are regarded to-day,
as they were in 1776, or in Jeffersonian times, as dangerous radicals; but while then they were in control,
to-day they are in a hopeless minority. A dominating
complacence, a comfortable obliviousness, an ignorant
pretense, mark the Babbittry of those who govern.
This is the best of all possible worlds; mine is the best
country in the world; mine is the best state in the country; my city is the best city in the state; my school is
the best school in the city. Rah! Rah! Rah! Rotary!

Gradually, so slowly that it is hardly noticeable, the
foundations of our institutions, the ideals for which
America stands, the rights guaranteed to the citizen in

the Constitution, are slipping away. There is no such thing as freedom of speech or assemblage concerning any subject that really matters. That was clear during the war when snoopers, spies and informers encouraged, if not induced, by the Government, made even private conversation dangerous to the timid citizen. To-day you can talk on any subject you please in Tennessee, except religion; in California, except the I.W.W.; in Boston, except the Sacco-Vanzetti case; in any place, except on a subject which, as a burning issue, would most profit by untrammeled discussion. Speech and assemblage are free in New Jersey, West Virginia and Pennsylvania, except to union men in time of strike. If you talk labor unionism then, you land in jail. I know it because I've tried it and I landed in jail. The press is free, unless attack upon some particular paper becomes safe because of its unpopular viewpoint. There are Espionage acts, criminal syndicalist laws, obscenity statutes—with the Post Office department, district attorneys, and sometimes judges, ready to intimidate and prosecute. We are guaranteed against arrest without warrant, and yet, in the year 1920, the notorious Mitchell Palmer on one night caused the arrest of thousands of people, without warrant of law, for alleged crimes many of which were instigated by his *agents provocateur*, and only a few years ago thousands of Chinamen all over the country were rounded up and jailed as a convenient method of investigating tong activities, an act which aroused not a ripple of public excitement. Some States deny the right to vote because of color; others have

expelled from the legislature the chosen representatives
of the people. There are guarantees against unreasonable searches and seizures, and yet in the holy name
of Prohibition the houses of citizens are ransacked
without search warrant. Double jeopardy is prohibited, yet the same acts are made crimes in different
jurisdictions, and under different laws. There are
guarantees against excessive bail, yet in New Jersey
during the Passaic strike, bail of ten, twenty, even
thirty thousand dollars was demanded where the
trumped-up charges would at most have amounted to
"disorderly conduct"—and this in an endeavor to
break a strike. Men are guaranteed trial by jury,
yet padlock and labor injunction proceedings rob them
of liberty and property. Trial is guaranteed before
an impartial judge, yet two men go to death with the
approval of the "respectables," after trial by a judge
who was stamped by an official committee as having
been guilty of a "grave breach of official decorum";
and who is reported to have declared during the trial,
"Did you see what I did to those anarchist bastards!"
Star chamber proceedings are abhorrent to our institutions, yet we deport and bar defenseless foreigners
after arrest by a government agent who acts as policeman, prosecutor and judge. Even our own people are,
in their callings and properties, subject to judgment in
a variety of ways, by executive boards, license bureaus,
and petty bureaucrats without hearing or opportunity
for judicial review.

We occupy Hayti, San Domingo, we land marines
in Nicaragua and deny civil liberty; we buy the Vir-

gin Islands and establish military, not civil, government.

We no longer welcome the downtrodden and oppressed of other lands. Once it was our proud boast that America was a haven for political refugees. To-day we deport anti-Fascists to Italy because perforce they came here without a passport and this in spite of the fact that they return to prison or torture. Only recently, a naïve Italian, one Chiassone, protested to the Department of Labor against deportation, but in vain. When tried in Italy for spreading anti-Fascist propaganda, the chief evidence used against him was his letter to the Department. He was sentenced to twelve years in jail. We have in the past refused, even on demand and charge of crime, to return political refugees; to-day we deport them without demand or charge of any crime.

Once Louis Kossuth, a political exile from Hungary, was welcomed by Congress and the whole country, to the annoyance of the Austrian Government. To-day, Count Karolyi, the first president of Hungary and a democrat, is barred, and even the Countess Karolyi was refused admittance. There is little doubt that the instigator was the reactionary Horthy Government. It was sought to bar Countess Cathcart from America because she wasn't chaste. Hypocrisy was never better illumined than when she indignantly retorted to the Board at Ellis Island, "Do you men mean to say you have never committed adultery?" to which they responded, "We are American citizens." Madame Kollontay, Soviet Ambassador to Mexico, was forbidden to set foot in the United States during her journey to her post. Bolsheviks, bewhiskered and be-bombed, might spring from the earth her footsteps should tread! Saklatvala, a member of the British Parliament, in spite of proper credentials, was excluded from an Interparliamentary Union in Washington, and likewise other Communists and Radicals, because forsooth those in power have so little faith in our institutions that they fear that Americans would be corrupted by radical propaganda to a point where they would rush to overthrow their institutions. How different from the Jeffersonian view:

"Truth is great and will prevail if left to herself. She is the proper and sufficient antagonist of error and has nothing to fear from the conflict unless, by human interposition, disarmed of her natural weapons—free argument and debate; errors ceasing to be dangerous when it is permitted freely to contradict them."

Again from Jefferson's Inaugural Address:

"If there be any among us who would wish to dissolve this union or change its republican form, let them stand undisturbed as monuments of the safety with which error of opinion may be tolerated where reason is left free to combat it."

How different is to-day from the confidence displayed by Lincoln in his first inaugural:

"This country with its institutions, belongs to the people who inhabit it. Whenever they shall grow weary of the existing government, they can exercise their constitutional right of amending it, or their revolutionary right to dismember or overthrow it."

On one occasion this was quoted by Allen McCurdy, a noted Liberal. The audience hissed. "I should first have mentioned the author," said McCurdy. "I never thought I should live to hear an audience of Americans hiss the words of Abraham Lincoln:"

The Declaration of Independence has become so radical that the mere reading of it has led to arrest. "I didn't say that," said one victim, "Thomas Jefferson said it." "Where is that guy?" said the policeman. "We'll get him too."

Molly Abrams and others were sentenced to twenty years in jail (Holmes and Brandeis, as usual, dissenting) for publishing a leaflet which Mr. Justice Holmes said they "had as much right to publish as the Government has to publish the Constitution of the United States, now vainly invoked by them." [1]

The dissenting opinion reads in part:

"But when men have realized that time has upset many fighting faiths, they may come to believe even more than they believe the very foundations of their own conduct that the ultimate good desired is better reached by free trade in ideas—that the best test of truth is the power of the thought to get itself accepted in the competition of the market; and that truth is the only ground upon which their wishes safely can be carried out. That at any rate is the theory of our Constitution. It is an experiment, as all life is an experiment. Every year, if not every day, we have to wager our salvation upon some prophecy based upon imperfect knowledge. While that experiment is part of our system I think that we should be externally vigilant against attempts to check the expression of opinions that

[1] Abrams *vs.* United States, 250 U. S. 616 (1919).

we loathe and believe to be fraught with death, unless they so imminently threaten immediate interference with the lawful and pressing purposes of the law that an immediate check is required *to save the country.* . . ."

A new theory of government based on human cussedness and need of legal restraint, is displacing liberty. A Declaration of Dependence represents the attitude of a large part of the community:

"All men are created wicked and are endowed by their Creator with certain limited Privileges—that among these are Life (if you don't drink), Liberty (if you conform) and the pursuit of Gloom. That to secure these privileges, Governments are instituted among Men, deriving their just powers from the consent of the Ku Klux Klan, the Anti-Saloon League, the W.C.T.U., the Lord's Day Alliance, the American Defense League, the Key Men of America, the Watch and Ward Societies, the Anti-Vice Associations, and every variety of Crusader, Vigilant, Reformer and Crank."

I don't want to be misunderstood. I should not deny to any of these people the right to express their views; or to persuade others. I don't want to control them. But I don't want them to control me.

This book narrates some half dozen cases with which the writer happened to be connected. They all occurred between the years 1922 and 1927. Differing in fact, background and motivation, they have one common characteristic—fear. They represent a type of mind. All exhibit different phases of ignorance, bigotry and intolerance. None of these cases can or should be considered by itself. They are all manifestations of the same spirit. In one a reader will find injustice, in another he will approve the actions of the authorities. In either case his attitude will merely show his own particular phobia or prejudice. One reader will commend every criticism, implied or expressed, except the comments on free speech as connected with labor unions. Perhaps he has had trouble with labor. Who hasn't? Another will agree with everything except that Negroes should not move into white neighborhoods. Perhaps his real estate has depreciated. Another will indignantly resent my attitude toward the obscenity laws. Perhaps he finds himself too much aroused over a salacious story. Another feels that anarchists should be hanged, drawn and quartered. He may be ignorant of what anarchism is, or he may fear unusual thought, or he may have a relative, perhaps a brother-in-law, who is an anarchist, or he may be just a plain, ordinary sadist. Another will find an emotional upset at what he will regard as my irreverence toward organized religion. Having sacrificed so much of human interest and enjoyment for his God, his compensation must naturally come from a comparison between his likely blessedness and my certain damnation. If only he could be sure of either, he'd be much happier.

I look over the publications of a representative group of men of eminent respectability and notorious piety. What are the subjects considered? The necessity of enforcing Sunday observance laws, the menace of automobiling and playing golf on the Sabbath, the "horror" of Sunday newspapers, the demoralization of youth not sent regularly to Sunday school;

the importance of Bible reading in public schools; the
sin of dancing and the theater; the danger of free
association between boys and girls; the immodesty of
short sleeves and skirts in women's dress; the indecency of bathing costumes and beach lounging; the
obscenity of the movies which require strict censorship;
the increasing number of divorces; the laxity of law
which fails to compel a hating couple to keep on mat-
ing, or which does not properly crucify those seeking
relief elsewhere; the horrible Bolsheviks who have not
only abolished private property but have attempted to
alienate people from a devouring church; foreign missions and other methods of persuasion or control over
heathens; prohibition and the demon rum; the necessity
of summary search and immediate punishment; references to the number of fires caused by cigars and cigarettes. These evils are all to be dealt with by law.
Every article indicates new modes of suppression.
There is naturally no reference to human freedom.
And yet, history has been largely a struggle for the
right of the individual to be damned in his own way.

To the people of Tennessee, salvation is important;
they fear the teaching of any doctrine that will destroy
faith. It doesn't occur to them that there is something
wrong with a faith which is endangered by knowledge,
and that fear and threat, fable and irrationality will,
among intelligent people, upset faith more surely than
intellectual freedom. The people of Boston and New
York, ridiculing Tennessee, find their conventional
morals and their economic order—matters of this
world—of supreme moment; they fear the teaching of

doctrine that will question the status quo. So we have the "American Mercury" and the Sacco-Vanzetti cases in Massachusetts, and in New York the Lusk laws of odious memory, the expulsion of Socialists from the legislature, the "Captive" case. Tranquillity of mind and security of social structure are the goal. This is exhibited in the free speech cases in Pennsylvania, West Virginia and New Jersey. The demand for Negro segregation, illustrated by the Sweet case in Detroit, is merely another phase of the same attitude of mind. Prejudice, intolerance, bigotry in whatever form, are merely on the obverse side of the shield on which Liberty is written.

Societies founded on tyranny still exist though many have passed away. Ours is an experiment with a society based on freedom. It is an experiment in democracy which has been described as a method of determination by counting heads instead of cracking them. The Constitution of the United States, with the exception of the Eighteenth Amendment, contains only one kind of restraint—that on the government. This was thought necessary to preserve liberty. This latter-day legislation does not curb the government but adds to its powers and restricts the individual. Incongruous, unsound and unworkable laws show the tendency to protect the individual from himself, not through self-restraint developed by education, but through law.

There may be something to be said for political institutions, based on suppression, whether through uniformity, oligarchy, monarchy or martial law: even for tyranny based on the dictatorship of the Fascists or

the Proletariat. But whatever may be said for tyranny
or power in Government, that is not, or was not, the
American method. We should bear in mind the fact
that there may be no greater oppression than by rule
of majority, when it enters fields outside of the realm
of government as understood by practically all the
people. Tyranny no less exists when imposed by part
of a written constitution, particularly when, as a practical fact, that part is unchangeable.

Liberty has dangers. Our theory is that they are
not as serious as those of repression. But while doing
lip service to the ideal, yet in practical fact, few are
ready to face the dangers of freedom. They believe in
it lightly—when they think it works.

H. L. Mencken says ("Prejudices"—Fourth Series,
p. 226):

"It is perhaps a fact provocative of sour mirth that the
Bill of Rights was designed trustfully to prohibit forever
two of the favorite crimes of all known governments; the
seizure of private property without adequate compensation and the invasion of the citizen's liberty without justi-
fiable cause or process of law."

"The actual history of the Constitution, as every one
knows, has been a history of the gradual abandonment of
all such impediments to governmental tyranny. To-day
we live frankly under a government of men, not of laws."

Again ("Prejudices"—Sixth Series, p. 74):

" . . . There is no sign any more of the . . . vision
of liberty. The fathers saw it, and the devotion they
gave to it went far beyond three cheers a week. It sur-

vived into Jackson's time and its glow was renewed in Lincoln's. But now it is no more.

" . . . Liberty, to-day, not only lacks its old hot partisans and romantic fanatics in America; it has grown so disreputable that even to mention it, save in terms of a fossilized and hollow rhetoric, becomes a sort of indecorum. I know of but one national organization that advocates it with any genuine heartiness, and that organization, not long ago, was rewarded with a violent denunciation on the floor of the House of Representatives: only the lone Socialist, once in jail himself for the same offense, made bold to defend it. From the chosen elders of the nation, legislative, executive and judicial, one hears only that demanding it is treason. It is the first duty of the free citizen, it appears, to make a willing sacrifice of the Bill of Rights. He must leap to the business gladly, and with no mental reservations. If he pauses, then he is a Bolshevik."

There will be those who will interpret my statements to mean that I regard absolute freedom as feasible. Far from it. I know that liberty to swing my arm stops where the other fellow's nose begins. Liberty is a relative matter. I believe in those liberties contained in the Bills of Rights. I am willing to concede that these are subject to interpretation, but I object to nullification. Freedom of speech involves the right to express any opinion. The principle is not affected by border line cases where men might differ as to whether the speaker is expressing an opinion, or directly inciting to violence. None of the cases related here is in this misty field of doubt, so metaphysical speculation is not necessary.

Indignation boils my blood at the thought of the

heritage we are throwing away; at the thought that, with few exceptions, the fight for freedom is left to the poor, forlorn and defenseless, and to the few radicals and revolutionaries who would make use of liberty to destroy, rather than to maintain, American institutions. I am quite aware of my intolerance on this subject.

A story is told of a Northerner talking with a Southern patrician about a negro. The Southerner insisted that the colored man was better off under slavery. "Come here, Sam," he called to an old negro shambling along across the street. "You were a slave?" asked he. "Yes, sir." "Did you have to work as hard those days?" "No, sir," said Sam. "Did you have as good a home?" "Much better," said Sam. "Do you get as good food now?" "Ah, no," said Sam, "nothing near as good." "Well, then," said the Southerner, "I suppose you prefer slavery to freedom?" "Well," drawled Sam, "I'll tell ye. There's a sort of a *looseness* about this here freedom that I likes."

Those who believe in old American ideals are to-day regarded as dangerous innovators. In fact, they are quite conservative and old-fashioned. The others are the innovators. They believe in Liberty, but—

"You're damned unpatriotic," growled an old gentleman, on an occasion when I finished an indignant harangue on the spirit of repression in the United States. "Gentlemen, I propose a toast to our country."

I added to this, "Gentlemen, I join in the toast, but there are some of us who love our country so much that we are willing to fight for the ideals underlying our institutions."

FREEDOM OF EDUCATION

FREEDOM OF EDUCATION

The People of the State of Tennessee *vs.* John Thomas Scopes—With Darrow in Tennessee —the Anti-Evolution Law

The sleepy town of Dayton, Tennessee, snuggled in the hills. Robinson's Drug Store was on the main street, a broad quiet village center flanked by the Aqua Hotel, a moving picture theater, a barber shop where one could get a hot bath, a livery stable and establishments of like character. George Rappelyea, a mining engineer, the live-wire of the town, Thomas Scopes, a young tow-headed High School teacher, and three lawyers, gathered in the drug store, discussed the Anti-Evolution law recently passed by the legislature. They read the wording of the Statute as printed in the Chattanooga *Times:*

"Be it enacted by the general assembly of the State of Tennessee, that it shall be unlawful for any teacher in any of the universities, normals and all other public schools of the State, which are supported in whole or in part by the public school funds of the State, to teach any theory that denies the story of the Divine creation of man as taught in the Bible, and to teach instead that man has descended from a lower order of animals."

Suddenly Rappelyea pushed aside the paper and smote Mr. Robinson's glass-topped table.* Here was a chance to put Dayton on the map! Would Scopes agree to place himself and his munificent school-teaching job in jeopardy? Scopes would. Here was a magnificent opportunity to test an obnoxious law. The sensational character of the undertaking, which would make Dayton world famous, was not an unwelcome feature. No time was to be lost. Other communities, once they caught the idea, would compete for the attraction of a trial involving science, the Bible and Tennessee. Scopes, a bit amused by it all, marched resignedly to the sacrifice. He intimated to his class that there might be something in the theory of evolution. He was arrested when his friends pointed out to the local constabulary just what he meant.

The stage was set. William Jennings Bryan, then resident in Florida, long a proponent of restrictive law to induce faith, and responsible more than any other for the Tennessee Statute, volunteered his services to the prosecution. Opportunity could grant no more. The exultant Rappelyea sent an S.O.S. for legal aid to the American Civil Liberties Union in New York. Clarence Darrow, Dudley Field Malone and myself answered the request to join Dr. John Randolph Neal, a lawyer of Tennessee, in the defense. The luster of Bainbridge Colby shone on us for a time, but he was unable to accompany us southward.

Scopes was indicted. The show was on. At once Dayton took on the character of a revivalist-circus. Thither swarmed ballyhoo artists, hot dog venders,

---

* The American Civil Liberties Union had announced that it would back any school teacher who would test the law.

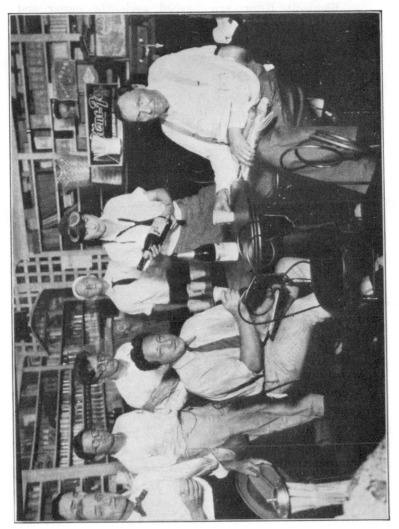

Robinson's Drug Store—where it started.

lemonade merchants, preachers, professional atheists, college students, Greenwich Village radicals, out-of-work coal miners, I.W.W.'s, Single Taxers, "libertarians," revivalists of all shades and sects, hinterland "soothsayers," Holy Rollers, an army of newspaper men, scientists, editors and lawyers. Dayton, Tennessee, had found its place in the sun.

Tennessee and its people were surprising to an unsophisticated New York lawyer. When, on occasion, Europeans have talked about the United States, I have been amazed at their misunderstanding and sometimes at their credulity. I have expressed what I thought was the American point of view, with more or less the assumption that as an American I understood it. And yet, with wider experience I realize more and more that there is no American type—that different sections of the country and various groups of people hold such diverse views that they might well be living not only in different hemispheres but almost in different periods of civilization.

Within a few years prior to and during 1925, many states were considering laws prohibiting the teaching of evolution in the public schools. Some states had adopted this legislation in one form or another. The question of the propriety or constitutionality of such laws had not been tested. Dayton provided the test-tube. The case derived its interest not only from the subject matter but because the main antagonists were William Jennings Bryan and Clarence Darrow. It was a battle between two types of mind—the rigid, orthodox, accepting, unyielding, narrow, conventional mind, and the broad, liberal, critical, cynical, skeptical and tolerant mind.

On one occasion during the trial, Darrow turned to me and said: "Isn't it difficult to realize that a trial of this kind is possible in the Twentieth Century in the United States of America?" I should have been startled and somewhat doubtful had any one told me that at this late date there were great numbers of people in the United States who held the religious views of the Middle Ages, who, in spite of railroads, steamboats, the World War, the telephone, the airplane, the radio, all the great mechanistic discoveries and all the advancement in science and philosophy, in spite of education in the public schools in geography, biology and kindred subjects, still thought that the earth was flat; that doctors were a menace; that lawyers were predestined to damnation, and that failure to observe literally every word of the Bible would send one to eternal Hell, a material region where the flames leap high and where the doors are sealed for eternity. Had any one suggested that there were millions of people who believed it possible to build up a theocracy in the United States under the leadership of Bryan, I should have thought the statement that of a madman—that is, before I went to Dayton.

Bryan actually felt that this was a fight between religion and atheism or agnosticism. He never realized that it was a fight merely between a literal interpretation of the Bible and common sense. His attitude was no different from that of the Church for centuries. He rested religion upon the precise verbiage of the

Book and insisted that religion would fail if those words were not accepted literally. Instead of accepting the spirit of religion or of Christianity, he accepted words, many of them the wrong words, many of them representing improper translations, all of them representing the ideas of men of thousands of years ago who spoke the language and expressed the ideas of their time. Such views lead to the downfall of religion, not to its growth. If to be religious one must believe things that his mind will not accept, he must, perforce, by human reasoning reject religion. Credulity may be a test of faith. It is not a test of rationality.

To the Fundamentalists faith is co-extensive with the Bible, the King James' version of the Bible. John Washington Butler, the farmer legislator, who introduced the Tennessee Bill, is reported to have said that he never knew there was more than one Bible until he heard this stated in Court. Apparently he had never heard of the Catholic Bible consisting of eighty books, or the Hebrew Bible consisting of sixty-six books, or of any other translation. It is doubtful whether he ever inquired as to the language in which the original Bible was written, whether he knew that the Bible in Hebrew was unvocalized, and that changes in vowels might have brought about important changes in the text. Apparently he did not realize that, before the age of printing, many priests made their own translations and did not hesitate to change a meaning for their own purposes. In the Fifteenth Century in England a law was passed making it a death penalty to read the Bible in the original tongue; under this law

thirty-nine men were hanged and their property confiscated to the Crown. Butler did not know that the
stories of the Bible constitute the folk lore of many
primitive peoples; that this is true of the story of
the creation, the flood, the Virgin birth and numerous
other tales. If one had suggested that there had been
no greater evolution than that of religion, and possibly that of the Bible itself, Butler would no doubt
have stamped that person as an atheist and unbeliever.
In fact, John W. Butler apparently thought, if indeed
he thought at all, that the King James' version of the
Bible was handed down by God in person to Moses,
in printed form and in the English language. Any
effort to enlighten Butler would have been met with the
words of one of the attorneys for the prosecution,
"If I must choose between religion and education, I
choose religion."

A little reading would have shown this legislator that
for centuries man, under the pretense of obeying the
teachings of a religion of love, had tortured and murdered for the glory of God. He would have learned
that in medieval times the Church lived on the backs
of the people, that theological power was constraining
and overwhelming; that priests sold relics and pre-
tended to perform miracles, and that it was to the
advantage of the reigning priestly class to keep people
in ignorance.

When Copernicus, around 1500, first proclaimed
the hypothesis that the earth and the solar system
moved around the sun, he dared not teach it in Rome
or Italy. In 1543 he went to Germany to publish his

book. The publisher wrote an apologetic preface presenting the material, not as a statement of fact, not even as a theory or a hypothesis, but merely as a wild guess. To assure a slight measure of safety, the book itself was dedicated to the Pope. Any Scopes of that day would have been subjected to torture and death. Giordano Bruno having traveled all over Europe, and having observed the same phenomena as Copernicus, returned to Venice. His patron delivered him to the Inquisition. His black-robed judges pointed out that his statements violated the word of God. Bruno spent seven years in a dungeon. Then the judgment read: "Thou shalt be put to death mercifully without the spilling of blood." So Bruno was burned. And then Galileo invented the telescope. Some one had said to Copernicus that if it was a fact that the planets moved around the sun, they should at times show shadows. Copernicus had answered that God in His own good time would show these shadows. Galileo found them with his telescope. He was likewise called before the Inquisition. He admitted that he was teaching heresy, and under threat of torture, recanted: "I, Galileo, being in my seventieth year, being a prisoner on my knees before your Eminences, having before my eyes the Holy Gospel, which I touch with my hands, objure, curse and detest the heresy of the movement of the earth." * So was Scopes expected to objure and detest the heresy of the theory of evolution.

Once witches, expressing the will of the devil, were tortured with the thumbscrew and the rack. Failure to confess was regarded as arrogance. On the other

* Galileo is reported to have muttered as he turned away, "Well, anyhow it moves."

hand, confession assured guilt. Those were the days
when it was argued that the earth could not be round
because, if so, people would fall off on the other side.
The heavens were a firmament in which the stars and
the moon were hung out at night to light the earth.
Earthquakes and comets were signs from the Almighty.

All of this was supposed to be a relic of a bygone
age until the Scopes trial indicated that the hold of
fundamentalism, or a belief in science as expounded in
the Bible, was still held by a large portion of the
people, particularly in those parts of the United States
which Mencken designates as the "Bible Belt."

It is strange that a world which accepts the helio-
centric theory should be troubled about the theory of
evolution. If the earth is not the center of the universe, but merely a small one of a myriad of planets,
it is hard to conceive man as the center of God's attention. He becomes infinitesimally small in an infinitely
large world, and his importance is proportionately
minimized. Yet in the course of time the Church
agreed to this peculiarly shocking phenomenon, not,
however, without the usual obstructive tactics. First,
denial; secondly, acquiescence; thirdly, agreement,
coupled with an agitated insistence that there was
no inconsistency between its doctrines and science.
Astronomy measuring in billions of miles, geology cal-
culating in millions of years, are incomparably more
dangerous to medieval faiths and dogmas than the
theory of evolution.

On one side then, Bryan with his Fundamentalist fol-

Is Education?

lowers. On the other, Scopes, Darrow and the rest—the old order against the new.

A word about Scopes. Had we sought to find a defendant to present the issue, we could not have improved upon the individual. Popular in the community, a leader in school athletics, intensely interested in science, clean-cut, typically American, he handled himself with much the same decorum that was shown by Lindbergh after his flight. I saw telegrams to Scopes offering him thousands of dollars for a lecture tour, for appearance in the movies or on the stage. He steadfastly refused to commercialize the case and this in spite of the fact that he was so poor that his father, a carpenter, having come from Paducah, Kentucky, to attend the trial, was forced to return for lack of funds after a few days. Scopes' only expressed wish was for educational opportunity. Through the efforts of the scientists at the trial, a fund was raised to provide him with a scholarship at the University of Chicago. He thereupon became the envy of the young school teachers in the State of Tennessee.

On the seventh day of July, in the year of our Lord 1925, Dudley Field Malone, Charles Francis Potter, a Unitarian minister whose knowledge of theology was very helpful, and myself started from New York, accompanied by a number of newspaper men. We had hardly reached Trenton before Ike Shuman, of the *Times*, having been picked by some genial fellow travelers, informed us that he had already lost his bankroll at draw poker. Though this seemed a bad omen, we arrived safely at Dayton, Tennessee, and joined the throng at the Hotel Aqua, renowned for its purity and bird dishes of varied vegetables. It also had rooms with bath.

As we approached the courthouse on the day of the trial, our attention was first caught by a sign on the fence reading, "Sweethearts, come to Jesus," and conveying other advice of like kind. In the courtyard were various groups of people, some singing psalms, some apparently engaged in a hair-splitting discussion of a phrase in the Bible, some menacing in attitude, muttering and mumbling. At the entrance to the building was a large sign "Read your Bible daily for one week." I never passed that sign without mentally transposing the words, "Read your Bible weakly for one day."

Court opened with prayer, not just an ordinary prayer, but an argumentative one, directed straight at the defense. We were told that "every perfect gift comes from God, the Father of Lights,"—that He was acquainted with the secrets of our hearts, with the motive back of every thought and act. The preacher hoped that the power and presence of the Holy Spirit might be with the court and the jury and all the attorneys—even the "foreigners." Thereupon we were introduced to the Judge, who stated that he was glad to have with him the "foreign" lawyers for both the state and the defense. We then learned a fact that was new to us of the North. We were reminded throughout the trial that the Civil War was over, that there was no feeling in the South against the North, that the same flag covered us all, but— This was a pertinent

introduction to unpleasant comment. The peroration
of any offensive speech was that the speaker had come
to love us all, but—

The courtroom was mobbed. Hundreds of newspaper reporters gathered at the tables; telegraph in-
struments clicked; camera men were in all corners.
Judge Raulston, ruddy-faced and important, entered
the courtroom followed by various members of his
family bearing flowers. We went to the bench to pose
for the ubiquitous photographers with the attorneys
for the other side. There were Clarence Darrow, Dudley Field Malone, John Randolph Neal, W. O. Thompson, and myself, for the defense. For the prosecution
appeared William Jennings Bryan, Sr., and William
Jennings Bryan, Jr., the McKenzies, father and son,
the Hicks brothers and the Attorney General, Thomas
Stewart. Scopes was almost forgotten. The Judge
called, "Come up here, Scopes." Whereupon the defendant charged with a. crime, which the court referred
to as "a high misdemeanor," became part of the picture. Somebody suggested that the usual procedure
was, "Court opens, prayers said, pictures taken, court
adjourns."

There had been some technical doubt about the
original indictment, which was natural in view of the
hurry with which Dayton had sought to beat out its
competitive neighbors. A new grand jury was called.
One of the jurymen protested that he wanted to get
away but the court assured him that the proceedings
would not take more than half an hour. In charging
the jury, the Judge read a large part of Genesis,

although he afterwards held Scopes was guilty merely if he taught evolution, and that the Bible had nothing to do with the case. The grand jury returned with a new indictment.

Jurymen were then called. In order to assure fair play, names were drawn from a hat by a child perched on the corner of the Judge's bench. It soon transpired that it made little difference to us who was called. The prosecution would ask to which Church the venireman belonged. The answer invariably came back "Baptist" or "Methodist." Whereupon Stewart, the Attorney General, would sing out, "Pass him to you, Colonel," which meant that Darrow was to proceed with the examination.

We of the defense had by that time acquired titles of "Colonel." Those on the other side were known as "Generals."

Every talesman assured us that he would give Scopes a perfectly fair trial; that he would in no way be influenced by the attitude of the community or by his preacher.

There was a great desire to get on the jury, for it meant a grandstand seat for the performance. It afterwards happened that the jury were excluded from the courtroom during most of the trial. On one occasion the judge remarked that it had been reported that jurors listened to the proceedings at the amplifiers in the courtyard, but the foreman assured the Judge that they merely sat around and read the newspapers.

One of the veniremen, J. P. Massingwell, swore that he had no opinion on the case and that he could try it without prejudice. On inquiry it appeared that he was a Fundamentalist preacher. Did he know anything about evolution? "Yes," he had "preached about it." "Did you preach for or against evolution?" "Well, I preached against it of course." Whereupon there was loud applause. Mr. Darrow turned to the prosecutors and asked if they thought the man was a fair juror. They answered they were satisfied with him, that we should bear in mind that he had promised not to be prejudiced.

One venireman was Jim Reilly, a simple man who wore dark blue glasses. He was asked if he had ever read about evolution, to which he answered that he could not read. We accepted him of course. Darrow commenced, "Well, you are fortunate. You can be a perfectly fair juror, can you?" "Yes, sir." It was suggested to Darrow that Reilly's inability to read was probably due to his eyes, whereupon Darrow said: "You said you could not read. Is that due to your eyes, Mr. Reilly?" A. "No, I am uneducated." "Q. Have your eyes bothered you?" A. "No, I am uneducated." It was said with such plain simple dignity that we felt that we had at least one honest man.

Of the jury as finally chosen, eleven were church members, one of whom did not go to church as often as he ought, the twelfth having slipped in by an oversight. The prosecution reëxamined him when this curious fact appeared, but he had been accepted and there was no way to unseat him.

We made our motions on demurrer and to quash the indictment on constitutional grounds. The jury was dismissed during the argument although the constitution of the State of Tennessee states that in criminal cases the jury shall be the judge of the law as well as of the facts. We pointed out, among other things, that the Tennessee constitution provided that the caption of a bill should be germane to the substance, that the caption of this bill referred to the teaching of evolution, whereas the bill itself forbade the teaching of anything concerning Creation contrary to the Bible.

We then referred to a section of the State constitution which reads:

"Knowledge, learning and virtue being essential to the preservation of republican institutions . . . it shall be the duty of the general assembly in all future periods of this Government to cherish literature and science."

A further provision is that "no preference shall ever be given by law to any religious establishment." When we suggested that this was violated by a law favoring the Fundamentalists, the answer of the Attorney General was, "Oh, that is all foolishness."

We contended that under the Fourteenth Amendment to the United States Constitution, no law was sound which was so indefinite that one could not tell what was forbidden, that no man could be in a position where he might "guess" himself into jail. In the first place, the act referred to the theory of Creation as set forth in the Bible. There is no statement of what Bible is intended. Then, there are various stories of Creation in the Bible. Is the test based on the Bible literally interpreted? The word "teach" leads

to further difficulty.   Does it mean teach "as a fact" or
does it mean "to expound information"?   For, obviously, if it doesn't mean to teach as a fact, then one may
teach, or expound information, on all theories.

We made the further contention that the law did not
come within the police power of the State.   The liberty
of the individual can be limited by the State only
under the police power.   No law which is unreasonable
can be justified by the police power.   As a test, we
presented a parallel law that it should be unlawful for
any one to teach in the public schools any theory contrary to the Bible that the earth is not the center
of the universe, and to teach instead thereof that the
earth moves around the sun.   We suggested the death
penalty for violation.   We insisted that the only difference between the supposititious law and the one in
question was that the scientific fact of the earth's movement was to-day accepted.   We thought the illustration was far-fetched but back in the hills of Tennessee is a sect called the Holy Rollers who would
regard such legislation not only with favor but who
would feel that it represented the word of God.   Yet I
have never observed more sincere and deeply religious
people than the Holy Rollers.

A group of them camped outside Dayton during the
trial and many of us were wont to observe their weird
ceremonies, not realizing perhaps that those in the
Court were almost as weird.   The services are held
at night under huge trees from which swing oil flares.
The people gather in a circle on benches.   The ceremonies are led by one, two or three holy-looking, un-

kempt, unlettered men. One thanks God that he has no education and owns no more than the tattered rags on his back. Working himself up into a fervor, another joins in, then a third, then the women in the crowd and the youngsters, until every one is praying and shouting vehemently. Every few words are punctuated by "Glory be to God. Precious be Thy Name, Glory be to the Lamb!" They shout the horrors of Hell to the unbelievers. The whole crowd becomes increasingly incoherent. One by one they get the "tongue," which means that they have been seized by the spirit of the Holy Ghost. Men and women shriek and roll in hysterical agony. Hour after hour the meetings continue.

On a Sunday morning we attended a baptism. The worshipers sat, kneeled or stood at the side of a stony creek bed. Children were throwing pebbles into the water and were happily dancing around. The adults were tense and nervous, keyed up for an emotional spree. We hear shouts—"Thank God I got no education, Glory be to God!" "Preachers are the lowest-down class we have in the country." "Precious be Thy Name, Sue for the Salvation of God." Then, turning to us, "Maybe God sent you here. He that believeth in Baptism, he shall be saved. Glory to the Lamb. He who believeth not shall be damned. They shall take up serpents. I got something there with teeth in his mouth. They shall speak under mean tongues. The Lord hates lawyers and no lawyers' names shall be written on the book of the Angels, Glory be to God! And He hates doctors and their sins should be washed away. Precious Little Lamb." In the midst of the speaker's harangue, another preacher broke in along the same line. "Some folks works their hands off to the elbows to give their young ones education and all they do is to send their young ones to Hell, Glory to His Name!" "I know my young ones are in glory because I never learned them nothing, Glory to our Lord!" A third one breaks in, then the crowd, then they burst into song.

Ready for the baptism, they were led along the stream by one carrying a branch of an olive tree. Every once in awhile, he poked the water. Having found a deep place, the leader, fully dressed, walked in, up to his armpits. He was followed by others pulling along a pale-looking girl, giggling with hysteria. She stumbled and fell, raised her head and shrieked. The crowd on the bank sang. The preacher took the girl's two hands, folded them over her breast and with one arm around her waist, threw her under. He called her to the Lord. She struggled and wept and shrieked. Brought to land she was surrounded by the older people, gesticulating and shouting their joy. Suddenly a woman yelled, "I'm falling, save me," and down she went rocking on the ground. She kept shrieking, "Glory to the Lamb, Blessed be His name," while others jigged and danced, yelled and sang.

All this means preparation for Heaven. Of course this doesn't represent the religious attitude of Dayton folk who, though more civilized, take their particular brand of religion quite as seriously.

We have wandered from the issue, just as we did at

Dayton, Tennessee, but the real significance of the Scopes case cannot be gathered without a realization of the background.

Our argument, ridiculing the law, aroused General McKenzie, the old war horse of the Tennessee Bar. He insisted that any boy of sixteen knows all about evolution and also about the Bible, *i.e.*, any boy of sixteen born and raised in Tennessee. In reference to our hypothetical act he said, "No such act as that has ever passed through the fertile brain of a Tennesseean. I don't know what they do up in their country." Malone objected to allusions to geographical location and suggested that we were there as American citizens. The Court tried to smooth the troubled waters by suggesting that General McKenzie loved us all and that we should always remember that we were guests. Mr. Malone answered with some asperity that in the courtroom we were lawyers and not guests.

The argument for the law was simple and persuasive. The public owned the schools and paid the teachers. The public had a right to direct what the teacher should say or do. The teacher is their employee. Certainly the people should not be compelled to hire and pay a teacher to destroy the faith of their children. The agnostic insists that the public supply not only the schools and the teachers but even the pupils, and demands the right to teach doctrines of which the people disapprove. Appallingly unjust! Those who in New York State approved the infamous Lusk laws will have no difficulty with the reasoning.

Of course, the answer is that the State may deter-

mine what subjects shall be taught, but if biology is
to be taught, it cannot demand that it be taught
falsely. If astronomy is to be taught, the State could
not legislate that no one teach that the earth moves
around the sun; if geography, that the earth is round;
if arithmetic, that two and two make four. The State
may decide that physiology should not be taught. If,
however, that is a prescribed subject, the State could
hardly provide by law that children be taught that
men and women have all of the same physical characteristics.

Sue Hicks, a young Tennessee lawyer, assured the
court that our contentions were ridiculous, that the
prosecution failed to see that there was any religious
issue whatever involved, and that certainly the act in
no way interfered with the promotion of science and
learning. Personally, I doubt whether at any time
the attorneys for the prosecution caught our point on
the religious question. Every word, to say nothing of
emotions, in the court made it clear that there was
really no other question. The constitution provided
against preference to any religious establishment. We
insisted that the Fundamentalist Church was a religious establishment and that preference was given to
Fundamentalists by making their Bible, and their interpretation of the Bible, the yardstick of education.
When General Stewart asked how the law interfered
with the constitution, Mr. Darrow answered, "Giving
preference to the Bible." General Stewart replied,
"To the Bible?" Mr. Darrow: "Yes, sir. Yes, over
the Koran." General Stewart: "What is there in this

that requires you to worship in any particular way?" But we insisted that the law preferred the Bible to the Koran. The Koran was not popular in the State of Tennessee.

It then appeared that the State of Tennessee prescribed the textbook from which Scopes had taught. For Scopes to have used any other textbook would have been a misdemeanor, and yet it was likewise a crime for him to have used this.

Then rose the well beloved and well hated Darrow, tall with stooped shoulders, lined face, lanky figure, in shirt-sleeves and lavender suspenders. At times he spoke in soft tones, then sardonic, then indignant. He started quietly, pointing out casually that while we came from Chicago and New York, yet Mr. Bryan, Sr., a foreigner, from Florida, and Mr. Bryan, Jr., from California, were responsible for this "foolish, mischievous and wicked act." He quoted the statement of Bancroft that "it is all right to preserve freedom in constitutions, but when the spirit of freedom has fled from the hearts of the people, then its matter is easily sacrificed under law."

"Here we find to-day as brazen and as bold an attempt to destroy learning as was ever made in the Middle Ages and the only difference is we have not provided that malefactors shall be burned at the stake. But there is time for that, your Honor. We have to approach these things gradually."

He pointed out that the State of Tennessee "has no more right to teach the Bible as the Divine Book than the Book of Mormon or the Book of Confucius or the

Essays of Emerson or any one of the ten thousand books to which human souls have gone for consolation and aid in their troubles." Again he referred to the statute as indefinite; nobody could tell what it meant, it might be a trap to get some one who did not agree with you.

"Does this statute state what you shall teach and what you shall not? Not at all. Does it say that you cannot teach that the earth is round because Genesis says that it is flat? No. Does it say that you cannot teach that the earth is millions of ages old because the account in Genesis makes it less than six thousand years old? Oh, no. It does not state that. If it did you could understand it. It says you shan't teach any theory of the origin of man that is contrary to the Divine theory contained in the Bible.

"It makes the Bible the yardstick to measure every man's intelligence and to measure every man's learning. Are your mathematics good? Turn to Elijah i:2. Is your philosophy good? See II Samuel 3. Is your astronomy good? See Genesis, Chapter ii, verse 7. Is your chemistry good? See—well, chemistry, see Deuteronomy 6, or anything that tells about brimstone. Every bit of knowledge that the mind has must be submitted to a religious test."

(A later check-up showed that Darrow's verse references were not accurate, but this did not detract from the argument.) Finally, in a burst of fire and eloquence came the peroration:

"If to-day you can take a thing like evolution and make it a crime to teach it in the public school . . . at the next session you may ban books and newspapers. Soon you may set Catholic against Protestant, and Protestant against Protestant. . . . Ignorance and fanaticism are ever busy and need feeding. Always they are anxious and gloating for more. . . .

"After awhile, your Honor, it is the setting of man against man and creed against creed until with flying banners and beating drums we are marching backward to the glorious ages of the Sixteenth Century when bigots lighted fagots to burn the men who dared to bring any intelligence and enlightenment and culture to the human mind."

This was the high spot of the day and the message went flying throughout the country.

That night the water supply of Dayton did not function, and the electric lights were not working. Next morning, the denizens commented, with furtive looks Darrow-ward, upon the miracle that the water had ceased to flow, the lights had ceased to burn, and some suggested that the rivers flowed with blood!

We looked upon the day's work and found it good. There was morning and there was evening that day and a ray of light had been flashed in Tennessee.

We have alluded to the fact that proceedings in court opened with prayer. We did not object to this until the second day. Then we quietly asked the Judge to dispense with this amazing procedure claiming that it was conceivable that it might prejudice the jury. This having had no effect, we made our objection in open court. Now, the idea that prayer should not be indulged in, any time, any place, under any circumstances, was extremely novel to Dayton, Tennessee, and a gasp of shocked awe went through the courtroom. General Stewart referred to the agnostic counsel for the defense. Mr. Malone objected that we had heard prayers daily; that they were "argumentative and helped to increase the atmosphere of hostility," to which General Stewart retorted that he would advise Mr. Malone "that this is a God-fearing country." The court finally stated that he was "pleased to overrule the objection" and Dr. Stribling thereupon prayed that all of us be blessed.

We waited for a decision of the court on the demurrer and the motion to quash the indictment, but Judge Raulston stated that "he had not worked last night; that the lights were out until 8:30. . . ." Thereupon the court adjourned until the afternoon session. A petition was then presented from Unitarians, Jews and Congregationalists, that if prayer was to be said, there be a selection of clergymen to include others than Fundamentalists and a motion was made that the petition be granted. The decision on the motion was referred by the court to the "Pastors' Association of this town." We objected that we were entitled to a judicial determination of the motion, but the court held to its ruling.

Still we awaited the court's opinion on the constitutionality of the law, but Judge Raulston remarked that he "had a very serious matter to speak of"; that he had been informed that newspapers had already published his decision; that no one except his secretary and himself knew his conclusion, and that before reading his momentous opinion he intended to conduct an investigation to find out how there had come a leak of the news. Thereupon one of the reporters suggested to the Judge that the way to go about the matter was to appoint a committee of newspaper men to look into the matter. A list of proposed members was handed to the Judge, who promptly appointed the nominees. It was generally known that the "scoop" had been made by a youngster named Hutchinson, representing the International News Service, but in the evening the Committee, with great hilarity and some disregard for the Volstead Act, held a mock trial. They reported to court that Hutchinson had come by his information in a legitimate manner. The court insisted upon knowing the source. Whereupon, Mr. Beemish, the chairman, remarked. "Upon investigation we find that the information came from the court." Judge Raulston interjected a startled, "What"? Whereupon Mr. Beemish continued: Hutchinson had met the Judge the day before upon his way to the hotel. The Judge had said that a stenographer was making a copy of the decision He was asked whether he would read the decision in the afternoon, to which the Judge's answer was that such was his intention. The next question was whether the court would adjourn until to-morrow, to which the reply was, "Yes, I think so." The inference was clear. If the motion to quash was granted, the trial would be at an end. An adjournment meant the denial of the motion. Hutchinson drew the obvious deduction. Whereupon the court with great dignity delivered a homily to these hard-boiled reporters, stars of the profession, drawn from all over the country. He informed them that he did not expect them to ask him questions without giving him direct notice of the purpose of the inquiry and that to draw deductions seemed to him to be a scurrilous betrayal of the hospitality of the South.

We were impatient for the court's opinion, but the question of prayer was still dominant. Our associate, Neal, insisted that the court should take judicial notice of the fact that the people of the world were divided into numerous sects and that we differed from the Attorney General in his statement that the case did not involve a religious question. This aroused Sue Hicks. "I have set over here and remained quiet these three days," he said, but on behalf of the court he wished to point out that during a period of five years every time he had been in a court where a minister had happened to stray, proceedings were opened with prayer. He wanted to know why we objected to prayer if evolution did not contradict the Bible. The Judge explained that he had had no purpose "to influence anybody wrongfully" and hoped that prayer might "influence somebody rightfully. . . . I do not think it hurts anybody and I think it may help somebody."

The next order of business was a request by General Stewart to be permitted to apologize for rude words to myself in court the day before. He was permitted. He apologized. Thereupon Neal insisted that Stewart likewise apologize to Mr. Darrow for having called him an "infidel" and "agnostic." Stewart replied, "So long as I speak what I conceive to be the truth, I apologize to no man." (Loud applause from the audience.)

Darrow explained that he did not except to General Stewart's statement; that as to the word "agnostic" he was proud to admit that he knew nothing of subjects on which so very many ignorant men were sure. As to the word "infidel" Darrow insisted it had no meaning whatever; that everybody is an infidel who does not believe in the prevailing religion. "Among the Saracens," he continued blandly, "everybody is an infidel who does not believe with them. In a Mohammedan country everybody is an infidel that does not believe with them, and among Christians everybody is an infidel that is not a Christian, or at least does not profess to be." Further, Darrow added that he hated to be accused of such a foolish thing as infidelity, because everybody at some time or another is guilty of that. The court asked General Stewart what he thought of this. Stewart answered that he thought "we were wasting a lot of valuable time."

This débris having been cleared away, Judge Raulston was ready to read his opinion. He requested order and turning to the photographers said, "If you gentlemen want to make my picture, make it now."

The motion to quash was overruled; the demurrer was denied.

The jury was then called in. Several days had passed. We were now about ready to proceed with the evidence. A newspaper reporter, however, interrupted: "Can we have chairs, Judge?" The court: "Gentlemen, I don't believe the whole courtroom should expect the Judge should look after chairs. Let the

Sheriff do that, appeal to the Sheriff." General Mc-
Kenzie objected that people carried off the chairs of
the attorneys and remarked that "we are a necessary
evil in the courtroom." The sheriff announced that
no chairs should be purloined from attorneys or from
the press. Juror Thompson then requested electric
fans, "if it ain't out of order."

General Stewart opened for the prosecution, Malone
for the defense. Dudley Field Malone, one-time dar-
ling of the Democratic party, a former aide of Bryan—
Malone, spruce and well-groomed from his trim shoes
to his unwrinkled soft silk collar even in the heat of
Dayton, rose to speak. The newspaper men remarked
upon his well-fitting Metropolitan shirts. They were
made in England. Mine came from the same shop, but
they received no public commendation: "Hays was
thick-set, stocky, democratic-looking, with rough shirt,
open at the neck."

Malone did not proceed far without interruption.
General McKenzie objected to the explanation of the
defense case to the jury, insisting that Malone could
not discuss evolution or the Bible, since the only question in the case was whether man was descended from
a lower order of animals. For Malone to discuss
other issues, said McKenzie, "would be like a couple of
gentlemen over in my country where they were engaged
in a lawsuit before a Justice of the Peace. There were
a large number of witnesses. Finally, after conference, the lawyers came back and one of them reported
'if your Honor please, the witnesses in this case, some
of them are not very well and others are awfully igno-

rant, and we have just agreed among ourselves to dispense with the evidence and argue the case.' " General McKenzie informed Malone that "the only mistake the good Lord made is that he did not withhold the completion of the job until he consulted you." Mr. Malone: "I rather think you are right."

The witnesses were sworn. Little boys in short trousers, girls in pinafores, all brightly polished for the occasion, the school superintendent and other leading members of Dayton's intelligentsia stood on one side. On the other, Maynard Metcalf of Johns Hopkins, Kirtley F. Mather of Harvard, Wilbur Nelson, State Geologist, Dr. Jacob Lippman, Winterton C. Curtis, Charles Hubbard Judd, Fay Cooper Cole, Horatio H. Newman, and others of the most eminent scientists of the day.

Walter White, school superintendent, testified that Scopes had used the book "Hunter's Civil Biology." Scopes had said that he could not teach the book without teaching the part pertaining to evolution.

The prosecution offered in evidence and asked the court to take judicial notice of the King James' version of the Bible. Objection was made on the ground that the King James' Bible could not be accepted in evidence unless some witness was ready to testify that that was *the* Bible. We pointed out that there was the Douay version of the Bible used by the Catholics, and the Hebrew Bible; that the original manuscripts, in Hebrew, Aramaic and Greek, had been lost for hundreds of years, and that all one had to-day were translations of translations; that the earliest copy of the

Old Testament in Hebrew now in existence was made
in the Eleventh Century, although there were partial
copies made in the Ninth and Tenth Centuries; that
the oldest Greek manuscripts, except a few fragments,
belonged to the Fourth and Fifth Centuries. Each
part claims its own version to be inspired. We argued
that the statute did not refer to the King James'
version. There was no law under which the court could
take judicial notice of that or any other version in
a case which involved *the* Bible.

The Court: Mr. Hays, would you raise the same objection if they attempted to file any other Bible?

Mr. Hays: Not if some one testified that the King
James' or any other version is *the* Bible; then the jury
could believe or disbelieve the statement.

The Court: Let your objection be overruled. Let it be
introduced as *the* Bible.

Howard Morgan, a clean-cut youngster of about
fourteen, thereupon testified that he was in Scopes' class
and that Scopes taught the following:

"He said that the earth was once a hot molten mass, too
hot for plant or animal life to exist upon it; in the sea the
earth cooled off; there was a little germ of one cell organism formed, and this organism kept evolving until it got
to be a land animal, and it kept on evolving, and from
this was man."

Scopes also had classified man as a "mammal." Darrow took up the cross-examination:

Q. Now, Howard, what do you mean by classify?

A. Well, it means classify these animals we mentioned,
that men were just the same as them.

Q. In other words, he did not say a cat was the same as a man?

A. No, sir; that man had reasoning power, that these animals did not.

Q. There is some doubt about that, but that is what he said, is it?

Darrow inquired whether Scopes had not taught that mammals were animals that had hair and suckled their young, and that among them were dogs and horses, monkeys, cows, man and whales.

A. Yes, sir; but I don't know about the whales. He said all those other ones.

Q. Well, did he tell you anything else that was wicked?

A. No, not that I remember of.

Darrow asked benevolently about the development of life, the teaching that the first life was in the sea; that it developed into life on the land and finally into the organism known as man. And then to Howard, "It has not hurt you any, has it? A. No, sir." The witness testified that there was nothing in the book that said that man was descended from monkey, not that he "knew of."

The next day Bryan arose and absolutely and unequivocally refused to be a mammal. Other people could do about it as they pleased, but as for him, he would have none of it. He pointed out a diagram in this corrupting textbook classifying animals beginning with the protozoa indicating different varieties in separate species—protozoa, sponges, insects, fishes, amphibia, reptiles, birds and mammals, some 3,500 of them, "and among them," said Bryan, "is man. They

left him there with 3,499 other mammals, among them
skunks and other animals that smell bad. They have
an odor that extends beyond the circumference of this
circle." No, Bryan would not admit he was a mammal.
One of the newspaper wags afterwards pointed out
that according to Darrow's test, perhaps Bryan was
right, for he neither had hair nor did he suckle his
young.

Bryan protested further. According to the scientists, man was not even descended from American monkeys, but from Old World monkeys. In order to make
his argument clear, Bryan dragged in the famous
Leopold-Loeb case, quoting the words of Darrow that
children were the product of their environment. Darrow objected. The court asked on what ground.
Darrow said this was obviously intended to create
prejudice. Mr. Bryan denied this, whereupon Darrow
interjected: "What's the use of it then?"

Dr. Maynard M. Metcalf, witness for the defense,
took the stand. Objection was made to his testimony
on the ground that the theory of evolution had nothing
to do with the case. We were permitted, however, to
examine him in order to raise the question of the mate-
riality of the evidence. As Dr. Metcalf testified to some
of the wonders of science, giving a modest guess of the
age of the earth at six hundred million years, as he
traced through the countless ages the development of
life on earth, the crowd in the courtroom, awed and silent, listened tensely to the words of science which they
feared might upset their faith. He explained that
"evolution and the theories of evolution are funda-

mentally different things. The fact of evolution is . . .
perfectly and absolutely clear. There are dozens of
theories . . . as to the methods by which evolution has
been brought about. . . . The term evolution in general means the whole series of changes which have taken
place during hundreds of millions of years which have
produced from lowly beginnings . . . organisms of
much more complex character."

The statements of various scientists sought to clear
up the misunderstanding as to what evolution is. It
was "the most satisfactory explanation of the observed
facts relating to the universe, to our world and all life
on it" or "a great scientific generalization, the only
relational explanation of an overwhelming mass of
facts."

Then we settled down to tell the story of evolution
in as bizarre and breath-taking a setting as that amazing story has ever had. The geologists read from the
rocks "the procession of life on the long road from the
one-celled bit of primitive protoplasm to the present
assemblage of varied creatures, including man." How
many varieties have there been? According to Herbert
Spencer, "we may safely estimate the number of species
that have existed, and are existing on earth, at not less
than ten million." Which is the most rational theory
about these ten million of species? "Is it most likely,"
said Dr. Winterton Curtis, "that there have been ten
million of special creations? Or is it most likely that
by continual modifications, due to a change of circumstances, ten million varieties have been produced, as
varieties are being produced still? And if the evidence

indicates that all other species have arisen by evolution, is it probable that man—whose bodily structure and functions are so nearly identical with those of the mammalia and particularly with primates—that man arose in a different fashion?"

The four bespectacled old ladies who sat in the front row next to the amazed correspondent of the London *Daily News* shook their bonneted heads in stern disapproval of such nonsense.

Rocks of one hundred million years ago show no traces of plant and animal life. Fifty million years elapse and then in the Paleozoic era are found strata containing fossils in abundance, but as yet there are no signs of backboned animals. Then in somewhat younger beds are fragmentary remains of primitive fishes. Toward the end of this era the rocks, formed of desert sand and swamps, contain footprints and petrified bones of amphibians and reptiles, the first animals with backbone that breathed through lungs. Another twenty-five million years and we come to the Mesozoic era, the age of reptiles, when petrified remains tell of large and ferocious animals with feathers to fly, claws on their forelimbs and teeth in their jaws—a transition form between reptiles and birds. And in those same rocks are signs of very primitive mammals.

The four bespectacled old ladies in the front row clutched their Bible as though indeed the Rock of Ages were splintering.

In answer to the usual suggestion that the theory of evolution is based on the survival of the strongest, Kirtley F. Mather, Harvard geologist, said:

"For the most part the reptiles were small brained and large bodied, they placed their trust in strength of talon and claw, rather than in mentality or agility. Observing the earth at that time one could not help but feel that no good could possibly come from that welter of blood-thirstiness and cruelty. Yet the small minority of puny mammals, present then, was so endowed with instinct, such as parental love for offspring, that at the end of the Mesozoic era it became the dominant form of life on land."

Millions of years bring the Cenozoic era, when the rocks show traces of a variety of mammals and the first record of a primate appears. It was a small rat-like quadruped, with toes terminating in horny nails and with teeth adapted not for tearing flesh, grinding grain, or gnawing nuts, but for eating herbs, fruits and eggs like those of man.

A fragment of jaw has been found in the banks of an Indian stream, the jaw of an animal which lived over two million years ago and which had teeth resembling those of a great ape or man.

Four gold-rimmed spectacles on the front row glittered ominously. Fundamentalist storekeepers and farmers saw the danger.

In Java, some thirty years ago, were found fossil remains consisting of a skull cap, two or three teeth and a left thigh bone. The fossil-bearing rock was over a half million years old. The specimens were scattered over twenty yards of space and were discovered at different times. There is no proof that they belonged to the same individual. But the anatomical characters were human. The brain ca-

pacity was somewhat greater than that of the brainiest
apes, but less than that of the smallest-brained man.
The forehead receded, there was a heavy ridge of bone
above the eyes, but the being stood and walked erect
upon his hind limbs.

A relic of four hundred thousand years was found
in Germany in 1907 in gravels deposited by the rivers
flowing from the melting ice of one of the interglacial
periods.   It consisted of the single lower ape-like jaw
of the so-called Heidelberg man.   But the jaw was too
narrow to have admitted of articulate speech; the teeth
were large and the creature had no chin.   Another hundred and fifty thousand years and there lived the Dawn
man, remains of which were found at Piltdown, Sussex,
England.   These consisted of the crushed skull of a
woman and a jaw scarcely distinguishable from that
of a chimpanzee.

A shirt-sleeved bailiff with a revolver butt protrud-
ing from under his gallus-strap pushed past the four
ladies on the front row to stop "one of them city-
slicker writin' men" from New York from smoking in
the courtroom.

The evidences thereafter are clearer.   By the fourth
interglacial period men in Europe were compelled to
make their homes in the caves of the rocks and for
fifty thousand years we can read their story from the
débris around their ancient hearths.   They buried their
dead, and more than a score of practically complete
skeletons and hundreds of fragmentary bones have been
found in France, Spain, Germany, Belgium and Aus-
tria.   These people, known as the Neanderthal race,

were massively built, with long arms and short legs, in height averaging five feet three for the men and a little less for the women. The head was long and narrow; above the eyes was a heavy bony ridge, back of which the forehead retreated abruptly. The nose was low and broad, the upper lip projecting; the jaw was retreating. The head hung forward on a massive chest. The thigh bone was curved, the knee bent, showing that this man walked in a. semi-erect position.

Then came the Cro-Magnons, living in Southern Europe. Five essentially complete skeletons testify to this race which lived perhaps twenty-five to fifty thousand years ago. They were tall, strong and intelligent and had prominent cheek-bones like the North American Indian. They manufactured implements and that they had artistic ability is indicated by pictures on the walls of caves in Southern France. About ten thousand years ago they were displaced by the first races of mankind in existence to-day.

The first row four turned expectant eyes upon their Defender. Surely Brother Bryan could suffer in silence no longer.

There were other phases of the story.

Like structures show a fundamental unity in animals in spite of the diversity of form or function. The flipper of the whale, the wing of a bird, the foreleg of a horse, show on close examination the same structure as the human arm. Anatomically man bears a striking resemblance to the anthropoid apes: bone for bone, muscle for muscle, nerve for nerve, and in many other details

they are similar. Man is many degrees closer anatomically to the great apes than these are to the true
monkeys.

All animals show vestigial attributes. Man has been
said to be a veritable museum of antiquities, containing
in his body no less than one hundred and eighty structures, probably useful at some stage of development,
but functionless to-day. Among these are the vermi-
form appendix, an abbreviated tail with a set of caudal
muscles, scalp muscles used by other animals to erect
the hair, gill slits, miniature third eyelids (these function with reptiles and birds). "Heredity is stubborn
and tenacious, clinging persistently to all that the
race has once possessed." Even in a whale, deeply
buried beneath the thick cushion of blubber in the pelvic
region, lies a little handful of bones, immovable and
useless.

"What's that about a whale?" utters one of the bespectacled old ladies, thinking of Jonah.

The development of the fœtus in the mother's womb
shows the various ancestral forms, the earliest stages
suggesting the most remote ancestors. Step for step,
the embryology of man is almost precisely like that of
other primates, especially anthropoids. Only in the
later stages does it take on distinctly human characteristics. The parts begin to appear at first without
resemblance to those of a human being. The arms and
legs start as little rounded knobs without fingers or
toes. They grow for months and are wholly dispro-
portionate. Gradually they elongate and toes and fingers appear. At an early stage, perhaps at the end

of a month, the embryo has a tail about one-fourth as long as the rest of the body. It also has gill slits which later come to play an important part in connection with the function of hearing. At six months the body is covered with a complete coating of hair which it loses before birth. The embryo becomes a human being when born, but the changes are significant.

"Obscene, that's what it is," murmurs the chorus.

Man himself is a witness of, and plays a hand in, the present-day evolutionary process. Sportsmen breed race-horses; farmers—even Fundamentalists— are breeding types of pigs; Luther Burbank has changed vegetables and flowers.

After all, questioned the scientists, why the excitement? No one is surprised at evidences that animals, other than man, are related. Sometimes the evidence is clear. One can directly trace the development of the horse through a series of intermediate forms, from Eohippus, of lower Eocene times, an animal eleven inches high, living in North America, with forefeet containing four-hoofed toes. Dr. Winterton 'C. Curtis said:

"The great antiquity of man, the existence of an earlier period of beings, man-like, but intermediate between man and the other primates, together with the facts of man's anatomy, his embryology, his physiological reactions, even his mentality, all point to bodily kinship with the rest of living nature.

"It is not that men come from monkeys, but that men, monkeys, and apes all come from a common mammalian ancestry millions of years in the past."

This was a thrilling fairy-tale to the natives of Tennessee. They were fearful, they were skeptical, but they listened with bated breath. A letter dated August 29, 1922, from Woodrow Wilson to Professor Curtis was quoted:

"May it not suffice for me to say in reply to your letter of August 25th that of course, like every other man of intelligence and education, I do believe in organic evolution. It surprises me that at this late date such questions should be raised."

"Must be a forgery," was the whispered comment. "Woodrow Wilson was a Democrat."

The marvelous story got into the court record either through testimony on the stand of Dr. Metcalf or through statements read and presented to enable the Appellate Court to determine whether or not the evidence was material. For in this case in Tennessee, involving evolution and the Bible, it was held by Judge Raulston that evidence on either subject was immaterial since the only question involved was whether Scopes had taught that man was descended from a lower order of animals. Anyhow, what could be the purpose of this evidence for, as General McKenzie said, "Every schoolboy knows the Bible in Tennessee." The doctrine of evolution is clear—"God threw a piece of protoplasm into the sea and said, 'Now be a good boy and behave yourself and in six million years I will come around and make a man of you.'" In moving words General McKenzie referred once more to his love for counsel for the defense, alluded to the men from Tennessee who had become great lawyers in New York, and in a fiery peroration advised the court "we have done crossed the Rubicon." The court asked him if his position was that reasonable minds could not differ as to the method of Creation, "that is, that man was created complete by God and in one act?" to which McKenzie replied that that was exactly right. Darrow interjected, "Let me ask a question: When it said in His own image, do you think that that meant the physical man?"

McKenzie: I say that, although I know it is awfully hard of our Maker to look like a lot of fellows who are profusely ugly, to say he favored the Master.

Darrow: Wait a minute, Colonel, do you think the physical man is like God and when you see man you see a picture of God?

McKenzie: Like unto Him and made in His image.

"In other words," Darrow inquired, "do you think God looks like you?"

Malone entered the fray with a speech on freedom of education, which was one of the high spots of the trial. He contended that we had a right to introduce evidence to show that the theory of evolution is not necessarily in conflict with the Bible, "also we maintain we have the right to call witnesses to show there is more than one theory of creation in the Bible. Mr. Bryan is not the only exponent of the Bible; Judge McKenzie is not the only defender of the word of God." Malone told the story of the burning of the great library at Alexandria by the Mohammedans. It is

said that one of the generals had asked his adversary
not to "destroy this great library because it contains
all the truth that has been gathered," to which the hostile general replied that the Koran contained all the
truth; that if the library contained the same truth,
the library was useless. If it contained anything else,
it did not contain the truth. Mr. Bryan had said that
the trial was a duel to the death. "Does the opposition
mean by duel that our witnesses shall be strapped to
the board and that the opposition alone shall carry
the sword; are the witnesses who testify to the accuracy
of our theory—our only weapon—to be taken from us?

"There is never a duel with the truth. The truth always
wins and we are not afraid of it; the truth is no coward.
The truth does not need the law. The truth does not need
the forces of government. The truth does not need Mr.
Bryan. The truth is imperishable, eternal and immortal,
and needs no human agency to support it. We are ready.
We feel we stand with progress. We feel we stand with
science. We feel we stand with intelligence. We feel we
stand with fundamental freedom in America. We are not
afraid. Where is the fear? We defy it; we ask your
Honor to admit the evidence as a matter of correct law,
as a matter of sound procedure and as a matter of justice
to the defense in this case."

The courtroom rang with acclaim. The bailiff was
pounding his desk. "I'm not rappin' to keep order,"
he explained, "I'm poundin' this desk for applause."
H. L. Mencken strode up the aisle. While we gathered
around Malone with our congratulations, it was clear
to us that the approval of Mencken would be particu-

larly gratifying to the orator. "Dudley," said Mencken, clapping him on the back, "that was the loudest speech I ever heard." Somehow the atmosphere was changed by this fervent appeal. People even forgot that Malone and his wife had registered at the Hotel Aqua as Dudley Malone and Doris Stevens.

Malone's Gaelic eloquence was aroused on the technical question of the admissibility of evidence. In connection with the Judge's apparent determination to prevent the jury from hearing the evidence, we referred to the peculiar procedure in the State of Tennessee, first that the defense is obliged to try the case on the theory of the prosecution; secondly, that the jury is excluded, both during hearings on the law and during evidence on the facts. It was suggestive of an occasion, we said, when a plaintiff, having finished his argument, the court with a fine Irish wit, turned to defendant's counsel:

"The court doesn't wish to hear from the defendant. To hear both sides has a tindency to confuse the court."

The discussion was closed by General Stewart. He insisted that if he had to choose between religion and science, he would choose religion:

"I say scientific investigation is nothing but a theory and will never be anything but a theory. Show me some reasonable cause to believe it is not. They can't do it."

Defense Counsel: Give us a chance.
Gen. Stewart: A chance to what?
Defense Counsel: To prove it, to show you what it is.
Gen. Stewart: . . . That charge strikes at the very

vitals of civilization and of Christianity and is not entitled to a chance. . . .

  (Applause and laughter.)

The following day the court promptly held that the
scientific evidence was not admissible. An exception
was noted on the ground that "for the Court of Rhea
County to try to determine whether or not this law is
unreasonable without informing itself by evidence, assumes plenary knowledge of matters which have been
the subject of study of scientists for generations."

Mr. Bryan then insisted that he wished to cross-
examine the witnesses whose statements had been read
into the record. Our objection was based on rather
an interesting reason. While, if the testimony had
been admitted, cross-examination would of course have
followed, yet we had merely presented the statements
to show what testimony we could have adduced. Cross-
examination would have shown that the scientists, while
religious men—for we chose only that kind—still did
not believe in the Virgin birth and other miracles. It
was felt by us that if the cause of free education was
ever to be won, it would need the support of millions of
intelligent churchgoing people who didn't question theological miracles.

Then occurred the interesting colloquy for which
Darrow was cited for contempt. The court asked the
purpose of cross-examination, to which Darrow responded, "to create prejudice, your Honor." The
court reminded Darrow that he must always expect
the court to rule correctly, whereupon Darrow said
that we were taking our exceptions in order to pro-

tect our rights in some other tribunal, adding, "Now, that is plain enough, isn't it?"

The Court: I hope you don't think the court is trying to be unfair.

To which Darrow, hitching up one suspender strap, drawled out the caustic retort, "Your Honor has the right to hope." A prolonged but electric silence ensued. The hearing was adjourned.

During the week-end the atmosphere seethed with excitement. The Tennesseeans have considerable regard for the dignity of the court. It was felt that Darrow's remarks had been willfully contemptuous. On the one hand respect for the court seemed to demand that something be done about it. But there was the haunting fear that if Darrow were cited for contempt the court might have to punish him. Darrow in jail would be a fearful antagonist. The case was sufficiently dramatic without adding dynamite. Darrow had intended to apologize but learning that the court wished to take action, felt that he should wait.

On Monday, at the opening of court, the Judge read aloud his version of the occurrence. When the matter appeared in consecutive fashion, it seemed to us of the defense even more satisfactory than did the original colloquy. Darrow was cited for contempt and was held, pending the return of the citation, under bond of $5,000.

Later in the day Darrow rendered his apology. The purport was that whatever a lawyer might think of a judge as an individual, or of his acts or decisions,

yet, as a member of the bar, he should never fail to show
respect for the institution of the court. The apology
was accepted. Judge Raulston showed mercy. He
gazed benignly upon Mr. Darrow and spoke solemnly:
"The Man that I believe came into the world to save
man from sin, the Man that died on the cross that man
might be redeemed, taught that it was godly to forgive
. . . the Saviour died on the cross pleading with God
for the men who crucified Him. I believe in that Christ.
I believe in these principles. I accept Colonel Darrow's
apology. . . . We commend him to go back home and
learn in his heart the words of the Man who said, 'If
ye thirst come unto me and I will give thee life.' "

The defense offered in evidence the message of Governor Peay approving the anti-evolution bill. There
was intimation here that probably the law would never
be enforced. Then we offered a new textbook called
"Biology and Human Welfare," by Peabody & Hunt,
recently adopted by the State Commission. This book
referred to Darwin, also to mammals. It was contended that all of this threw light on the public policy
of the State.

Thousands of people had come to court to listen to
the summation of the case. The room was jammed.
There was some question about its safety. A rough
platform had been erected next to the courthouse, and
proceedings were adjourned to the courtyard. On one
side of the platform were the attorneys for the defense;
on the other, the prosecution; in the middle, the
Judge's bench. Below, under the spreading trees, was
the audience. And what an audience! In the front

rows the newspaper men sitting on the bare ground and
scribbling furiously away, using knees, platform props
and the shoulders of their neighbors for copypaper
rests. On one side were adherents of Darrow, youngsters for the most part (some from the vicinity, some
from far away who had hitch-hiked the distance). Now
and then Darrow would glance down at them over his
spectacles, as if drawing strength from his supporters.
And on the other side of the square, beneath the platform, were the Bryanites, gnarled farmers, their brows
knit with the struggle of following the swift battle
of the giants; tight-lipped women with weary lines of
drudgery around their eyes, confused but confident that
Righteousness would prevail; stern visaged Men of
God, some of them clothed in stifling broadcloth beneath a pitiless Tennessee sun, which shone alike on
believers and skeptics.

The jury was called to the box. Another quarrel
arose over a side issue. Fronting the twelve good men
and true, was a sign about ten feet long: "Read your
Bible." We objected. The prosecution protested our
disrespect. Discussion was long and heated. The sign
was removed. Tennessee farmers were shocked. The
case proceeded. The defense offered in evidence a
Catholic Bible. The court asked whether it was in
English. The court accepted it. The Tennessee farmers were stunned. A Catholic Bible and on the Judge's
bench! Judge Raulston, after a little cautious scan-
ning, remarked that the story of Genesis there was not
very different. We contended that if any word differed from the King James' version, we could argue to

the jury that the Bible was a man-made, not a God-made, document. Then was offered a Hebrew Bible, not in English. This was accepted. But to our surprise we were not permitted to call a witness to translate the story of Genesis. The judge was wiser than he knew.

To the Mansion—the euphonious name for the ramshackle dwelling which we of the defense occupied—Rabbi Herman Rosenwasser of San Francisco had brought a chart of Hebrew characters. It was the story of Genesis. Night after night he conducted a class made up of the assembled body of scientists and lawyers. His method was as follows: He would translate the Hebrew into German and we had a choice of perhaps six German words for each Hebrew word. He then translated the German into English and we had a choice of perhaps six English words for every German word. By the time we got through we could make Genesis say pretty nearly what we wanted. Thus, God did not "create" the earth—he "evolved" it, or "set it in motion," which would do quite as well. The words in Psalms, usually rendered, "He hath made a decree which shall not pass," are properly translated, "He hath made a law of nature which He doth not transgress." Our new translation would have startled the faithful.

In response to a query as to whether the defense had any more evidence to offer, I stated that we wished to call Mr. Bryan as an expert on the Bible. I have never yet discovered whether this was a greater surprise to Darrow or to Bryan. Darrow turned to

Malone: "You examine him, Dudley." Malone answered, "Oh, no." Darrow turned to me. I shook my head.

Then came the battle that was the quintessence of the whole case. Perhaps never before in the history of the world has a witness under cross-examination attempted rationally to defend beliefs not based on rational reasoning.

Bryan took the stand conditionally. "If your Honor please, I insist that Mr. Darrow be put on the stand, and Mr. Malone and Mr. Hays."

The Court: Call anybody you desire. Ask him any questions you wish.

Mr. Bryan: Then we will call all three of them.

Darrow started in. Slouching back in his chair at first, later on shooting forward as he hammered a question home across the deal table that separated him from his famous antagonist, Darrow, reading from the Bible on his knee, looked like a benign Sunday-school superintendent, a bit deshabille perhaps, lecturing a class on a hot Sabbath afternoon. Bryan assured him that he accepted the Bible literally; that he believed that a whale swallowed Jonah, although Bryan thought it was a fish rather than a whale. Darrow asked whether this was a "mine" run of fish or made specially for the purpose. Bryan was not prepared to say. When he was asked whether the Lord purposefully made a fish big enough to swallow Jonah, he answered affirmatively, adding, "One miracle is just as easy for me to believe as another," to which Darrow responded, "It is for me too." When asked whether

he thought that Joshua had made the sun stand still,
Bryan replied that he accepted the Bible literally.
Bryan had never pondered what would have happened
to the earth had the sun stood still; the God he believed
in would have taken care of that.

Darrow: Don't you know it would have been converted
into a molten mass of matter?
Bryan: You testify to that when you get on the stand.
I will give you a chance.
Darrow: You have never investigated that subject?
Bryan: I don't think I have ever had the question asked.
Darrow: Or ever thought of it?
Bryan: I have been too busy on things that I thought
were of more importance than that.

Bryan thought the world was created in 4004 B.C.,
the date appearing in the King James' version of the
Bible. The calculation was made by Bishop Ussher
who figured it out from the ages of the prophets.
Ussher fixed the time more definitely. According to
the Bishop, the year was not only 4004 B.C. but the
date was the 23rd day of October, and at nine o'clock
in the morning, to which some infidel voice in the audience added, "Eastern Standard Time." Darrow inquired how long ago the flood occurred. Bryan,
cautious, first wished to see Ussher's calculations.
From this he figured the date as 2348 B.C.

Darrow: When was that flood?
Bryan: I would not attempt to fix the date. The date
is fixed as suggested this morning.
Darrow: But what do you think that the Bible, itself,
says? Don't you know how it was arrived at?

Bryan: I never made a calculation.
Darrow: A calculation from what?
Bryan: I could not say.
Darrow: What do you think?
Bryan: I do not think about things I don't think about.
Darrow: Do you think about things you do think about?
Bryan: Well, sometimes.

No evidence had ever satisfied Bryan that there was any civilization more than 5,000 years old. He believed that the human race did not run back more than 4,300 years. He did not know whether any scientist would agree with him but he was not sure that the matter was important. On one occasion when the crowd applauded, Bryan turned to Darrow: "And these are the people you call yokels," to which Darrow responded, "Those who are applauding you, I do call yokels." Bryan traced all language back to the fall of the Tower of Babel somewhere around 2218 B.C., never having seen any evidence that would persuade him that languages had developed otherwise. He had never studied philology. Bryan was sure that the world was created in six days, but not that these were 24-hour days. That was helpful to our case for if a Fundamentalist concedes anything to interpretation, he concedes his whole case.

As the drama developed, the amazing chorus below the actors sighed and groaned, laughed and grumbled, "hurrahed" or "amened" in alternate triumph or despair.

Continually Mr. Stewart objected to the examination, calling it a harangue. Mr. Bryan bravely insisted upon proceeding, stating that he was simply trying "to protect the word of God against the greatest atheist or agnostic in the United States,"—a statement which brought loud applause. Bryan believed that the first woman was Eve; that she was actually and literally made out of Adam's rib. When asked if he had ever discovered where Cain got his wife, he answered sharply: "I leave the agnostics to hunt for her." He did not know whether there were other people on earth at that time. He believed the sun was made on the fourth day and that there was evening and morning without the sun. Yet creation might have gone on for a long time—millions of years—for a day is to the Lord as a thousand years. He believed the story of the temptation of Eve by the serpent and that all the troubles of man arose from that little *contretemps* in the Garden of Eden. Women suffered torture in childbirth because of Eve's dereliction, which reminds one that when opiates were first known objection was made to their use until some one reminded the theologians that God put Adam to sleep before he removed his rib. Bryan was asked whether he thought that God had made the serpent crawl on his belly because of his participation in the temptation. He did. "How do you suppose the snake got along before that?" queried Darrow.

The day ended with Bryan protesting that

the only purpose Mr. Darrow has is to slur at the Bible. . . . I want the world to know that this man, who does not believe in a God, is trying to use a court in Tennessee—

Darrow: I object to that.

Bryan: to slur at it. . . .

Darrow: I object to your statement. I am examining you on your fool ideas that no intelligent Christian on earth believes.

The Court: Court is adjourned until nine o'clock tomorrow morning.

The examination, starting calmly, had grown in tensity. At times Darrow and Bryan rose and glowered at each other, shaking their fists. There were constant interruptions by State Counsel, General McKenzie once stating that we would "no more file the testimony of Colonel Bryan as a part of the record than they would file a rattlesnake and handle it themselves." In unison we shouted, "We will file it. We will file it. File every word of it." But we didn't. The Supreme Court of Tennessee attended to that.[1]

This was the evening of the seventh day.

Several times there was cheering from one side or the other and when at last it was over, the followers of Darrow rose up and swarmed on the platform, keen to seize the hand of their champion.

Few came to Bryan. The man who, up to then, had everywhere been followed as a conquering hero, stood apart, almost alone, a strange tired expression on his face as he looked into the twilight that was closing all about him. One could not but feel a deep pity for the fallen Commoner.

Much had been accomplished by this examination.

[1] John Thomas Scopes *vs.* The State of Tennessee, 152 Tenn. 424 (1926).

Bryan had conceded that he interpreted the Bible in at least one respect. He must have agreed that others have that right. We had expected to force Bryan to admit that there was nothing in the Bible contrary to evolution. In fact, much can be found to support that theory—which should not be surprising— since almost all causes, however contradictory, can find support.

At one point, Stewart, in objecting, had expostulated that the examination "is not worth anything to them, if your Honor please, even for the record in the Supreme Court"; to which we answered, "Is it not worth something to us on the Story of Creation, if Mr. Bryan, as a Bible student, agrees that you cannot take the Bible as literally true?" Stewart: "The Bible speaks for itself." "But," we countered, "do you mean to say the Bible itself tells whether these are parables? Does it?"

When, on the morning of the eighth day we appeared in Court ready to continue the examination, the Judge not only refused to permit us to proceed, but stated that he was "pleased to expunge this testimony, given by Mr. Bryan on yesterday, from the records of this Court, and it will not be further considered."

Since, according to the interpretation of the Court, the only question in the case was whether Scopes had taught that man was descended from a "lower order of animals," a fact that was conceded from the beginning, we were ready for the verdict of the jury. These involuntary exiles were called in. Indignant at their regular exclusion from the courtroom, many of them would have voted to acquit Scopes had there been the slightest loophole. Darrow told the men of the jury that he was glad to see them, that he had missed them during the trial; that he hoped that nobody would stand out against a verdict of guilty because that would interfere with our appeal.

The Court instructed the jury. There was some discussion about the amount of the fine, which under the Tennessee Constitution is fixed by the jury. It appeared that the usual fine for transporting liquor was $100, and it was suggested that there should be no greater fine for transporting information. The Court told the jury that if they wished to assess the minimum fine, this would be implied merely by a verdict "guilty" without naming a figure. The Court would then impose a minimum as "that is our practice in whisky cases." Darrow said we did not care who named the fine, that we would not take an exception either way. The matter later turned out to be of vital consequence.

Scopes was found guilty. Before judgment was pronounced he stood before the Judge and said calmly:

"Your Honor, I feel that I have been convicted for violation of an unjust statute. I will continue in the future, as I have in the past, to oppose this law in any way I can. Any other action would be in violation of my ideal of academic freedom."

Many, including a Canadian newspaper correspondent, made speeches of felicitation; the Court itself made a little oration, referring among other things to the fact that "truth crushed to earth will rise again." I asked his Honor to permit me to send him a copy of Darwin's "Descent of Man" and "Origin of Species." I came back from Tennessee with a copy of the Bible. When the Court reads Darwin, he will discount every scientific statement in it. I shall do the same with the Bible.

Within a few days of the trial, William Jennings Bryan died. Had this happened to Darrow, Tennessee would have regarded it as a judgment of God. As it was, Bryan was gathered to the angels. Inquiry is often made as to the effect of the trial on him. Did he die from age, disease, disappointment or overeating? It is a moot question. No doubt he was much upset. His first entry into the courtroom was greeted with applause; his every word in debate was accepted as from a prophet. Then came the revealing encounter with Darrow. Probably he himself never realized the depth of his humiliation, for he had had the support of a large quantity, and rather a fair quality, of ignorance and bigotry, but undoubtedly he was chagrined.

The youngsters of the Dayton High School gave a dance in honor of Clarence Darrow. He attended, danced and even smoked cigarettes with them. They seemed to recognize that this was their battle; that, although perhaps fought on different lines, it represented the issue between the eagerness of youth and the fear of age. Any pleasure, unconnected with the church, had been condemned by their elders. Smoking, dancing, free association between girls and boys,

games and movies on Sunday had been their issues at
home. Here were champions indeed. And we of the
defense seemed to enjoy some popularity in Dayton.
We "mixed" more than the Bryanites. And when the
boys came to us from the telegraph office, they received
liberal tips. A dollar gratuity in Dayton was widely
heralded by the recipient, and not wholly disapproved
by the denizens.

Argument on the appeal was heard in June, 1926.
Tennessee lawyers, at first hesitant, flocked to our
standard. Robert Keebler of Memphis, and John R.
Neal of Knoxville, had been with us from the beginning,
but we were joined by other leaders of the bar, among
them, Thomas Malone and Edward E. Colton of Nash-
ville. Our arguments in the court below were developed
on appeal, but our local associates laid particular
stress upon the indefiniteness of the law. This would
give the court a way out. A decision on that ground
would not offend public sensibilities.

Argument before the Supreme Court was in a far
different atmosphere from that of the trial. Everything was calm, dignified and quiet, though intense.
Bryan had passed away, public interest had largely
subsided, Tennessee resented the world-wide ridicule
the case had aroused.

As was expected, the court disregarded the contentions concerning religious preferences and the police
power of the State. It dealt chiefly with the question
of the indefiniteness of the law. Two judges, in a
prevailing opinion, held that the law was definite. A
third judge, concurring in the opinion, likewise held

that the law was definite but interpreted it quite differently from the other two and to the effect that the law merely prohibited the teaching of materialistic theory. The fourth judge dissented on the ground that the law was indefinite and thus unconstitutional. Had the court rested there, we should have been well satisfied. We should then have appealed to the Supreme Court of the United States, our final goal. But the decision was a subtle one. Determined to prevent an appeal, the court, having decided that the law was constitutional, nevertheless reversed the conviction on the ground that the fine had been improperly imposed by the judge, a question not raised on appeal and on which no exception had been taken. And this, in spite of the fact that, in prior cases which arose in connection with fines for violation of the liquor laws, the Supreme Court had justified the imposition of a fine by the presiding judge where the minimum had been imposed.

The court did more than this. It not only reversed the verdict, but it also directed the Attorney General to *nolle prosse* all proceedings in this "bizarre" case, thus practically agreeing with Governor Peay in his message accompanying the passage of the law that it was a statute which was not to be enforced. For obviously, if the Supreme Court disapproved enforcement against Scopes or prosecution of Scopes as a violator, it could not intend that the law should be enforced against others.[2]

[2] John Thomas Scopes *vs.* The State of Tennessee, 154 Tenn. 105 (1926).

Thus ended the Scopes case, and with it ended at least for a time—the passage of anti-evolution laws. What the future will bring no one can foretell, but the ridicule heaped upon Tennessee leads one to believe that no state would be likely to follow its example. When an anti-evolution bill was pending recently in the Kentucky legislature, one of the legislators introduced a companion measure reciting that there were other natural phenomena more important to the State of Kentucky than evolution; that every one knows that it is too cold in winter and too warm in summer; and that laws should be passed to compel an even temperature. The bill further referred to the fact that the power situation in Kentucky would be greatly improved if a law were passed that water should run uphill as well as downhill. The Kentucky measure failed.

Those engaged in the Scopes case will ever be grateful to the thousands of people all over the United States who overwhelmed the mail-carriers and the telegraph offices with offers of help and information. One man telegraphed, "Have found missing link. Wire instructions." Another, from San Francisco, "Civilization is at stake. Telephone me at once."

The memory of the Scopes case will undoubtedly live on. The Appellate Court was correct in designating it as a "bizarre" case. Its most intense interest was derived from the clash of the two types of mind. But to-day the statute is generally disregarded in Tennessee. Not only this, but interest in the scientific theory of evolution has been greatly increased. Forbidden theories, like forbidden fruit, arouse curiosity, curiosity leads to investigation, investigation to learning. Even though this may result in the specter of skepticism, and in the weakening of faith, the process of mental development cannot be reversed. The stifling of freedom of thought or education often has this effect. Repression always feeds the enemy.

The Anti-Evolution laws provide that certain things should not be taught. Many groups in the community, while ridiculing this type of law and while not favoring the teaching of religion as such, do by various methods attempt to support religion to some extent through the schools. It is an endeavor to bootleg a forbidden product into the public schools. It may be a good product; it may be a bad one. It may be an article of tolerance, mercy and love, and undiluted. It may have in it nothing of bigotry, hate and ignorance. It may be of the ambrosial variety containing not more than one-half of one per cent of human wickedness whose sanctified imbibers may become useful citizens, but with its strength or weakness, its value or its harm, we are not concerned. We are interested chiefly in the type of mind which promotes the undertaking.

In many communities laws have been passed providing for the reading of the Bible or parts thereof in public schools. Where the law is general, this raises a question as to what Bible is intended. Some of the statutes refer to the King James' version of the Bible. Laws of this character have been subject to attack on many occasions. While one hesitates to admit that courts are influenced by any consideration other than that of the law, yet it is a peculiar circumstance that in those states where the Catholic or Jewish influence is strong, the law seems to have been held unconstitutional; otherwise constitutional. Practically all constitutions provide substantially that public monies shall not be devoted to religious purposes and that no preference should be given to any religious establishment. Where the Bible is read in public schools, it would seem that a preference of some kind is given; for instance, to Christians over Mohammedans, and that at least a modicum of public monies, to the extent that the teachers are paid for a few minutes devoted to this purpose, are used for religious purposes. Cases in court must be argued on questions of law involving the interpretation of the statutes and constitutions. The real objection to Bible reading lies deeper. Some parts of the Bible might be objectionable to none. Others might offend the sensibilities of persons of one religious sect or another. Where parts of the Bible are read, discretion must be lodged with some one and thus there is a possibility of religious division. But far transcending the effect of Bible reading in itself, is the principle that public institutions should be free from sectarian influence.

Along with the agitation for Bible reading is that which would promote the teaching or reading of the Ten Commandments in public schools. In the judgment of many there is an added objection to this. As a modern moral code the Ten Commandments can be greatly improved, both by elimination and addition. This should certainly be clear to those who, during the

war, tore down the commandment "Thou shalt not kill,"
or even to those who demanded that Ruth Snyder and
Judd Gray pay the extreme penalty of the law.   One
would have difficulty explaining to children the commandment "Thou shalt not commit adultery."   The
admonition that one shall not covet his neighbor's
house, nor his wife, nor his manservant, nor his maid-
servant, nor his ox, nor his ass, seems somewhat a
reflection upon women through their general inclusion
with other animals.   The commandment "Six days
shalt thou labor and do all thy work" could hardly
have been intended to apply to workers in delicatessen
stores and barber shops—institutions probably unknown at the time of Moses.   It can hardly apply to
the police.   One approves of the suggestion that a
child honor his father and mother, though one may
question the reason therefor, to wit, "that thy days
may be long in the land that Jehovah, thy God, giveth
thee," and one rather speculates about whether something should not be said about the attitude of fathers
and mothers toward children, and as to whether the
honor that is due should not to some extent depend
upon the parents.   In general, one would say the Ten
Commandments were rules made by a jealous God for
a world in which the homo, male (whether sapiens or
not), was all important.

In the general thought that immorality is due to
the weakening of church influence, there has been recently a widespread movement towards excusing children in public schools for a period in which to attend
religious instruction.   The claim is made that week-

day religious instruction is necessary, and that the
schools monopolize too much time. If this is true, the
situation might be remedied by shortening the school
hours for all children, but such a plan would lose the
advantage of a release from school as an inducement
to attend religious instruction, or of using the school
as a "bait." This matter has been the subject of litigation in New York State during the past year. The
case first came up in Mount Vernon, where it appeared
that children, at the request of their parents, were excused from school for a half hour on Wednesday
afternoons in order to attend a named institution for
religious instruction. The teacher kept a record of
whether a child stayed in school or went to church;
either was noted as school "attendance." Mr. Justice
Seeger of the State Supreme Court decided, in a case
involving the City of Mount Vernon, New York, that
such procedure was illegal.[3] The State Superintendent
of Education, Frank Pierrepont Graves, was called
upon to follow the decision in other places throughout
the State. On his failure a mandamus suit was brought
against him. The regulations in White Plains were
cited as an example. The school law provided that
children should attend school for the entire time in
which the school should be in session, although "occasional absences not amounting to irregular attendance"
were permissible. The State Constitution provided that
public monies should not be used for religious purposes,
and that no preference be given to any religion. The
proponents of the procedure were frank in their posi-

[3] Stein *vs.* Brown, 125 Misc. 692 (1925).

tion. They admitted that the half hour of instruction was of no great moment, but insisted that it would establish a desirable connection between religion and the schools. The Freethinkers' Society, which through Joseph Lewis as president brought the suit, agreed that the principle rather than the half hour, was important; that the regulation tended to bring sectarian influences into the schools; that presumably if children might be excused for half an hour one day a week, they might be excused for an hour a day. That in time the hours of release from the repression of education might occur during the biology, geology or astronomy hour, so that a youngster might learn Bible biology, Bible geology and Bible astronomy. It was contended that at 2:30 on Wednesday afternoons Catholic children were herded or herded themselves together from whatever class in school they might come, the Protestant children likewise, the Jewish children likewise; the Hindus, the Chinese, the Mohammedans, and the infidels remaining in the classroom. Children are not always tolerant and considerate of one another. The Catholics become the "Micks"; the Jews become "Kikes," the Protestants become "Ku Kluxers," and the rest remain infidels. And the lines of division through the school not formed by harmonious relationship from class association become perpendicular, dividing children according to sect or religion. Yet the Court of Appeals held that, so long as such methods were reasonably applied, such school regulations were not illegal.[4]

[4] People *ex rel* Lewis *vs.* Graves, 245 N. Y. 195 (1927).

On the other hand, within the last few years, effort has been made in some States to prohibit parochial and other denominational schools. The Oregon statute was held unconstitutional by the Supreme Court of the United States.[5] Any such effort represents the same intolerance and fear as does that devoted to bringing religion into the public schools. Bigotry is not necessarily limited to church people, or to any class or creed of church people. Freethinkers, in attacking religion, often show the greatest intolerance. Just as one sect attacks another, they attack all. Charles H. Tuttle, representing the church element in the White Plains case, referred to the "bigotry of irreligion."

It should be clear to those who would bring religion in any form into the public schools, as well as to those who would prevent private denominational establishments, that a majority group always endeavors to exercise tyranny over the minority and that the only protection for any one in his religion or lack of religion is absolute equality, without discrimination arising directly or indirectly from civil government. Any particular group is in the minority. Every sect should itself be anxious to avoid the meddling of religion with the schools. All men should know that toleration was not found sufficient for the framers of our Constitution, but that equality was their goal—that there was to be such an absolute separation of church and state, that civil establishments should be free from any connection with religious establishments.

[5] Pierce vs. Society of Sisters and Pierce vs. Hill Military Academy, 268 U. S. 510 (1925).

Sensitive on many subjects, human beings always become most aroused concerning matters of which they know not.   And the very precepts of the Christian religion, of mercy, love and brotherhood, are violated in our most sacred institutions when we permit the introduction therein, directly or indirectly, of those matters of religion which necessarily create division.

FREEDOM OF SPEECH AND ASSEMBLAGE

FREEDOM OF SPEECH AND ASSEMBLAGE

THE VINTONDALE CASE IN THE PENNSYLVANIA COAL
MINES—WEST VIRGINIA—SUPPRESSION OF SACCO-
VANZETTI MEETINGS IN MASSACHUSETTS AND
ELSEWHERE—PASSAIC DURING THE STRIKE—PAT-
ERSON AND OTHER CASES

"FREEDOM of opinion, of speech, and of the press is our most valuable privilege, the very soul of republican institutions, the safeguard of all other rights. . . . Nothing awakens and improves men so much as free communications of thoughts and feelings.

"If men abandon the right of free discussion; if, awed by threats, they suppress their convictions; if rulers succeed in silencing every voice but that which approves them; if nothing reaches the people but what would lend support to men in power—farewell to liberty. The form of a free government may remain, but the life, the soul, the substance is fled."

—WILLIAM ELLERY CHANNING (1780-1842)

Sic Semper Dissenters [1]

"In the town of Hottentottenville an aged Hottentot,
    Whose name was Hottentotten-Tillypoo,
Was feebly hottentottering around a vacant lot,
    With a vacant look upon his higgaboo.

[1] Published and copyrighted by Alfred Knopf (1926) in book by Clarence Day, Jr., entitled "The Crow's Nest."

93

Now 'higgaboo' is Hottentot, as you may know, for
    'face,'
And to wear a vacant look upon your *face* is a disgrace.
But poor old Mr. Tillypoo, he had no other place,
    Though I understand it grieved him through (and
    thru).

"He was grubbing up potatoes in an aimless sort of way
    (Which really was the only way he had),
And an officer was watching him to hear what he might
    say,
    And arrest him if the thing he said was bad.
For it seems this wretched Tillypoo had gone and had
    the thought
That his neighbors didn't always do exactly as they
    ought;
And as this was rank sedition, why, they hoped to see
    him caught;
    For it naturally made 'em pretty mad.

"So the men of Hottentottenville, they passed a little law,
    Which they called the Hotta-Shotta-Shootem Act,
Which fixed it so the postman was a kind of Grand
    Bashaw,
    Who determined what was false and what was fact.
And the postman sentenced Tillypoo, and wouldn't hear
    his wails,
But kept him twenty years apiece in all the local jails,
And said he couldn't vote no more, and barred him from
    the mails,
    And expressed the hope that *this* would teach him
    tact.

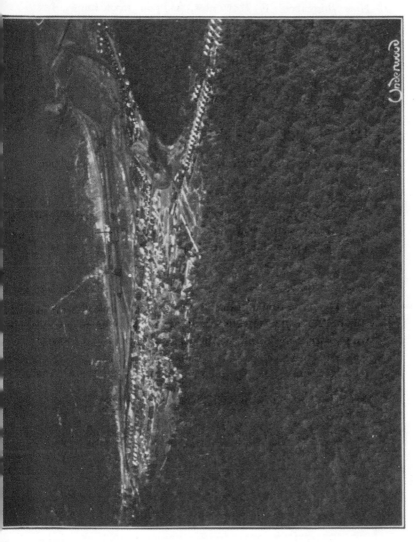

Vintondale, Pennsylvania, 1922.

By geography inside; by order of the coal company outside, the United States of America.

"Well, the last I heard of Tilly, he was trying not to think,
    And he'd tied a piece of string around his tongue,
And he never went within a mile of either pen or ink,
    And he always stood when *any* song was sung.
And maybe you are thinking that his fate was rather
        tough,
But what I say is, 'Not a bit, they didn't do enough';
When anybody differs with you, dammit, treat 'em rough;
    Why, they ought to be bub-boiled alive and hung."
                                —CLARENCE DAY, JR.

One can hardly conceive of democratic institutions
which do not recognize the *right* of free speech and
free assemblage. I say "right"—not privilege. And
the test of a right is whether there is interference when
the persons involved are the most pitiful, the most defenseless class in the community, when the occasion is
one of stress and when the views expressed are violently unpopular.

There are those of us who believe that this freedom
of speech should apply in war time as well as during
peace. The guarantees in the Constitution make no
distinction. In *Schaefer vs. United States*, 251 U. S.
466, 494-5 (1920), a case based on publication made
in 1917, Mr. Justice Brandeis in a dissenting opinion,
in which Mr. Justice Holmes joined, said:

"Nor will this grave danger end with the passing of the
war. The constitutional right of free speech has been
declared to be the same in peace and in war. In peace,
too, men may differ widely as to what loyalty to our country
demands, and an intolerant majority, swayed by passion or
by fear, may be prone in the future, as it has often been

in the past, to stamp as disloyal opinions with which it
disagrees. Convictions such as these, besides abridging
freedom of speech, threaten freedom of thought and of
belief."

The First Amendment to the Federal Constitution
says that Congress shall make no law "abridging the
freedom of speech, or of the press" without excepting
periods of war when the right is of the greatest importance. In fact, it has even been suggested that
a war which people disapprove ought to be opposed
by them even at the risk of national defeat. And when
one considers the tremendous weapons of propaganda
controlled by the ruling power, the effect of social
pressure, and that any specific war (as opposed to
war in general) is always popular, it would seem that
a war whose success is jeopardized by free criticism
or opposition has little ground for support. Yet
one can understand the reason approving an "Espionage" Act which abridges freedom of speech in
times of "clear and present danger," to use the words
of the Supreme Court, even though one can scarcely
forgive its vindictive misuse. One becomes impatient
when a Court says there is no conflict with the Constitution in the Espionage Act. We should feel happier if there was no evasion—if the Court would
simply say that the Constitution and Bill of Rights
are scrapped during war. At least this would be
more agreeable to one's intelligence. A Government
must assure order and maintain itself. Without our
fundamental rights, it wouldn't maintain a de-

mocracy; it wouldn't maintain "America" as we know or would like to know America, but it would maintain government in America. Why not admit that in times of stress, when the country is in danger or rather when those in power think it is in danger—quite a different thing—we have tyranny. Tyranny in war, democracy in peace would be understandable and less nauseating if we were honest about it.

The freedom of speech and assemblage to which I refer has to do with propaganda, expressions of opinion and exhortations and not with direct incitement to violence. From the opinions of Mr. Justice Holmes and Mr. Justice Brandeis of the Supreme Court, one can easily determine the legal line of demarcation. (Although the views expressed by these judges often appear in dissenting opinions, yet the difference between them and the majority of the Court, is not so much as to the law, as to its application to the facts of the particular case. Where there is a difference, I prefer to take my stand with Holmes and Brandeis.)

It is often said that the guaranties against abridging freedom of speech contained in the First Amendment to the Federal Constitution, apply only to Federal action and that we must look to the Constitutions of the States for limitation upon State action. This leaves out of consideration the Fourteenth Amendment. As was said by Mr. Justice Brandeis, dissenting on another point, in *Gilbert vs. Minnesota*, 254 U. S. 325, 336 (1920):

". . . The matter is not merely of State concern. The State law affects directly the functions of the Federal government. It affects rights, privileges and immunities of one who is a citizen of the United States; and it deprives him of an important part of his liberty."

Again, Mr. Justice Holmes in *Gitlow vs. New York,* 268 U. S. 652, 672 (1925), said:

"The general principle of free speech, it seems to me, must be taken to be included in the Fourteenth Amendment, in view of the scope that has been given to the word 'liberty' as there used. . . ."

Although this comes from a dissenting opinion, the Court does not seem to disagree on this point, for in the prevailing opinion Mr. Justice Sanford said:

"For present purposes we may and do assume that freedom of speech and of the press—which are protected by the First Amendment from abridgment by Congress—are among the fundamental personal rights and 'liberties' protected by the due process clause of the Fourteenth Amendment from impairment by the States."

The matter, therefore, is one of Federal law (as well as State law where the guarantees exist in State Constitutions as is the case with practically all of them), and the question remains as to what is the test. Referring to the Schenck [2] case, Mr. Justice Holmes said:

"The question in every case is whether the words used are used in such circumstances and are of such a nature as to create a clear and present danger that they will bring about the substantive evils that (the State) has a right to prevent. It is a question of proximity and degree."

Referring to the conviction of Gitlow,[3] he said:

[2] Schenck *vs.* United States, 240 U. S. 47, 52.
[3] Gitlow *vs.* New York, 268 N. Y. 652, 673 (1925) *infra.*

"If what I think the correct test is applied, it is manifest that there was no present danger of an attempt to overthrow the government by force on the part of the admittedly small minority who shared the defendant's views. It is said that this manifesto was more than a theory, that it was an incitement. Every idea is an incitement. It offers itself for belief and if believed it is acted on unless some other belief outweighs it or some failure of energy stifles the movement at its birth. The only difference between the expression of an opinion and an incitement in the narrower sense is the speaker's enthusiasm for the result. Eloquence may set fire to reason. But whatever may be thought of the redundant discourse before us it had no chance of starting a present conflagration. If in the long run the beliefs expressed in proletarian dictatorship are destined to be accepted by the dominant forces of the community, the only meaning of free speech is that they should be given their chance and have their way."

In a later opinion (*Whitney vs. California*, 274 U. S. 357) where Charlotte Anita Whitney was convicted under the California Criminal Syndicalism Act for membership in the Communist Labor Party, Mr. Justice Holmes and Mr. Justice Brandeis joined in a concurring opinion, written by the latter. He said (pp. 376, 377):

"Fear of serious injury cannot alone justify suppression of free speech and assembly. Men feared witches and burnt women. It is the function of speech to free men from the bondage of irrational fears. . . .

"To courageous, self-reliant men, with confidence in the power of free and fearless reasoning applied through the processes of popular government, no danger flowing from speech can be deemed clear and present, unless the incidence of the evil apprehended is so *imminent* that it may befall before there is opportunity for full discussion. If there be time to expose through discussion the falsehood and fallacies, to avert the evil by the processes of education, the remedy to be applied is more speech, not enforced silence."

It would seem from this that where there is an opportunity for discussion so that there is no imminent danger to the State through peaceful processes, freedom of speech and assemblage cannot lawfully be abridged. The limitation refers to conditions where the State is in danger.

". . . this freedom does not deprive a State of the primary and essential right of self preservation; which, so long as human governments endure, they cannot be denied." [4]

Gitlow *vs.* New York, *supra.*

But

"The fact that speech is likely to result in some violence or in destruction of property is not enough to justify its suppression. There must be the probability of serious injury to the State. Among free men, the deterrents ordinarily to be applied to prevent crime are education and punishment for violations of the law, not abridgement of the rights of free speech and assembly." [5]

[4] Gitlow *vs.* New York, 268 U. S. 652, 668, *supra* (prevailing opinion of Mr. Justice Sanford). This proposition is, of course, not controverted in the dissenting opinions there or anywhere else.

[5] Whitney *vs.* California, 274 U. S. 357, 378, *supra* (concurring opinion, Mr. Justice Brandeis).

When I refer here to freedom of speech and assemblage, I have in mind normal conditions; that is, conditions where the Government, as such, is not in danger. It would not be far from the truth to say that in the United States to-day, in spite of constitutional guarantees in every state, that where a matter involves unpopular expression on a matter that is close to the hearts of the people, freedom of speech and assemblage is fast disappearing, or has disappeared. There exists neither an official nor social attitude upholding the Voltairian view, "I do not agree with a thing you say, but I would die for your right to say it."

The indirect effect of suppression of free discussion is perhaps more important than the direct effect, because the general atmosphere is permeated by either a free or a timid spirit. Travel in an undemocratic country and you at once find that along with prohibition of public free expression comes a general hesitancy to talk freely, even in private conversation. We all had this experience during the War. A year ago I felt it in Russia where it seemed that frank social intercourse is interdicted by something rather sinister lurking in the background. During the War I often traveled in Germany and England. When I came to Scandinavia, I felt a relaxation, a lack of restraint, which resulted, not from any specific pressure in the war countries, but from a feeling of once again breathing free air. In times and places where freedom of speech and assemblage is met with force, one finds diffidence and hesitancy in private relations. Tensity is a by-product of intolerance. Along with it comes suspicion.

Particularly this affects those questions which, being closest to the people, are the subjects of greatest interest and should be subject to freest discussion. Thus a force which prohibits public expression and assemblage spreads like the ripples on a pond to repress the spirit of freedom everywhere. As witness Vintondale, Pennsylvania.

On a pleasant spring day in 1922 I was busily engaged in my prosaic duties, when I received a telephone call from the American Civil Liberties Union, Roger Baldwin speaking, "We want you to go down to Cresson, Pennsylvania, and arrange to hold a meeting in a non-union town—yes, the strike is on. No, it won't take long. You'll arrive in the early morning, hold your meeting and be back in the evening." One doesn't like to refuse such a simple request. By nature I am inclined to be timid, but never having been in a tight corner, I have always managed to cover this with a respectably dignified front.

Arrived at Cresson in the morning, I joined some union men in the small office of the *United Mine Workers' Journal*. Naturally, I inquired why a lawyer's attendance was necessary to assure a public meeting. My auditors smiled indulgently. "Well, let's hold a meeting," I suggested. "We'll go to one of these closed towns. Tom, here, will make the first talk. Jim will carry on. If there's any trouble, I'll take care of you." This didn't arouse much enthusiasm. But, when some one suggested that Attorney Hays do the talking, there was unanimous and spirited approval. I regarded the attitude as a tribute to my eloquence, though I was a little disturbed by a certain jocularity which animated two rather hard-boiled youngsters. "Where shall we go?" was the next inquiry. That seemed to be a matter of indifference. Somerset County where union organizers were arrested on sight, Cambria County filled with State Troopers and Coal and Iron Police, organized to maintain order with machine guns, clubs and rifles? We'd get the same reception anywhere. "What's the toughest town?" "Well, there's Vintondale; we haven't been able to get near the place," said a union organizer. "Welsh here was thrown out at the point of a shotgun a few weeks ago. A New York *Herald* reporter was turned back on the public road by an armed guard within a few days. No one can get into that town without the consent of the Coal Company. There's not been a meeting there in years." "And," added Welsh, "the United Mine Workers' Union owns a house there so if they won't let you talk on the street, you can speak from the veranda."

We drove along beautiful highways marred here and there by squalid villages, with coal dumps and tipples marking the mines. We passed through Nant-y-Glo, neatly set among the hills, continuing along smooth roads with mountains and woods on both sides. There were two automobile loads, Attorney Clarence Loeb from Philadelphia, J. J. Kintner, the union lawyer, Julian Rosenberg from New York, and myself. Then there were John Gieger and Art Shields, newspaper men, William Welsh, union organizer, and some of his followers.

Suddenly around a turn in the road we reach Vintondale, in the State of Pennsylvania,—by geography inside, by order of the coal company outside, the United States of America. Trees flank one side of the road; on the other dips a deep, dirty hollow, dotted by slag and slate dumps. Railroad tracks run here and there, broken by piles up which crawl little cars dumping their burdens at the top. On the piles and at other points of vantage are mounted powerful searchlights to warn of strangers at night. Machine guns? No doubt. An armed guard stands near a sentry booth. In the road are obstructions squarely planted to hold up traffic.

In New York I had hardly pictured this scene. I had been skeptical when told that no stranger could enter Vintondale without molestation. This doubt had been emphasized in the drive along the peaceful Pennsylvania hills, through the quiet orderly union towns where the only signs of the strike were little groups of men loafing around, playing cards, throwing jack-knives under the trees, working in the vegetable patches or whipping up the quiet streams.

"Stop" is the order. Our machines sweep by. "We'll get you yet," shouts the guard. I wondered what for. We'd done nothing but drive along a public highway. No doubt it was lese majesty to ignore an order from this armed ruffian.

We speed up the road across the railroad tracks. Clattering hoofs resound behind. The coal and iron police, wearing awe-inspiring gray uniforms, belted with ammunition, armed with gun and blackjack, are in chase. We round up at the general supply store. Other troopers having no insignia but carrying arms close in on us. "We know you, you ——— ——— ———! You're union organizers from Nant-y-Glo. Get the hell out of this town." We pile out of the machines. "Who are you men?" we demand. "Where is the Post Office?" "Where is the Mayor's office; we'd like to see the ordinances of this town." One trooper rages at me, "Take a look at this sign," pointing to a Sheriff's placard opposite on a corner frame building. The placard reads that, in the event of public disorder, the Sheriff shall order a crowd to disperse and if they do not do so immediately, may place them under arrest. There is no disorder here. "I see that—what of it?" I ask. Around us the troopers, jeering, yelling and threatening, spur their skittish horses. I take my stand on the sidewalk, announcing, "I am going to stand here as long as I damn please." I didn't. The high-bred horses seemed to be almost as nervous as I was. I dodged their hoofs with the activity of a mountain goat. We shout inquiries as to who these Cossacks are, what laws we are violating, and the cause of all the excitement.

"Bust this up or we'll bust you up," shouts one while hoots, threats and curses come from the others. Finally, one Arbogast, the Coal Company Comptroller, with the assistance of one of the troopers and a bystander, grabs me by the nape of the neck and the seat of the trousers while others are busy with my companions. There was then impressed on me a clear conviction, verified by other experiences, to wit:—

when one is in that position he may talk constitutional law, insist upon his rights as an American citizen, he may proclaim the Declaration of Independence, but all the dignity is on the side of the authorities. "Now, then, into the machine and about your business." Shoving, pushing and hauling, they force us along. Finally, as they were about to throw us over the side of the car, they desist. "Now get the hell out of here; you're collecting a crowd." It was the troopers who collected the crowd.

We left Vintondale, accompanied to the outskirts of the town by cursing mounted men. When we were stopped by an obstruction in the street, they would pull up their horses whose forelegs would hover ominously over the automobile.

Nant-y-Glo was a union town. William Welsh was a union organizer. Justice of the Peace Robert Harnish was a union miner elected by union men. We soon had warrants for the arrest of John Doe, Richard Roe and other members of the well-known "oe" family. The Constable was not at his blacksmith's shop. With the High Constable he had gone fishing. Before long we collected them and started back for Vintondale.

Again the obstructed road. Again the entrance guard. Again the thundering hoofs behind the machine. The railroad crossing was blocked by a long freight train. "Back up, Walter: we're in a hurry," shouted Cooney, a union engineer who, on a day off, was driving our car. Like a toy train, the cars obediently moved away. We sped over the tracks, down the narrow dingy street, around the corner, pulling up short at the town center,—the company store.

"What the hell are you doing here now?" yelled the mounted men.

"You're under arrest," said the Constable. As armed guards, one after another, galloped up to initiate and quell a disturbance, they were served with warrants. The coal and iron police of Vintondale were pained and surprised. This was not according to Hoyle. The Vinton Colliery Company did not pay them for this. The Company Comptroller arrived in his machine. This situation was unique. Outsiders causing trouble in his peaceful community! The Comptroller sped away.

How he got back to the company supply office we never knew, but there must have been a rear entrance, for presently we heard rumors that the Company Superintendent, the Comptroller, Justice of the Peace Blewett and Justice Daly were closeted in the office with the Constable. The Constable reported that a voice on the telephone, claiming to be the County District Attorney, advised that Justice Daly might accept bail for the arrested policemen. We did not know till later that the voice was unauthenticated.

As a lawyer, representing the Union, I made my way up the outside steps of the building to make inquiry about the date for trial. "Get out of there," shouted the Comptroller, mysteriously appearing below. "Arrest that man for trespass,"—this to two troopers who unexpectedly loomed on the landing above. "I want to see the Justice," I said. The troopers grabbed me, hustled me off to the lock-up and into a three by six cell, littered with scraps of paper, cigar butts and refuse, and containing an iron bed covered with a filthy blanket, and a toilet. "And you call yourselves men!" said I. "What the hell you want to stir up a row for? The people here are satisfied," was the answer. "What would they do if they weren't?" I asked. "You talk like a lawyer," was the reply.

I have often thought that the civilization of a town may be judged by its jails. If so, that of Vintondale was very low in the scale.

After a time it was discovered that they had locked up a lawyer, not just a coal miner. I wondered why this should make any difference. Soon came a trooper to the cell holding out a paper. "Here's a warrant for your arrest." "You can't serve that now; I've already been arrested." "Do you want to see the Justice?" We proceeded to the front of the garage-like structure where Mr. Justice Blewett, collarless and unshaven, appeared, having just finished personally providing bail for my defendants. The next paper he signed was the warrant for my arrest. The Justice's signature was a power. It bailed the company men and jailed me. "We want to get through with this," said Justice Blewett. "I am ready for trial." Then the following:

Justice Blewett: All right, I find you guilty and fine you $5.

Prisoner: I insist on a trial.

Justice: I was near enough; I know what happened.

Prisoner: I want a trial. There are people all over the United States interested to know what happens in these closed towns.

Justice: You don't have to pay the $5 if you get out of town.

Prisoner: I won't pay the $5 and I won't get out of town. I want a trial.

Justice: Well, it's all over.

Prisoner: I won't let a verdict of guilty stand against me.

Justice: Then you're not guilty.

The court adjourned.

As I came out of the jail the troopers were clattering up and down the street while curious onlookers scuttled into the byways.

The chief of the coal and iron police, a handsome figure smartly uniformed, belt bulging with ammunition, shook his club at me, and shouted: "You needn't think you can intimidate me." He and the others, out on bail, pursued our machines to the outskirts.

As we reached the end of the street, I noted an American flag, emblem of freedom, at the top of a tower mast, flying bravely over the Borough of Vintondale. I wondered what significance it had for the foreign-born miners.

A few days later the coal and iron police came up for arraignment. The striking vocabulary of forceful profanity, exhibited by them on our excursion to Vintondale, was not superior to that displayed by the union miners of Nant-y-Glo when their traditional enemies appeared. In originality, variety and vigor,

epithetical honors were about even. "We'll cut your
heart out," was the miners' promise to the police.
Considerable persuasion was required to stop stoning
of the visitors. The defendants were enthusiastically
held for the Grand Jury by Justice Harnish, the union
Justice of the Peace. They had about as much chance
as union miners have before a Justice of the Peace
in a non-union town.

All of which goes to show—if proof is necessary—
that men are much alike; and that courts—or at least
some courts—are not unmindful of the pervading atmosphere. The tensity of feeling engendered by force
finds much the same expression everywhere. The cause
of the massacre at Herrin, Illinois, is readily understandable to one familiar with the spirit of outrage
resulting from the bullying and repression on the part
of armed guards there. Through the course of history,
it has been found that freedom is safer than repression;
that conditions are actually more stable where each side
recognizes the fundamental rights of the other; that
disorder springs from emotions; that force and brutality result from anger and hate; that free expression, assemblies and parades are a safety valve, a
method of letting off steam; that democracy as
a philosophy, giving the individual a sense that he
has some power over his conditions, is sounder than
a tyranny which arouses resentment and provides no
form of release.

On many occasions I talked this over with members
of the State Constabulary, the coal and iron police,
mine owners and operators. "Why did they interfere

with meetings, prevent the distribution of literature, break up groups of men and parades?" The answer was always the same,—and plausible. Why should they permit incitements to disorder? They knew that any meeting would lead to lawlessness and the destruction of property. In time of strike the unions always raise "hell." Why give them the chance? I was not surprised at the attitude for I have heard the same view expressed by learned judges from the bench. "Do you mean to say, Mr. Hays, that if the police have reason to believe that a meeting will be disorderly, or that a speaker intends to incite a crowd to violence, that they have no power to interfere?" My reply that I meant just that has often been met by a growl. I would refer to Thomas Jefferson's distinction between words and "overt acts," and insist that freedom of speech and assemblage meant that or nothing. I find Jefferson's name is a tradition, his words an aggravation. The fallacy of these fearful gentlemen lies in their assumption that freedom will mean disorder, which implies the right to determine just where the line of demarcation lies, and how far it is safe to recognize the rights of other men. Those in power, whether they be capitalists, mine operators, labor-leaders, mayors or police officers, appear to believe not in liberty, but in order. The business of the police, or at any rate their psychology, is to maintain order, not necessarily to protect rights, particularly rights of men so unreasonable as to wish to exercise them whatever the consequences. Such men appear to be on the lunatic fringe anyhow. To a policeman, concussion is more effective

than discussion. And it is naturally difficult for a coal
and iron policeman to imagine that union organizers
have any purpose except to cause trouble. In a non-
union town this is perhaps true in a sense, since the
object is to unionize the men. And these officers, paid
by the coal companies, intend to prevent that, or any
other disorder. But interference, induced by fear of
what might happen, cannot be justified if freedom is to
endure. Tyrants are always induced by fear. Democracy assumes that there is more safety in taking a
chance.

As was said by J. G. Brooks in an article on "Problems of Police Administration" (Vol. 8, Papers and
Proceedings of the American Sociological Society):

" . . . No lesson is clearer than the danger of permitting average officials to act on 'tendencies,' to guess that
some violence will befall unless assembly or speech is
choked off in good time. From few causes has public
security suffered more than from hysterical pre-judgments
as to what is likely to occur unless somebody is first knocked
about. This is invariably the mark of the crudest and
least efficient policing of assemblages."

The fact is, curious as it may seem to policemen, that
"what might happen" seldom does, if they let people
alone. We taught this lesson.

While these proceedings were pending, we were busy
preparing papers to enjoin interference with meetings.
Fortunately the United Mine Workers owned a house
and lot in Vintondale, so that we could base our petition for an injunction on the violation of a tangible

property right. Also the barber of the town and a storekeeper averred that business was not as good as it might be in Vintondale; that they had a right to the custom which union men would provide, particularly if these men were permitted to come freely and hold meetings. Thus we had a readily understandable business proposition. It is unfortunate that one should be obliged to make this kind of presentation, for the wrong lay in the denial of civil right, which in itself has often been held to be a property right. But real estate and barbering (shaves, haircuts, and bobs) seem stronger pillars of support in court than liberty. The Chinese have rioted to save their queues (in fact, a Supreme Court decision has disapproved a San Francisco ordinance pursuant to which if a person was arrested, his hair should be cut, as discriminating against the Chinese) and when Peter the Great tried to Europeanize the Russians by cutting off their beards, there was great resentment. I am not aware, however, of any important revolution in history caused by the "hair" question. There has been bloodshed over real estate, but by and large the great political revolutions have concerned liberty. But these revolutions were not strictly legal.

Having prepared the papers for an injunction I went home, to return some days later to Ebensburg, Pennsylvania, the county seat. We appeared before the Grand Jury which then and there brought in an indictment for assault and battery against the coal and iron policemen of Vintondale. Also, I came to argue the injunction.

Word had been passed around, among the coal diggers, to attend court on the hearing. The circular courtroom was crowded with union miners, some sitting, some standing, some crouched on their haunches in true miner fashion through two long hours of technical argument. The bill was objected to on various grounds. It was claimed that there was a "multifariousness of parties plaintiff"; that the American Civil Liberties Union, members thereof, the barber shop proprietor, the feed-store man and the United Mine Workers had no legal right all to join in one complaint; that the rights violated were different as to each. We countered with the argument that riparian owners might join in a suit against one who fouled a stream. Our audience approved the answer. Objection was made that no injunction would lie to prevent police officers from enforcing the criminal law, and as policemen never do anything else, no injunction should be granted against them. We retorted that we merely wished to enjoin them from violating the law. We quoted Judge Gaynor's memorable remark that "a policeman is merely a citizen in blue clothes with brass buttons," and is amenable to an injunction to the same extent as any private citizen if there is reasonable cause to believe he intends to violate the rights of others.

The defendants insisted that they were acting within the Sheriff's proclamation which provided that meetings might be broken up under certain circumstances, assuming, as is usually done under these circumstances, that the Sheriff's proclamation was law. We asked

the court to make a definite ruling to the effect that
the Sheriff did not make the law and that the proclamation had no effect other than to give notice. We
referred to an early statement from "Coke Reports"
(Vol. 12):

" . . . The King cannot create any offense by his
prohibition or proclamation which was not an offense
before, for that was to change the law, and to make an
offense which was not; for . . . that which cannot be
punished without proclamation cannot be punished with
it . . . but never was seen any indictment to conclude
contra regiam proclamationem."

The court interjected: "Of course, the Sheriff's proclamation is not the law," to which we responded that
we knew that and the court knew that and the miners
knew that, but public officials did not seem to know it.

As Judge McCann indicated approval or disapproval, the response of the miners in the courtroom was
instant. If the Judge showed a favorable view on
some point, the audience brightened; if the tendency
were the other way, the dissatisfaction was evident.
Patiently the union miners waited. They did not express themselves volubly, but there was no mistaking
their attitude.

We argued that the law was the only answer to
force; that property rights were inviolate; that the
court should be no less jealous of the right to human
liberty. We pointed out that where courts are power-
less to prevent improper acts of repression, history has
shown that citizens will be driven to take the law into

their own hands; that radicalism and revolution have always been so induced. We referred to the Pennsylvania Bill of Rights which says:

"The free communication of thoughts and opinions is one of the invaluable rights of man and every citizen may freely speak, write and print on any subject, being responsible for the abuse of that liberty."

We referred to the Pennsylvania case of *Spayd vs. Ringing Rock Lodge*, 270 Pa. 67, where Chief Justice Moschzisker said as to these rights:

"The rights above noted cannot lawfully be infringed, even momentarily, by individuals any more than by the State itself. . . .

"The Constitution does not confer the right, but guarantees its free exercise—without let or hindrance from those in authority, at all times under any and all circumstances.

" . . . Chief Justice Waite in *U. S.* v. *Cruikshank*, 92 U. S. 542, 551, speaking of the closely related privilege of the people to assemble for lawful purposes, said: 'The right . . . with the obligation on the part of the states to afford it protection, existed long before the adoption of the (Federal) Constitution; in fact, it is, and always has been, one of the attributes of citizenship under a free government.' "

All this seems clear enough, yet it must be admitted that the procedure was unusual. Injunctions were common against the miners. In fact, one was outstanding at the time. But injunctions against a coal company, and the police, that was another matter. Judge McCann refused to enjoin · interference with members of the American Civil Liberties Union or with newspaper men who alleged that their business was interfered with by their inability to obtain news, or to shopkeepers who alleged that they had lost customers. But the good fortune of owning a piece of real estate in Vintondale led to the granting of a preliminary injunction on behalf of John Brophy, David Cowan, William Welsh and James Mark to restrain interference with the holding of a meeting on the mine workers' property.

This served the purpose admirably. The miners were pleased with Judge McCann. We were then informed that Mr. Justice Kephart of the Supreme Court had stated that he feared that any meeting in Vintondale would lead to bloodshed and that if application was made to him he would grant a writ of supersedeas. This would practically restrain the operation of the injunction. Knowing, however, that it would take time to prepare the papers to make application for such a writ, we concluded to hold a meeting immediately in the Borough of Vintondale.

Word was sent to miners in the vicinity and automobiles loaded with cheering, exultant union men made their way to the little house owned by the United Mine Workers' Union at Vintondale. The guard at the entrance of the village, the coal and iron police were served with the court paper. They accepted it without enthusiasm.

We crowded on the grass in front of the veranda from which various speakers addressed the crowd. Below, in a small space, were packed these brawny, swarthy, determined union men. Across the street in a thin line backed up against the coal company buildings were non-union miners. At the window in the company office were the superintendent and the secretary of the coal company. Up and down the street rode coal and iron policemen sitting their horses with an aggrieved dignity. Not a non-union man dared cross the road, but our voices were loud enough to reach them as well as the coal company officers.

To the joy of the union workers we referred to the company officers as un-American and Bolsheviks, men who would rule by force and overturn the institutions of this country. We pointed out that Vintondale was still in America and suggested that our pilgrimage was in a sense a vanguard of the march of freedom to this little town.

Was there disorder? Of course not. Was there bloodshed? Of course not.

They had the guns. We had the law.

Ordinarily the coal and iron police, paid by the company, and contemptuous of the coal miner, have both guns and the *power* of the law. The power is more potent than the law itself. Restraint and respect for the liberties and rights of others would be too much to expect under such circumstances.

We reflected with amusement that had our original meeting been permitted, there would have been no excitement and our crowd, consisting mainly of lawyers and newspaper men, would have constituted both speakers and audience. Whereas through the violent actions of the police we had an opportunity to hold a meeting which aroused considerable public interest. Ordinarily one can trust tyrants to make these issues clear. Almost invariably they provide a good show.

I had occasion to note this some time later, when with two others I arrived in Vintondale at about six o'clock in the evening to hold another meeting. The street was dark, the night was cold. There were few people about. I mounted the steps to talk, but it was dull and uninteresting to express oneself in those surroundings to men who were in absolute agreement. After about two minutes I suggested to one of the others that he take my place. This seemed useless. We agreed that we had made our point and somewhat ingloriously went our way.

Returning to Ebensburg after the meeting, we were served with the writ granted by Justice Kephart. When the Supreme Court later considered the propriety of this, they dismissed the proceeding,[6] but the writ itself took the keen edge off our victory. The strike was over before the court passed on the question of whether the injunction had been properly granted.

Some time later we appeared against the coal and iron police in the criminal prosecution for assault. The defense claimed that we had gone to Vintondale with the express purpose of violating a Sheriff's proclamation, apparently entirely unmindful of the fact that it had already been held that a Sheriff's proclamation is not the law. They contended that though we were

[6] Welsh vs. Vinton Collieries Co., 71 Pittsburgh Legal Journal (Pa.) 209.

ordered out of town, we were handled with great propriety and the utmost gentleness, by the host of armed guards hired to keep peace in this town of about a thousand inhabitants. Some thirty witnesses testified for the defense as against six or seven for the prosecution. The Judge charged that the question was one of credibility.

After about two hours' delay the jury returned, having found the defendants guilty of assault. They were sentenced to small fines and ordered to pay the costs of prosecution. The moral effect was salutary and the victory heartening to the union miners. On the jury had sat two coal operators and yet they had joined in the verdict. The union men were so accustomed to playing the parts of defendants that when on this occasion they were prosecutors and were successful, they felt a new interest in the possibility of court processes. In place of a cynicism which ordinarily led them to ask "What's the use," they came to see that after all the courts were not invariably on the side of the employer.

While the issue was one of fact, the real interest centered around the question raised by the defendants' attorney, Percy Allen Rose of Johnstown: "What business is it of yours?" Since none of us lived in Vintondale, this query seemed a crushing retort to any charge of assault.

It was a hard question to answer. I wondered really what business it was of mine. I am a New York attorney. My business chiefly centers in corporate and commercial matters. Prior to this little adventure, I had known none of the union miners and little about the strike. But then I reflected that anything in which one is interested becomes his business, and this to the extent that he interests himself. I told the jury that every once in a while a man is moved to do something from which he does not derive direct benefit. Of course, this is true. He acts because his nervous system responds pleasurably to the altruistic emotions aroused. In other words, he gets a "kick" out of it. Yet I put the thought before the jury in words of far nobler expression. I said that, as a lawyer and citizen, I was sworn to uphold the laws and Constitution of the United States, and that that was what I was doing when I went into Vintondale and was manhandled by a crowd of gunmen.

I am not proud of having put the proposition just that way, but it got across with a Cambria County jury. To a group of rationalists I probably would say that I had for some time been a member of the American Civil Liberties Union: that I believed in liberty and that I would feel uncomfortable if I just did nothing about it. I would probably add that I had made speeches on the subject of the Constitution and the Bills of Rights; that the matter had become more or less of a hobby and that a request from the American Civil Liberties Union to take some part would be difficult to ignore. After all, one's activities in matters that do not seem to concern him personally are perhaps most intensely personal.

Largely through the instrumentality of Samuel Untermyer, the noted New York lawyer, we induced

Governor Pinchot of Pennsylvania to investigate the tyranny of the coal and iron police. We suggested that a Governor's proclamation, restating the fundamental rights guaranteed the citizen, with special reference to violations by police officials, would be effective. The Governor declined to take this course, but the mere fact that he was looking into the matter was of value in bringing to public attention the lawlessness of the coal and iron police.

An injunction suit, a criminal prosecution and an investigation by the Governor, were the satisfactory product of our activities on that one day, and to them we added a civil suit in New York against the Vinton Collieries Company, claiming damages for assault, battery and false imprisonment. By the time the case came to trial the issues were dead. We lost the case, the skeptical New York jury concluding that we had provoked the assault. Doesn't government depend upon obedience to the police? Had we stopped at the entrance to the town at the command of the officer, there would have been no trouble. They were right. There would have been no trouble. Nor would there have been trouble had we peacefully stayed at home.

My visits to the Pennsylvania coal fields were punctuated by interesting incidents. Ordinarily when I arrived I would find that Powers Hapgood, ardent union organizer, had just been locked up. The usual charge was trespass. As an answer I would have a warrant issued against the arresting officer. The cases would appear before the same Justice of the Peace. I would point out that if Hapgood was not guilty of trespass, then the officer was guilty of assault.   The Judge would reserve decision until he had heard both cases.   Then, against my expostulations, he would trade one for the other and both defendants would be acquitted.

Powers Hapgood is a Harvard graduate of distinguished family, interested in practical economics, unionism and freedom.   Though young in years, he is reasonably familiar with the inside of various jails. He has achieved distinction as a union organizer and to him, in the strike of 1922, was entrusted the care of union tent colonies.   He had difficulty "getting men out" when his persuasion was met by counter-argument on the part of the operators.   But when lawlessness prevailed, when he was thrown out of town or jailed, he found a fruitful field.   On one occasion an operator told me he quite understood my activities.   After all, I was a lawyer employed to represent the side that retained me.   "But that fellow Hapgood," said he, "comes of a good family, has a good education and doesn't have to earn a living by stirring up dissatisfaction.   He's just a plain, lowdown S.O.B."   I asked him what would be his opinion if he thought I was an unpaid volunteer.   "I couldn't believe it," he answered. "You seem like a reasonable fellow, but if you're not getting paid for it, you're just as bad as he is."

The position of the Pennsylvania operator is admittedly difficult.   He must compete ·with the non-union field of West Virginia; nor is he permitted to "conspire" with the union to organize those fields.   He might well paraphrase Lincoln—"You can't run an industry half slave and half free."

Following our visits, the Borough of Vintondale decided to prevent undesirable meetings in a lawful way. The new method was that of the "municipal ordinance" —a device declared constitutional in New York and Pennsylvania, supported (though weakly) by precedent of the United States Supreme Court in a case where the facts were somewhat dissimilar.[7] A town regulation provides that no meeting may be held without a permit from the Burgess or Mayor—whatever that important functionary may be called. This is claimed to be within the police power, for a city has the right to control its streets in view of traffic requirements, or its halls because of the necessity for fire protection. No Mayor, in denying permits to union men, Socialists or radicals, while granting them to Republicans and Democrats, is moved by any consideration other than public safety. Certainly this is so when the case gets to court. It is a clever method and effective.

A union meeting was broken up in Duquesne, Pennsylvania, and the speaker arrested. The Mayor stated that Jesus Christ himself could not speak in Duquesne on the labor question, the evident and probably true assumption being that Jesus would be on the side of the workers. The constitutionality of the ordinance was upheld in that case.[8] Yet the Pennsylvania Bill of Rights guarantees free speech and assemblage. In New York State, the same situation arose in Mount

[7] Davis vs. Massachusetts, 167 U. S. 43 (1897).
[8] Duquesne City vs. Fincke, 269 Penn. State Rep. 112 (1920).

Vernon. Socialists were denied a permit. John Haynes Holmes, Norman Thomas and Rose Schneiderman took up the challenge. On the streets of the city they read the Bill of Rights of the New York Constitution. "Where's your permit?" "We don't need one." "Come along." A writ of habeas corpus was granted; on appeal this was reversed. The ordinance was held constitutional.[9] The city was within its rights, for were not the streets and traffic thereon a proper subject for municipal regulation? The United States Supreme Court refused to interfere. It is, of course, possible that one may obtain a writ of mandamus to compel the granting of a permit. No doubt a meeting can wait while the matter is pending before the courts. But a practical way immediately to raise the question by writs of habeas corpus after arrest, is disapproved. The Supreme Court of Connecticut, in a test case with McAllister Coleman as the victim, found such an ordinance unconstitutional, but that is a small part of the United States.[10] Boston used the municipal ordinance to prevent meetings to discuss the Sacco-Vanzetti case. Probably people may still hold meetings without permit where such ordinances are in force. They need merely hire a lot and gather the assemblage by airplane.

When the general strike was over, the wages of the non-union miners of Vintondale were materially re-

[9] People *ex rel* Thomas F. Doyle, William C. Chambers and Blanche M. Hays *vs.* George C. Atwell, Chief of Police, 197 A. D. 225 (1921); 232 N. Y. 96 (1921); 261 U. S. 590 (1923).

[10] The State of Connecticut *vs.* McAllister Coleman, 96 Conn. 190 (1921).

duced. Promptly the men went on strike. Interested, we decided to hold a public meeting. No guard obstructed the public highway. Butalla, my former trooper jailer, was found in the main street in front of the company store. "What can we do for you?" he inquired. "We want to hold a meeting." "We haven't much of a hall," said he, "but we can arrange for a field near-by." The meeting was held. There was no excitement and little enthusiasm. Auditors were few in number. "We don't have any trouble any more," said Butalla as we drove away. "Perhaps you fellows were right after all."

The issue of free speech and assemblage is never settled through any particular effort. Liberty is in the spirit. Unless people believe in freedom, unless it is of the atmosphere a community breathes, the rights of citizens are not recognized. While in Pennsylvania I endeavored to form branches of the American Civil Liberties Union, realizing that Vintondale could not exist were a public sentiment opposed to such conditions. I approached business men and lawyers. Most of them were somehow connected with the railroads, oil companies or coal operators, or if not, they hoped to be. Rarely did they give this as a reason for refusing to join. They would scan the list of directors of the union, names of Conservatives, Liberals, and Radicals, Republicans, Democrats, Progressives, Socialists and Bolsheviks. They would be associated with no movement with which William Z. Foster or Elizabeth Gurley Flynn was connected. They failed to see that an organization confined to the issue of civil liberty and sincere in its pursuit must necessarily be composed of people of different views; that its efforts would be mostly devoted to the protection of the unpopular. A suggestion that they form their own organization was met with complete indifference and apathy.

The American Civil Liberties Union in almost every case is on the unpopular or disapproved side. We are seldom called upon for assistance otherwise. Therefore, in California, we are associated in the public mind with the I.W.W.; in the South with the negroes or the atheists; in Pennsylvania, West Virginia and New Jersey with labor "agitators"; in Michigan and elsewhere with the Workers' Party; in Albany with birth control; in Boston with the Ku Klux Klan and anarchists. Our enemies have little doubt that we are financed from Moscow.

Usually when an issue of importance arises, one fights not only for the thing immediately involved, but he again takes up the battle for liberty supposed to have been won hundreds of years ago. I have before me a report of the Cheswick case in Pennsylvania, where on August 22, 1927, a meeting, held to discuss the Sacco-Vanzetti case, was scattered by State Troopers. More than two hundred persons, including women and children, were injured when troopers used poison gas and clubs brutally to disperse this meeting which was proceeding peaceably on private property some distance from the highway. One trooper was killed in the fracas, stirred up by this unprovoked assault. Several workers are now in jail.

This narrative of the Pennsylvania coal mines in

time of strike is valuable only in so far as it reflects a general condition. The situation is by no means confined to the Pittsburgh district, nor to Pennsylvania. In 1923 we took a jaunt to Logan, West Virginia, a non-union territory under the control of Sheriff Don Chafin, himself a coal operator and swaggering autocrat of the county. He advised us over the long-distance telephone that no meeting would be permitted. Logan is a quiet community set in the hills at the end of a narrow gauge railroad line. On the way we passed drab, colorless shanties, the so-called homes of the workers. Logan was jammed with miners and railroad men from many parts of the county, attracted by the unusual spectacle of a public meeting. They had come with the eager expectation of seeing us assaulted and hustled to jail for braving "Two-Gun" Don. Arrived in town we tried to find this terror. A mountaineer in the corridor of the courthouse said, "Don's in there." We rapped at the door. No answer. We went to Don's house where his bright-faced boy said, "Sure, Dad's at the courthouse." Our efforts were fruitless. Don wasn't around. In the evening we mounted the courthouse steps. Dr. Huntington, associate editor of *Christian Work*, talked on free speech: "Christ practiced free speech and they killed Him for it." He drew the parallel between ancient Pharisees and modern coal operators. Behind him prowled Don Chafin and a number of deputies.

When we flung the question, "Do you know that the name of Logan is a national scandal?" there came a roar of cheering approval from the crowd. "Free speech in Logan," said one of the speakers, "means talking in public about the very things that interest Logan County. It means talking about the rights of representatives of the Miners' Union: it means talking about the representatives of the operators' association, what they do and how they do it." There was no disorder, although we were later informed that had we talked a few minutes longer, Don Chafin's cohorts, already sorely tried, would have taken action. After the meeting, a disapproving bystander remarked: "Why don't you fellows stay in New York and attend to your own evils? I understand there are lots of prostitutes up there who might require your attention."

The American Civil Liberties Union held its meeting, but a few weeks later we learned that one of our supporters, Maston White, had been beaten on the street late at night by one of Chafin's deputies and lay in the hospital seriously wounded.

Don Chafin is now in jail, not for assault, not for tyranny, not for any of the serious crimes he committed against the poor miners in the name of the law, but for bootlegging. Perhaps in modern civilization this is a more serious crime.

Boston is more elegant, cultured and dignified than Logan, West Virginia. There the authorities prevent public meetings by exercising pressure upon owners of halls and by use of the municipal ordinance requiring a permit in advance. The American Civil Liberties Union was once called to the assistance of the Ku Klux Klan who insisted upon their right to hold a meeting in Boston. We responded, not, however, without first pointing out to the Grand Dragons that, although as Americans we believed in their right to hold meetings, yet as individuals we felt a sneaking satisfaction that they should feel the hand of oppression. Also in Boston we came to the assistance of Margaret Sanger, who wished to hold a meeting to discuss birth control. In Albany, New York, we likewise found meetings on this subject prohibited.

But Boston most clearly showed its hand in the prohibition of meetings to discuss the Sacco-Vanzetti case and this at a time when there was real reason why people should want to discuss this case. Superintendent of Police Crowley said, "You can hold a meeting on the Commons, but you need a permit." "Where can we get a permit?" "Well, I am not sure about that." "Can we use the permit of some other organization?" "I won't answer those questions." The Socialists allowed their annual permit to be used by Sacco-Vanzetti sympathizers. The permit was revoked. Powers Hapgood, to whom I have referred before, laid down his mining tools, and came to Boston. He was arrested for speaking without a permit. The arrest was lawful. The courts had held in the case of *Davis vs. Massachusetts*, passed on in the United States Supreme Court,[11] that the Municipal authorities had the right to demand a permit, as the protection of the lawns and flowers of the park was within their purview.

The Sacco-Vanzetti case aroused the furor of the world. Thousands of people in practically every coun-

11 Davis *vs.* Massachusetts, 167 U. S. 43 (1897) *supra.*

try held meetings of indignation, outrage, resentment and protest. Boston was quiet, though tense. After Powers Hapgood was arrested for speaking on the Common without a permit, a new and more serious charge was laid against him, worded that he

". . . together with divers other evil-disposed persons to the number of twelve and more, whose names are to the said McTiernan unknown, unlawfully, riotously and routously did assemble and gather together, to the disturbance of the public peace, and being so then and there assembled and gathered together in and upon said McTiernan then and there unlawfully, riotously and routously did beat, wound and ill-treat, and other wrongs to the said McTiernan then and there unlawfully, riotously and routously did, against the law, peace and dignity of said Commonwealth."

On analysis it appears that this is a common law charge of riot. Defense of Sacco-Vanzetti sympathizers was not conducive to a Boston lawyer's popularity, yet Joe Bierak and Frank Lichtenstein nobly answered the call. The case was carried to the Superior Criminal Court where it was later tried before a jury. The charge was that Hapgood conspired with twelve other like evil-minded persons, yet it appeared that only Hapgood and one Carvotta were arrested and this because no one else was disorderly. The charge itself was an afterthought, having been made a day after that of the original arrest. Superintendent Crowley of the Boston police, after stating that there was a large and menacing crowd, testified on cross-examination:

Q. When the arrest was made, when the police appeared on the scene, it attracted people there, didn't it?

A. Yes, sir. When the arrests were made then the people all surged or came there from all parts of the Common.

.   .   .   .

Q. There was a crowd around there when Hapgood was arrested?

A. A large crowd.

Q. And that increased hugely?

A. Yes, sir.

Q. Before that time Hapgood had been speaking, hadn't he?

A. Yes, sir, he had, but I didn't hear what he said.

Q. And the congregation was orderly before the arrest?

A. Orderly—as much as a large crowd usually is.

The police were there to preserve order, to arrest disorderly persons. They did not discriminate against Hapgood but:

Q. You say some one in the crowd shouted "Kill them" after Hapgood was in your care?

A. Yes, sir.

Q. You are Superintendent of the Police of Boston?

A. Yes, sir.

Q. Did you have the man arrested?

A. I do not get that question.

.   .   .   .

Q. Did it occur to you to arrest that man?

A. Well—

Q. Answer my question, did it occur to you to arrest that man?

A. No, sir.

Apparently, speaking on the Common without a permit was more serious than threats to kill. Excitement was created, so the police testified, by a cheering crowd. Mr. Mikolajewski testified:

Q. Officer, are people disorderly when they cheer?

A. I would call it such.

Q. Always?

A. Not always.

Q. It depends upon whether you approve of the thing they are cheering for, doesn't it?

A. It all depends.

Officer Murphy testified on cross-examination:

Q. Officer, I understand you had orders to circulate the Common and see that no meetings were held. Is that correct or were your orders that no meetings should be held concerning the Sacco-Vanzetti case?

A. No, to see that there was no speaking done on the Common that day.

Q. Wasn't speaking done on the Common that day?

A. Yes.

Q. By other people?

A. Yes.

Q. So you didn't obey your orders?

A. I did obey orders.

Q. Weren't your orders changed?

A. No, I didn't get any more orders.

The police testified that Hapgood had continued to

make his speech while in the hands of the police, and that Carvotta had attempted to rescue Hapgood when under arrest. There were different accounts of what Hapgood had said. There was no denial that he had remarked: "We fought a war for democracy for this." He had further said: "I insist on the right of free speech. The people must save Sacco and Vanzetti. We must not let Sacco and Vanzetti be murdered. Don't forget, comrades! Keep it up! Save the men!" But some officers testified that in addition to this Hapgood had said: "Don't let them take me."

Officer McTiernan admitted that Hapgood didn't routously or otherwise, beat, wound, ill-treat and otherwise wrong him, against the dignity of the Commonwealth. He had merely sworn to this because it was part of the complaint.

The jury were reminded of forgotten episodes in American history. In imagination they were called upon to make a tour of the Boston Common. While waiting for the patrol wagon Hapgood had stood with his back to a bronze tablet reading as follows:

"The site of Fox Hill.

"Fortified during the siege of Boston from the bottom of the Common.

"British crossed Charles River this eighteenth day of April, 1775, to proceed to Lexington and Concord.

"Erected by the City of Boston in the year 1925."

This tribute was to the Minute Men of 1775.

A plaque not far away read:

"Lafayette, who nobly served the cause of liberty on two continents."

And then, from the Bunker Hill oration of Webster:

"Heaven saw fit to ordain that the electric spark of liberty should be conducted from the new world to the old."

Near-by was a tribute to Paul Revere:

"May the youth of to-day when they visit the old home be inspired with the patriotism of Paul Revere."

And around the Common were mementoes of John Hancock and Samuel Adams. Hapgood stood up before the Court and Jury, while for him was quoted the wording on the base of the Commonwealth Avenue statue of William Lloyd Garrison—Garrison, who was dragged through the streets in Boston and threatened with hanging for espousing the cause of Abolition:

"I am in earnest. I will not equivocate. I will not excuse. I will not retreat a single inch—and I will be heard."

John Adams was called upon to speak:

"When kings, ministers, governors or legislators, therefore, instead of exercising the powers entrusted with them according to the principles, forms and proportions stated by the Constitution, and established by the original compact, prostitute those powers to the purposes of oppression to subvert, instead of supporting a free constitution; to destroy instead of preserving the lives, liberties and properties of the people, they are no longer to be deemed magistrates vested with a sacred character."

Daniel Webster made the peroration:

"The last hopes of mankind, therefore, rest with us; and

if it should be proclaimed, that our example had become an argument against the experiment for freedom, the knell of popular liberty would be sounded throughout the earth."

The Jury retired. Twenty-three hours later they reported a disagreement as to whether Hapgood and Carvotta had been engaged in rioting.

But during the excitement of the Sacco-Vanzetti case Hapgood had been dealt with even more summarily. On the night of the execution he was thrown into the Psychopathic Hospital of Boston to be held for observation as to his sanity. I went to the hospital and asked for the order of commitment. Dr. Barnett said that that was a private document. I asked what evidence there was that Hapgood was psychopathic. Had any doctor made a certificate? I was told none had. I asked that doctors, whom I had brought, be permitted to examine him. This was refused. I asked that examination be permitted by one doctor as Hapgood's own physician. My request was denied. Finally I stated I wanted to see Hapgood.

I was taken upstairs. A door was unlocked. We passed through. It was locked again. A few steps further another door was unlocked. We passed through. It was locked again. There, in a ward containing about eight beds, was Hapgood. Next to him was a patient who closely gripped a piece of paper, to which he had held for five successive days. In another bed was one who held his head in an immovable position, rigid. One was a negro held for observation because he had been found reading a newspaper while sitting on a curbstone. In the next room in cells were raving maniacs. Occasionally a shriek would rend the air.

I told Hapgood to take his clothes and come with me. He answered, "I can't. They have taken away my clothes." I went downstairs. I pleaded and stormed. I evinced my surprise that doctors had so little sense of the dignity of their profession that they would permit themselves to be used as tools by the police. The doctors of the Psychopathic Hospital observed me kindly. I have argued before juries, judges and commissions of all kinds, but never with the same feeling of futility as before these doctors, trained to observe emotional outbursts. They watched my gorge rise and fall; to them I was an interesting specimen, another case for observation. They listened indulgently and answered kindly, but they were immovable. I endeavored to obtain a writ of habeas corpus, but found that it would not be returnable for a day or two. We applied to Judge Sullivan to grant the writ, but were told he had no jurisdiction. We pointed out that Hapgood was a defendant in his court, in another case, about to be tried, whereupon the police withdrew the charge.

We had arranged with Dr. Myerson to go to the Psychopathic Hospital and examine Hapgood. Later we found that the full staff had met and had come to the conclusion that Hapgood was not only sane but exceptionally intelligent. He had been asked his views on society. He told us he made the best socialistic speech of his life. He also had had an opportunity to tell the staff the facts of the Sacco-Vanzetti case, which gratified him, because while he had wasted no time in relating the story of the case to the patients in his ward, yet he realized that this was not very effective propaganda. Some of the staff were apparently shocked into thought on the case, on democracy and social conditions in America. One of the doctors informed me that Hapgood was not particularly efficient in arithmetic. They had had him multiplying, dividing, adding and subtracting. They had tickled the soles of his feet. They had pressed pins into his body. They had scratched his breast. But it seems that he had all the normal reactions, even that of indignation. Poor Powers had tried hourly, but vainly, through the night, to get some information about what had happened to his friends, Sacco and Vanzetti.

This had been an original method of disposing of one of the minority who insisted upon being heard. True, a few rights had been violated. He had been denied the right of free speech; he had been arrested without warrant; he had been denied liberty; he had had no opportunity to provide bail. In the language of the street, he had been "framed." But this was Massachusetts in August, 1927, and the Sacco-Vanzetti case was on.

There were numerous arrests in those days. People from all over the country, unable to rest at home while the tragedy was being played in Boston, had come to make their protests. They held meetings or picketed before the State House, carrying placards and marching in single file. On August 23rd, the day following the execution, was set the trial of those who picketed.

At the Municipal Court masses of people stood outside the courtroom or sat on the stairs—all of them defendants, all of them awed, saddened by the execution. The officers passing me through the gate courteously permitted me to take into the empty courtroom Ellen Hayes, of Wellesley, and Ella Bloor, of San Francisco, the sweet old women who were our proudest pickets.

Ella Reeves Bloor was charged with a variety of crimes. She had not only picketed, but she had had the temerity to make a speech from a window the night before. Somebody in the crowd had shouted: "Go back to Russia!" Some one had answered: "She comes from generations of Americans." The two started a fight, so the police arrested "Mother" Bloor, charging her with inciting to riot.

In the dock was Polly Holliday, from Greenwich Village. She had spent the night in jail as a volunteer, since there had not been enough bail to go around. She was the young woman who, learning that the police were seizing placards, had had her message written on her slicker, knowing full well that in Boston the police would not undress a lady. In the corridor was Lew Ney, who had announced himself as the Mayor of Greenwich Village, dressed in knickers, high walking boots, and with a haversack swung over his shoulder, and passing around word that a ceremonial would take place later in the day at the home of William James. He started talking to the police of the delights of Greenwich Village and was encouraged to show them radical papers which he carried, whereupon he was arrested, charged with the possession of indecent literature.

Some of the cases were based on a charge of "loitering and sauntering." Some on a charge of "obstructing traffic." Where the individual had been arrested before, he was charged with "inciting to riot." It did not make much difference what the charge was, for, after all, it was necessary merely to find an excuse to oppress those who believed in the innocence of Sacco and Vanzetti.

The police suggested that they were anxious to get the whole business out of the way; that if everybody pleaded not guilty there would be merely a charge against all of "sauntering and loitering," which would mean a small fine. I stated that we wished to try some of the cases. I told Judge Sullivan that I did not think these people had violated the law, but that if after trial he found guilt in the test cases, the others would plead guilty, or, pleading not guilty, would waive trial so that he might find them guilty and assess a small fine. This seemed to be a practical procedure, so I chose my defendants.

Of course, I picked Ellen Hayes and Ella Reeves Bloor. I chose Edna St. Vincent Millay, the poet, Katherine Huntington, member of an old and distinguished Boston family, John Howard Lawson, eminent playwright, and William Patterson, a colored New York lawyer, always active in a just cause. I avoided choosing those who had been arrested before, in spite of the fact that another charge should not affect the question of guilt or innocence on this particular trial.

Strangely enough, I had come to believe that not only the police, but the judiciary as well, are not likely to look kindly on one who repeatedly and insistently asserted his rights.

In requesting the opportunity to test the law Judge Sullivan frankly told me that if the defendants had picketed (and I admitted they had), he would have to find them guilty under the statute. I still insisted upon trial.

The defendants stood to the right of the Judge's bench; behind them were the police witnesses. All were sworn at once. Sergeant Thomas F. Connolly, officer, was the first witness. He told of warning and arresting the defendants. He testified they carried placards. Holding up one, he said it was carried by Miss Millay. She interrupted and told him, in rather a decisive way, that he was mistaken. "The placard I carried said, 'If these men are executed, justice is dead in Massachusetts.'" The Sergeant was interrogated as to whether these people were walking continuously, to which the answer was "yes." "What is the difference between walking and sauntering?" A. "Walking is where people are walking about their business with a definite object in view," returned the Sergeant vigorously. Q. "Then, by your definition, if these people had in view the definite object of protesting, that would be walking and not sauntering?" The witness was in doubt. He was asked why he did not arrest other people who were standing around watching. He "arrested only those whom he had orders to arrest."

Q. But the others were loitering, were they not?

A. I don't know.

Q. Weren't they either loitering or sauntering?

A. They were told to move on.

Q. Is it not a fact that the only people in front of the State House who were not loitering or sauntering were those in the picket line?

A. I do not know.

The ordinance of Boston provided that it was a crime to loiter or saunter, without moving on after seven minutes, if so ordered by the police. But it provided that nothing therein contained should prevent peaceful persuasion or the exercise of rights guaranteed by other statutes. A State law specifically recognized the right to carry placards.

Miss Ellen Hayes, calm, grim, determined, seventy-six years of age, with white bobbed hair, was called to testify. She stood beside the Judge's bench. She stated she had been a professor of mathematics and astronomy at Wellesley College. Had she "come to Boston on business"?

A. Yes.

Q. Serious business?

A. Very serious business.

She had come to protest against the injustice to Sacco and Vanzetti.

Q. Was that your business?

A. It was the business of every decent American citizen.

Q. Did you lead the picket line?

A. Yes.

Q. Did you carry a placard?

A. Yes.

Inscribed upon it were the words "Hail, Sacco and Vanzetti! The élite of the world greet you as heroes!" She had walked continuously. She had not sauntered or loitered. She knew that as an American citizen she was guaranteed the right to petition the Governor. She was there for the purpose of petitioning the Governor for justice to these men. Part of her business as an American citizen was to express her views. She, of course, had not come to commit violence. There was no disorder. She was exercising the right of peaceful persuasion. She did not resist when two burly police officers arrested her. Why was she protesting? Because she thought Sacco and Vanzetti were innocent.

Miss Millay then testified. She was born in Rockland, Maine:

Q. What is your profession?
A. A writer.
Q. Poetess?
A. No, poet (she corrected, with a smile).
Q. You wrote "The King's Henchmen" produced at the Metropolitan Opera House of New York last winter?
A. I wrote the words to it.
Q. You are a college graduate?
A. A graduate of Vassar.
Q. Was your purpose peaceful persuasion?
A. It was.
Q. Was there any disorder?
A. I saw none.
Q. Did you loiter?
A. No.
Q. Saunter?
A. No.

Q. Did you have a purpose there or were you idling?

A. I was engaged in the most serious business of my life; that of protesting as an American citizen against a grave injustice.

The testimony of the others was to the same effect.

Our legal position seemed impregnable. Judge Sullivan interrupted the argument: "Suppose those who held the other view should likewise carry placards and the two groups should meet?" I answered that that was a civilized way for people to express themselves; that it would be the duty of the police to arrest only those who were disorderly. But, after all, that issue had not arisen. The question was whether these people, engaged in the legitimate business of peaceful persuasion, were guilty of crime.

As I finished my argument Judge Sullivan started, "I find these defendants—" Knowing what was coming, I interrupted and asked the Judge to state his reasons. I referred to the fact that while he had the power to impose sentence, yet it was due to the defendants, to lawyers and to the community that on an issue of this importance, he should satisfy us rationally.

"Guilty," tersely replied Judge Sullivan.

Miss Millay, convinced of her innocence by my persuasive appeal, commented: "The Judge just seemed not to pay any attention."

Miss Huntington read a statement in part as follows:

"I am an American citizen by inheritance. The name of my family appears on the Declaration of Independence.

When the liberties which my ancestors established are endangered as they have been in Boston during these recent horrible weeks, I consider it peculiarly my duty to protest. The right of free assemblage is denied to citizens who wish to discuss a grave national issue. Boston Common is denied to those who would use it for the very purposes for which that Common was set aside and dedicated. Terrorism by the police replaces law and order.

"Under these circumstances, I must exercise my rights as a citizen in the only manner which is left and make some demonstration of my sentiments in common with others who feel as I do.

"If it is unlawful to walk in silence before the State House, carrying a card mutely voicing a great injustice, then I am guilty. If it is unlawful to urge upon the public authorities in this manner, while there is still time to rectify a tragic mistake, the earnest wish of the citizens that the honor of the commonwealth be saved, then I am guilty. If it is unlawful to hold an opinion which happens to differ from that of some of the public servants whose salaries my taxes go to pay, then I am guilty. If believing in the innocence of two brave and unfortunate men charged with a crime which almost the entire civilized world believes they did not commit, then I am guilty.

"I don't believe that this is the sort of country which my ancestors tried to make—and that is why I walked in front of the State House yesterday."

Then old Ellen Hayes mentioned her stock, running back to 1630, and declared she would be untrue to her heritage should she not take upon herself at least this slight obligation of citizenship.

Miss Millay traced her ancestry, related the im-

portance to her of the issue at stake and declared herself ready at any time to do at least this much to
justify her ancestry and birth.

An appeal was taken.   In December, immediately
after the Powers Hapgood trial for rioting, and while
his jury was out, we empaneled twelve other men to
hear the cases against the picketers.   One of our defendants, Patterson, had been lost somewhere in the files
of the police department, but we picked up John Dos
Passos, George Teeple, George Kraske and one or two
others on the way to the Appellate Court.   Edna St.
Vincent Millay, having appeared in Boston on other
occasions when her case was called for trial, was then on
a lecture tour.   Her default was taken.   "Three times
I waited for them," she is reported to have said; "the
judges can now wait for me."   She had had little experience as a criminal.

All cases were tried together.   Many of the veniremen had sat in the courtroom and had watched the
earlier proceeding in which they had had some reminders of American history.   At about 4 P.M. the jury
retired.   We hoped for a disagreement at best.   Hour
after hour passed with no word from the jury room.
We were informed that they had come to a decision at
about midnight.   In the morning the verdict was read:
"Not guilty!"

Pennsylvania, West Virginia, Massachusetts!   The
roll would probably not be complete unless one enumerated most of the States.   In Oklahoma in order to
assemble, striking miners camouflaged their meetings as
religious revivals.   At the mouth of the coal pits would

stand groups of union men praying hard for the benefit of non-union men as they left the mines:

"We pray to God that a heavy bowlder won't fall from the skies to kill these snakes who are taking the food out of the mouths of our starving women and children. We trust the Lord that no unruly individual will rip their guts out. Amen!"

When arrested these men had the support of the church elements and were discharged.

New Jersey has within the last few years read itself out of a union of free states. A meeting was advertised in Paterson "for the purpose of protesting against unlawful acts . . . and supposed oppression by the police officers in excluding the strikers from Turn Hall, and in preventing their continuance with daily meetings." The Chief of Police forbade a meeting. Roger Baldwin, representing the American Civil Liberties Union, started from the hall with a procession of thirty persons marching in twos, led by two young women bearing an American flag. At the City Hall Plaza one Butterworth stopped to address the crowd: "Fellow workers, . . ." he said. The police asked whether he had a permit. He held up the Bill of Rights of New Jersey. "This is my permit." He was arrested. The police wrested the flag from the women who were likewise taken into custody. Roger Baldwin was not arrested but upon his insistence that he was responsible for the meeting, he was later held by the police, indicted, tried and sentenced to six months in jail.

On writ of error to the Supreme Court, the judgment was affirmed.[12]   Said Black, J., in the opinion:

"The testimony, a consideration of the background of the case and the subsequent events also clearly show, that the advertised meeting in the City Hall Plaza, the most conspicuous place in the city, laid out a program in defiance of the constituted authorities.   It was intended in a spectacular fashion, to emphasize a disapproval of the action of the police."

In view of the fact that "this would provoke police hostility" a consequent breach of the peace might result.   Therefore, said the Court, there was an unlawful assembly.   Yet the New Jersey Constitution provides that "no law shall be passed to restrain or abridge the liberty of speech . . ." and "the people have the right freely to assemble together, to consult for the common good, to make known their opinions to their representatives, and to petition for the redress of grievances."

The citizens had been denied access to their hall. They had gathered "in defiance of the constituted authorities, . . . to emphasize a disapproval of the action of the police."   They were dispersed and found guilty of crime.   Here is truly a death knell to liberty. Right of free speech and assemblage in New Jersey is limited to occasions when the police approve!   What are the constitutional guaranties worth?   How far have we advanced or retrograded from the principle

---

[12] State of New Jersey vs. Butterworth et al (N. J. Supreme Court), New Jersey Advance Reports and Weekly Law Review, Vol. V, No. 46, p. 1657.

enunciated by the Court in *United States vs. Cruik-shank* (92 U. S. 452):

"The very idea of a government, republican in form, implies a right on the part of its citizens to meet peaceably for consultation in respect to public affairs and to petition for a redress of grievances."

This meeting was called to discuss public affairs—suppression by the police. The case was appealed to a higher court where it is now pending.*

But Passaic, New Jersey, during the mill strike presented the most comprehensive picture of lawlessness. Here was obviously a spontaneous strike due to conditions. People of different origin, language, thought, poverty-stricken, cowed and with huge families, would not be interested in theoretical labor union ideas. Any unity was out of the question until the breaking point had been reached, yet within a few weeks some fifteen thousand people struck their jobs. Conditions in the mills were well known. Men worked days; women worked nights. The children carried placards: "We want milk!" "We want enough to eat!" "We want our mothers home nights!" Long hours, meager pay, labor under unsanitary conditions, work speeded up, sudden lay-offs for indefinite periods, spies infesting the factories, blacklisting, fingerprinting of employees, and in general conditions under which no decent human being ought to work or live! The answer was that Albert Weisbord, the leader, was a Communist. The workers in Passaic cared not a rap for this. When a

* The judgment was reversed by the Court of Errors and Appeals on May 15, 1928, after a four-years' fight by the American Civil Liberties Union, the highest court in New Jersey holding that there was "nothing in the statement of the facts * * * to have warranted the finding of the Trial Judge that the accused were guilty of the offense of unlawful assembly."

ten per cent cut brought a climax to conditions, the
disorganized workers found in him a man to lead them.
By unexpected good fortune in the early stages of the
strike, the police clubbed a few newspaper reporters.
The issue became one not wholly of conditions in the
mills, not of Weisbord the Communist, but one of civil
liberty. Cossacks make Communists. Weisbord had a
sense of the dramatic. Babies in carriages, women and
young children, headed picket lines. Disinterested
(and respectable) New York women were placed in the
forefront. Steel helmets and gas masks were worn by
strikers who not long ago had fought for democracy.
Police brutality continued. Tear gas, fire hose, rifles
and clubs were used to maintain a species of order.

On one occasion a group of us went to Belmont
Park, near Passaic, where Under-Sheriff Donaldson
and his armed gang were standing guard. "We'd like
to hold a meeting," we said. The answer was "Va-
moose!" "Well, if we can't hold a meeting in the park,
may we hold one inside the hall?" "I ain't got nothing
to say to you people; just get out of here." One man,
Robert Wolf, did not move fast enough. He was arrested. I appeared at the Police Court. He was
charged with not having dispersed "within an hour"
after the reading of the Riot Act. This would constitute a crime. No Riot Act had been read. He had
been arrested within five minutes of his arrival. Yet
Mr. Justice Hargreaves, whose business, on the side,
was real estate and insurance, held him in $5,000 bail.
I protested that that was supposed to be a court of
law, to which the justice responded, "This is a court of

martial law." Angered, I called the proceedings a mockery of justice. "One word more," said Hargreaves, "and I'll have you arrested for disorderly conduct." I said that we called it "contempt of court" in New York. A lawyer of Passaic, Joseph Feder, remarked, "This is worse than Siberia." He was thrown out of court.

Robert Dunn of the American Civil Liberties Union, was held in ten thousand dollars bail for marching in a picket line. Esther Lowell, a newspaper woman, taken into custody within three minutes after the reading of the Riot Act, was charged with failing to disperse within an hour. She had attempted to pick up a woman thrown down by the police. On another occasion, Norman Thomas had the audacity to address about thirty people in a vacant lot that had been hired. His pulpit was an apple tree. He made the seditious utterance that bail of thirty thousand dollars, held over Weisbord, was in contravention of the Constitution of the State of New Jersey, which provides that excessive bail shall not be demanded. He was thrown into jail. The bail for this heinous act was fixed at ten thousand dollars. The American Civil Liberties Union then obtained an injunction to prevent the Sheriff from interfering with peaceful meetings. Meetings were held. There was no disorder.

In New York City, school buildings are used as public forums in the evening. Yet the American Civil Liberties Union has been denied the right to hold a meeting to discuss the subject "Old-Fashioned Free Speech," with John Haynes Holmes, Nevin Sayre,

James Weldon Johnson and myself as speakers. Certain organizations and individuals are blacklisted. Samuel Untermyer, Louis Marshall, Morris Ernst and Newman Levy have enlisted as attorneys in the controversy, still undetermined, against the Board of Education. "It would be all right," said the Corporation Counsel, "if they would accept our limitations on free speech. These people do not object to expression of opinion on any subject." The American Defense League, the Lord's Day Alliance, Ladies' Good Government Clubs and other hundred per cent patriots nodded approval through their fearful representatives. Naturally they felt a schoolhouse should not be used for the expression of free or new ideas. The purpose of public education is regimentation, not individuality; acceptance, not doubt; complacent satisfaction and agreement, not stimulation of thought.

Are these instances exceptional? Not at all. Intolerance is in the saddle. Whether or not there is free speech and assemblage does not depend on whether I may express my views or whether my respectable reader (if there is a reader and if he is respectable) may express his. Naturally, our views are sound and wise. And we are ordinarily reasonable enough, or timid enough, to withhold expression in time of stress. The test is whether the guaranties protect the unpopular, those of wild or radical views, and at times when society disapproves of the expression of those views. Our doors are sealed against foreigners with radical ideas, because, say those in government, our people have so little belief in democracy, so little confidence in our institutions, that our government would topple had it to meet radical views in open forum, and this in spite of our pretense that in the free competition of ideas, truth will prevail. Liberty has dangers but they do not compare with those of tyranny. The recognition of rights more effectively maintains order than machine guns.

The ideal of America, as expressed in the Constitution and Bills of Rights, is liberty. Our institutions are based on the theory that order is best maintained through liberty. But people to-day merely do lip service to the ideals of free institutions. They are fearful.

As was said by Mr. Justice Brandeis:[18]

"Those who won our independence by revolution were not cowards. They did not fear political change. They did not exalt order at the cost of liberty."

And then these ringing words:

"Those who won our independence believed that the final end of the State was to make men free to develop their faculties and that in its government the deliberative forces should prevail over the arbitrary. They valued liberty both as an end and as a means. They believed liberty to be the secret of happiness and courage to be the secret of liberty. They believed that freedom to think as you will and to speak as you think are means indispensable to the discovery and spread of political truth; that without free speech and assembly discussion would be futile; that with them, discussion affords ordinarily adequate protection

[18] Whitney *vs.* California, 274 U. S. 357, 377, 375, *supra.* Separate concurring opinion in which Mr. Justice Holmes joined.

against the dissemination of noxious doctrine; that the greatest menace to freedom is an inert people; that public discussion is a political duty; and that this should be a fundamental principle of the American government. They recognized the risks to which all human institutions are subject. But they knew that order cannot be secured merely through fear of punishment for its infraction; that it is hazardous to discourage thought, hope and imagination; that fear breeds repression; that repression breeds hate; that hate menaces stable government; that the path of safety lies in the opportunity to discuss freely supposed grievances and proposed remedies; and that the fitting remedy for evil counsels is good ones. Believing in the power of reason as applied through public discussion, they eschewed silence coerced by law—the argument of force in its worst form. Recognizing the occasional tyrannies of governing majorities, they amended the Constitution so that free speech and assembly should be guaranteed."

We need a regeneration of the brave men and sound philosophers who wrote the Constitution and the Bills of Rights—of men who are not afraid of freedom.

FREEDOM OF THE PRESS

FREEDOM OF THE PRESS

The "American Mercury" Case—Commonwealth
vs. H. L. Mencken, Boston Municipal Court—
The American Mercury, Inc. vs. Chase et al.—
The American Mercury, Inc. vs. Kiely, Postmaster, New York Federal Court

By and large, there is less interference with freedom of the press than with other civil rights. I do
not refer to the responsibility for libel which exercises
a proper restraint, nor to the pressure on the part of
advertisers, bankers or the views of the community, nor
have I in mind the frequent complaints concerning
suppression of news by editors, editorial writers and
reporters. After all, the newspaper proprietor—and
he is the boss—usually is free from official restraint or
force. No doubt many newspapers, particularly in
small communities, are unduly cautious and lack independence. Though the public welfare may suffer, it is
the right of newspaper owners to choose their own
policies.

The reason for comparatively little official interference with the press is not hard to seek. Newspapers
require capital; ordinarily therefore they represent a
privileged class. Further, an attack on the freedom of

one paper is regarded by the press as an attack on all, so on this issue there is a tremendously powerful group to oppose violation. Yet in time of war, when a free press in a democracy would be a real safeguard, there is suppression. During the recent unpleasantness, this suppression was practiced sometimes directly by the Federal Government, often through the Post Office, sometimes by municipal ordinance forbidding the sale of certain papers, sometimes by force. Of course, the test of freedom is its recognition in time of stress. But in normal times the issue rarely arises—at any rate, not in political fields. True, we have occasional cases of charges of contempt of court. In places under our control, such as Hayti or the Virgin Islands, we jail editors. Not so long ago, Carlo Tresca, editor of an Italian paper in New York, having earned the enmity of the Fascists, found himself charged (it is said at the instigation of the Italian government) with having published in his newspaper an advertisement of a book on birth control. Two small lines offering the book had appeared in the corner of the paper. He was sentenced to a year in Atlanta. It would seem that the authorities were "after" him for something else, but the advertisement served their purpose.

During the War, *The Masses*, a radical publication, displayed a picture of a "cracked" Liberty Bell, and otherwise indicated some contempt for the Glorious Adventure. The Postmaster General ordered the issue of the magazine banned on the ground that it violated the Espionage Act. (The United States Supreme

Setting out "manifestly" to corrupt the morals of "youth."

Court held that the First Amendment to the Constitution, guaranteeing the freedom of the press, did not apply at a time when its protection was most needed.) *The Masses* sued out an injunction against the Post Office and their contention was upheld by Judge Learned Hand.[1] "Why," said he in substance, "if this is unlawful, the editors would be guilty of a criminal act," which reduced the proposition to a *reductio ad absurdum*. The Circuit Court found the issue unmailable but agreed with Judge Hand's reasoning.[2] The editors were indicted. They were men of old American lineage and great charm of manner. One of them, Max Eastman, by sheer force of personality, persuaded the jury to disagree. But the Post Office, having in the interim held up other numbers, then took the position that since the magazine had not been regularly distributed, it was not entitled to second-class mailing privileges. *The Masses* went out of business.

Sometimes the charge of "obscenity," the usual ground of complaint against offending publications, is made in good faith, but more often it is a method to "get" some one or something objectionable on other grounds. Obscenity is such a vague, indefinite proposition as legally construed, that it is often difficult to meet the charge. A court or jury often condemns in order to illustrate their own strict notions of morality or to sustain a doubtful sense of virtue. "Elmer Gantry," by Sinclair Lewis, attacks the church or

[1] Masses Publishing Co. *vs.* Patten, Postmaster, 244 Fed. 535 (1917).
[2] Masses Publishing Co. *vs.* Patten, Postmaster. 246 Fed. 24 (1917).

rather churchmen; "An American Tragedy," by Dreiser, reflects on the salvationist method of early education; "Oil," by Upton Sinclair, shows the corruption of the Harding administration. All are banned in Boston. *The American Mercury* attacks everything held sacred by Brahmin Babbittry; specifically, prior to 1926 it had aimed its shafts at the culture and morals of Boston, and the Watch and Ward Society, a self-appointed guardian thereof.

On April 5, 1926, a milling, enthusiastic and hilarious mob of thousands gathered at the corner of Park and Tremont streets in Boston, the crowd running over onto the Boston Common. Word had leaked out that at two o'clock in the afternoon the April number of *The American Mercury* was to be sold. There was a huge demand for the magazine and at almost any price. People were wildly waving one, five and ten dollar bills. One might imagine mobs of people gathered in a large American city to buy *Jim Jam Jems* or *Snappy Stories*. Be it known that *The American Mercury* is not ordinarily regarded as a thrilling or sensational publication. It is not illustrated. It is quiet in dress, dignified at times, and thoughtful in spots. The demand for *The American Mercury* was not due to any uprising of the intelligentsia of Boston. Quite to the contrary.

A few days before H. L. Mencken, editor of *The American Mercury*, and Alfred Knopf, the publisher, had visited my office. Mencken did not waste time in coming to the point:

"Those dogs in Boston have banned *The American Mer-*

cury. The swine don't read it. They read 'Hot Dog.'
And these wowsers aren't even in the cow country."

Mencken's words were characteristic, but not illuminating. On inquiry it appeared that the April number
of his magazine contained an article entitled "Hatrack," a chapter from "Up from Methodism," a book
by Herbert Asbury. The claim was made that this
article violated the obscenity laws. The real basis of
the objection was that it attacked a widely held religious concept, to wit, the power for "good" of revivalist meetings. In his piece, Asbury had told of
such meetings in the small town of Farmington, Mis-
souri, where professional devil-chasers imported for
the purpose, "proclaimed loudly and incessantly" that
the morals of the town "were compounded of a slice of
Sodom and a cut of Gomorrah, with an extract of
Babylon to flavor the stew." Particularly, the pious
brethren worried over the amorous activities of the
inhabitants. They would point out that men were
constantly engaged in attacking virgins and advised
the young women "to go armed to the teeth prepared
to do battle in defense of their chastity." They would
add that the town permitted dens of vice, full of
alluring women whose devices were aided by trappings
of luxury—red carpets, draped walls, settees largely
proportioned, all in a background appealing to the
senses. The effect of such information was to create an
unusual eagerness in the audience. Asbury suggested
that all this is more or less of a dream of fevered
senses; that in most of our small towns there is no
such thing as commercialized prostitution. He illus-

trated the actual situation with a woman descriptively called "Hatrack"—the occasional prostitute who plied her trade in Farmington. Hatrack was a household drudge, but on Sundays she would go to church to offer "her soul to the Lord." The respectable citizens of the town shunned her. So she went to the devil. As Asbury said:

" . . . For Hatrack there was no forgiveness. Mary Magdalen was a saint in Heaven, but Hatrack remained a harlot in Farmington. . . . She was hopeful always . . . that the brothers and sisters who talked so volubly about the grace and the mercy of God would offer her some of the religion that they dripped so freely over every one else in the town. But they did not and so she went back down the street to the post office, swishing her skirts and offering herself to all who desired her."

This isn't a pleasant story. It is nevertheless said to be true. One can easily conceive the effect of such a recital upon those whose chief emotional outlet is attained at revivalist meetings.

The test of violation of the obscenity laws is not measured by one's approval or disapproval of sentiments expressed, nor has it been thought that such laws are violative of a free press. They are not, when interpreted, as they have been time and again, to apply merely to matter that excites libidinous thought, impure imagination or sexual desire. Material, however sordid, shocking and unpleasant, which stirs thought, but does not have the above effect, does not violate these laws. Is the appeal to the mind or the senses? The distinction is a sound one. Thought and the ex-

pression of thought are free.   Emotions and the incitement to sexual impulses are not free.   One may admit that it is difficult to draw the line, yet however far
to the left, there is a point at which most men would
agree that, in the present state of civilization, anything
on the other side should be banned.

Of course nothing is in itself obscene.   The question
of whether or not one gets a sexual thrill out of certain
material, depends upon his or her experience.   It is
a matter of custom.   If we go far enough, we may
image a situation where almost anything will appear
pornographic to emotions oversensitized by repression.
In the course of history, and among different races,
every part of the body, from the top of the head to
the sole of the foot, has had an exciting effect.   Among
one tribe women might go naked, except for a head
covering, without stirring the emotions of men, but if
one removed the head covering, the thoughts of the
males would become unprintable.   A few years ago, if a
woman of the East were seen in the field with uncovered
face, up would go her petticoats to hide the face.   So
with the breasts at another time or place, the stomach
elsewhere, or the feet.   The Russians indulge in nude
mixed bathing—an awesome custom till one gets used
to it.   To-day women wear short skirts.   The sight of
an ankle or a knee does not now cause excitement, but
a few years ago, when the wind blew around the Flat-
iron Building in New York, the corner was a vantage
point for men whose eyes had long been starved for
such attractive and thrilling parts of woman's anatomy.
A fair deduction is that were mysteries removed, so-

ciety would become so clean-minded that there would
be no such thing as "obscenity"—in the present sense.

Would this make men and women less attractive to
each other? Not at all. A beautiful face is still alluring, though faces are not covered.

But the question to-day is where to draw the line.
Probably when these laws were written the legislators
had pretty clearly in mind what they wished to prohibit. Anthony Comstock, the famous Vice Crusader,
spent weeks in Washington with a suitcase full of vile
literature and pornographic pictures which he showed
to interested Congressmen in the cloakrooms. By this
method he induced the passage of the Federal Postal
Law barring obscene matter from the mails. It is
unlikely that men would disagree on the question of
obscenity when applied to Comstock's collection. It
has been remarked by Heywood Broun that self-appointed censors have an advantage over the rest of us.
They can eat their cake and suppress it too.

At any rate, the "wowsers" in Boston had suppressed the April number of *The American Mercury*.
The background shed light on the situation. Within
the past six months the *Mercury* had had the audacity
to publish an article by A. L. S. Wood, entitled "Keeping the Puritans Pure" and another article by Charles
Angoff entitled "Boston Twilight." In the former the
author exposed the system by which the Watch and
Ward Society of Boston kept its fingers on the throats
of the news and book dealers. The other article told
of the decline of Boston as a cultural center.

For years the Watch and Ward Society had exer-

cised an effective dictatorship under the leadership of
J. Frank Chase, whose sensitive emotional mechanism
determined what Bostonians might or might not read.
Anything which raised his temperature unduly was felt
to be dangerous to others—particularly to "youth."
Strangely enough as Chase grew older, he apparently
became more highly sensitized. To the old, youth always seems to need protection. This is a gross libel—
youth has its decent restraints and ideals as opposed to
a certain looseness which comes with the cynicism of
age. But when Chase felt that youth must be saved, his
method of operation was simple. He would merely
notify booksellers that he or his committee had read a
book; that in their opinion it was violative of the law;
that they took no responsibility for making the statement and would not give further advice. The Boston
book market responded nobly and with surprising
unanimity. Sale of the book was ended. Even the
newspapers would not comment on it. "I had it in
my power," once remarked Mr. Chase, "to prevent an
American edition of the 'Arabian Nights.' It is not
likely that if I had ordered a raid, any one else
would have risked another $25,000 for another set of
plates." As the author said in the "Keeping the Puritans Pure" article:

"The pleasant scheme that not only suppresses books,
but also suppresses all mention of those suppressed, permits the Rev. Mr. Chase to talk in his reports of 'waves
of obscenity' and the good work of the Court of Preventive
Criticism without the danger of having his tall talk con-
trasted with his short list. Almost every state in the

Union has a statute as umbrageous as that of Massachusetts. But no state can have as perfect a system of Preventive Criticism until it finds a J. Frank Chase."

Not only did the article "Hatrack" appear in the April number of the *Mercury*, but there was another piece referring to the Methodist endeavor to prevent magazine circulation as follows:

"In this benign work it has the aid of the Reverend J. Frank Chase of the Boston Watch and Ward Society and Methodist vice hunter of long practice and great native talent."

With a magazine the procedure of suppression was different from that of book-banning. It was merely necessary to notify the Boston distributing agency that the magazine, in the opinion of Chase, violated the law and that a warrant would be issued for the arrest of the manager if it was circulated. Mencken made it clear that, if action was not taken, a magazine of pugnacious opinion was in great danger of curtailment. Ordinarily the question of suppression involves the small book or news dealer who cannot afford to make a fight. He is naturally satisfied if the penalty is limited to a fine. Brazen defiance of Chase merited this at least. The authorities had already arrested a Greek named Felix Karagianes for "manifestly" corrupting the youth of Harvard by selling the April number of the magazine.

There was only one way squarely to raise the issue. Would Mencken go to Boston, sell the *Mercury* and submit to arrest? He would. I went along.

Arrived in Boston we found that no one could sell magazines without a peddler's license. Mencken made the necessary application. He had a choice of two licenses, one permitting the sale of bones, grease and refuse matter; the second giving leave to hawk anything one chose except fish, fruit or vegetables. We took the latter, although it did occur to us that possibly he should take the one applying to "refuse" matter.

Armed with the license, we approached the Reverend J. Franklin Chase and invited him to buy a copy of the *Mercury* on the Boston Common. Chase swallowed the bait. He did not realize that a smut-hunter's business is greatly prejudiced unless attended with due solemnity, nor did he anticipate that his action would provide such hilarious entertainment for the populace. Into the crowd on the Common we made our way carrying handfuls of *American Mercuries.* Oblivious to a demand that would cheer the heart of any publisher, we refused to sell except to Jason Franklin Chase, secretary of the New England Watch and Ward Society, and then at the fixed price of fifty cents. Chase bought and paid. Mencken is said to have bit the coin, although it seemed to me an unnecessary precaution. He should have had confidence that this eminent custodian of Boston morals would not offer a counterfeit piece. A bundle of magazines was passed to W. A. S. Douglas, Baltimore *Sun* reporter who, much to his astonishment, was promptly arrested for possessing indecent literature. Then began the parade of Mencken and his cohorts, followed

by a joyous crowd, to the Police Station. Bail was
fixed and the hearing set.

The next morning Mencken was brought before Mr.
Justice Parmenter on the charge of selling certain
"obscene, indecent and impure literature . . . manifestly tending to corrupt the morals of youth."
Mencken testified as to the character of the magazine
and made clear that he came to Boston to test and not
to defy the law.   Asbury, having qualified himself by
pointing out his descent from the brother of Bishop
Asbury, one of the founders of the Methodist Church,
testified that the facts in the story were true.   Douglas, also a defendant, testified that he was "hooked"
quite by accident.   The case against him was dismissed.

On careful perusal the Boston censors had found
another objectionable article in the magazine—"Clinical Notes," by George Jean Nathan.   The opinion was
there expressed that sex was a diversion and pastime
and that "civilized man knows little difference between
his bottle of vintage champagne, his Corona-Corona,
his seat at the Follies and the gratification of his sex
impulse."   This thought is obviously very damaging
to one's morals.   The inclusion of it was merely an indication of the desire to "get" Mencken and *The
American Mercury*, once the hunt was started.   In
court, we made the familiar argument that the Bible
or Shakespeare would not stand the test of Chase's
temperature.   Reference was made to the illiberal
spirit throughout the country pursuant to which small
groups of people gathered together to compel others

to accept their ideas. We did not fail to direct attention to the animus of the proceeding. We realized that
the decision depended not so much upon the law or the
article in question as upon the personal attitude of
the Judge. In decisions on these questions, involving
psychological reactions, the Judge expresses himself,
his backgrounds and habit pattern rather than the law.
The effect upon a reader can, of course, never be
measured. It has been said that determination of the
point involved depends upon the effect of the material
upon hypothetical, unknown individuals. Since the
court decision depends upon what the Judge *thinks* will
be the effect, the conclusion merely shows what kind of
a man the Judge is. Realizing that we were in Boston,
we little hoped that any case brought to court, particularly where a warrant had theretofore issued, would
bring a favorable result, but Mr. Justice Parmenter
acquitted Mencken, saying:

"I cannot imagine any one reading the article in question and finding himself or herself attracted towards vice."

Indirectly, of course, this was condemnation of Jason
Franklin Chase, for his reactions brought him to a
contrary conclusion. And the Judge's comment on
"Clinical Notes," to the effect that the article merely
pointed out that "sex is not nearly so important a
matter in life as it is often assumed to be," might have
been persuasive to one less interested in sex as a business than a professional smut-hound.

I know nothing of Chase's early background or
training. However, the attitude of mind of such an

individual causes reflection. Anthony Comstock, the most famous of this galaxy, was surrounded in his home by three women, a repressed wife, years older than himself, a bed-ridden sister-in-law and an adopted girl child who was weak-minded. Yet he would suggest himself as a test of the reactions of the ordinary healthy-minded individual brought up in normal surroundings. No wonder he thought that any modest woman would undress in the dark. One can imagine the dire results, if perchance his eyes should have alighted upon a woman engaged in this process.

While this case was pending, we busied ourselves with papers for an injunction to prevent further interference with the distribution of the *Mercury*. It was our theory that no group of people had a legal right to behave in such a way as to affect adversely the business of a third party. We had in mind that all over the country organized groups, the Ku Klux Klan, the Women's Christian Temperance Union, the Anti-Saloon League, the Lord's Day Alliance, Anti-Vice Societies and others, sought to impose their will upon the community, exercising a sort of extra-judicial restraint. The country was coming to be governed not by law and by courts, but by threat of ruination made by various irresponsible groups of imposing title and supposedly pious purpose.

We made our application for an injunction to Judge George A. Anderson. As he granted the order to show cause, he remarked that he would not let any one interfere with Mencken's constitutional right to "raise hell."

Justice Parmenter's decision acquitting Mencken came the next day. The Harvard Union had invited the pugnacious editor for luncheon expecting to greet a martyr. Thousands awaited him in a small hall. Thunderous applause greeted the welcome news.

The argument on the injunction was set for an afternoon about a week later. In the morning we blithely made our way to Cambridge to present the case of the Greek before Judge Arthur P. Stone. After endeavoring to shock the court by reading pointed passages, a procedure which left Judge Stone reasonably cool, Edmund A. Whitman, a dignified member of the Boston bar, retained by the Watch and Ward Society, assured the Bench that had Judge Parmenter been a married man he would never have dared to go home after rendering his decision on "Hatrack." Apparently this experienced Boston attorney was not unmindful of the fact that a Judge's wife may not be a pleasant critic. The argument seemed to appeal, and Mencken's prognostications that a book, lawful when sold by a publisher, becomes unlawful when sold by a dealer, were verified. It was found that "Hatrack," sold by Mencken, was moral in Boston, but was lewd, lascivious, libidinous and lecherous to the tune of $100, when sold by a Greek across the Charles River. But then Karagianes had sold some thirty-five copies to Harvard students and professors, many of them "youths."

The argument on the injunction came before Judge Morton of the Federal Court. The legal theory found an analogy in labor boycott cases. Here the Watch

and Ward Society having a complaint against the
Mercury, threatened not the magazine, but distributors and sellers. A further contention was based on
the claim that no one has the right to interfere with
the business of another except as part of an economic
dispute—the origin of a right so to interfere running
back to the Fifteenth Century, when a schoolmaster
who attempted to open a new school in Gloucester,
England, was met by injunctive action on the complaint of a family that had run the one school there
for many generations. This was regarded as poaching
on chosen territory, as unfair competition. The court
held, however, that one had a right to do this in his own
economic interest.[3] From that has developed the law.
The Watch and Ward Society had no economic dispute
with *The American Mercury*. They were volunteers,
prompted to activity by their dislike of the magazine.
Mr. Whitman argued that the Watch and Ward Society merely gave advice and that to give advice was
wholly legal. This was countered by the argument
that, although one person may in good faith give advice, yet when he associates himself with others and the
group acquires great power so that the advice comes
as a threat, the action is illegal. Mr. Whitman insisted there was no threat involved—that the booksellers, unable to read all the material on their shelves,
willingly subscribed to a control by the Watch and
Ward Society. We called J. Frank Chase as a witness.
Here is part of the testimony:

[3] Anonymous Common Pleas (1410), Year Book 11 Hen. IV,
fol. 47, pl. 21. Reported in Sayres Cases on Labor Law, p. 250.

Q. Ordinarily when a book is brought to your attention and you regard it as violative of the law, what do you do? What is your first step?

A. I don't quite understand your question.

Q. What is your practice, do you send out a notice or letter of any kind to the booksellers?

A. I send out a notice.

Q. In substance what does that notice say?

A. It says we have made an examination of the particular book in question and we find the same to be actionable.

Q. What was your practice, Mr. Chase, if a bookseller continued to sell?

Mr. Whitman: How is that important? [The interruption was ignored.]

A. We bring him into court for it.

Q. So that when a man receives a notice of this kind it is a notice that if he does not follow your opinion he will be arrested, is it not?

Mr. Whitman: Just a moment. [Counsel was trying hard to awaken Chase's thought.]

A. Not necessarily.

Q. Has a notice of this sort always been followed by arrest in the event that a bookseller continued to sell?

A. No, it depends on the circumstances.

Q. You mean sometimes you don't arrest?

A. No, we don't arrest the wholesaler—some one whose business it is to distribute.

Q. What do you do in the case of a wholesaler?

A. Why, the wholesaler stops.

Q. You mean that when he gets a notice from you, he stops?

A. Yes.

Q. Hasn't there ever been a case where a wholesaler has gone ahead?

A. I think not.

Q. Now, in this particular case you sent a notice to Mr. Tracy, did you not?

A. Yes, sir.

Q. And that notice threatened him with arrest if he continued to distribute the magazine, did it not?

A. Yes.

Mr. Whitman: Now, just a minute. [He had asked for only a "moment" the time before.]

Q. Now, there are some cases, I think you said, where a notice of this kind has not been followed by arrest. Is that correct?

A. I think the first October number of *Snappy Stories* did not follow the rule.

Q. No, I mean according to your practice, I think you said, a notice of this sort was followed by arrest, wasn't it? That has been your practice, hasn't it?

A. Yes.

Q. But there have been some cases where a notice of this sort was not followed by arrest, isn't that correct?

A. Yes.

Q. In those cases what was the purpose of sending the letter?

Mr. Whitman: I object to that, if your Honor please. [This little pleasantry failed to interrupt the examination.]

A. I don't know of any case where it has not been done.

Q. You mean in all cases, so far as you know, where you sent out letters, if the bookseller did something other than follow your advice he was arrested, is that correct— always, without exception?

A. No.

Q. There are exceptions?

A. There are exceptions.

Q. I want to know why the exceptions?

A. Well, the October first edition of *Snappy Stories* did not follow our advice, and they were indicted and brought into court and fined $1,000.

Q. Has there been any case where the man has failed to follow your advice, that you have not had him arrested?

A. I know of none.

Q. You know of none?

A. None.

Q. So that according to the practice of the Watch and Ward Society, when a bookseller gets a notice of this sort, according to your practice, it means, if he doesn't follow your judgment, he is going to be taken into court, doesn't it?

A. Yes, sir.

Q. Have there been many cases where booksellers have failed to follow your advice?

A. Not many.

.   .   .   .

Q. Well, in any case, Mr. Chase, is your letter a bluff or a threat?

No answer.

Q. In this case, Mr. Chase, you notified the news distributor, did you. The American News Company?

A. Yes, sir.

Q. Wasn't it under an arrangement with them, that they would notify the news dealers?

A. Yes.

Q. And you sent this letter in which you threatened

the arrest of whomever distributed the magazine, did you not?

A. Yes.

.   .   .   .

Q. You knew, did you not, that you and the Watch and Ward Society had been attacked in various issues of the *Mercury?*

A. Yes.

That is all.

We made it clear that we were not trying to enjoin the arrest of any distributor; in fact, we insisted that a claim of violation of the criminal law should properly be made by arrest. Our objection lay in the insidious, covert and suggestive method that might ruin a publication, while those involved assumed no responsibility.

The court was somewhat doubtful about granting a preliminary injunction. Mr. Whitman claimed it was not necessary. He stated that *The American Mercury* could avoid all difficulty if the publishers would submit future numbers to the Watch and Ward Society who would then notify them whether or not an issue was objectionable. This gave away the whole case. It indicated that no magazine could be distributed over the objection of the Watch and Ward Society.

Judge Morton's decision is so momentous on the general subject of restraint or pressure by groups, that it is worth setting forth in full.[4]

Judge Morton: The questions before me arise on the

[4] The American Mercury *vs.* Chase *et al.*, 13 Fed. (2d) 224 (1926).

defendants' motion to dismiss the plaintiff's bill, and the plaintiff's motion for an injunction *pendente lite*. As the facts alleged in the bill are accepted by the motion to dismiss, and those shown by the evidence on the motion for injunction are substantially the same, both questions can conveniently be considered together. The material facts are not seriously in controversy.

The defendant Chase and the society of which he is secretary scrutinize publications of various kinds, including books and magazines. If they believe that a book or article violates the law, they inform the large distributors of their opinion, with the intimation, express or implied, that if the book or magazine be sold or distributed prosecution will follow. Where this warning is ignored, it is their custom to institute prosecutions. Such notice or warning is generally sent to one Tracy, who is connected with the New England Newspaper Publishing Co., a distributor of periodicals, with the understanding that he will pass it along to other persons in the distributing trade, who are thus apprised that the article (or book) is considered unlawful by said defendants, with the statement or implication that prosecution will follow if it is sold or circulated. That course was followed as to the April number of *The American Mercury,* and said defendants avow their intention to follow the same course as to future issues which seem to them objectionable The effect of such notice is to interfere very seriously with the sale of the book or magazine objected to.

The important question is whether this is a legal course of conduct. May an unofficial organization, actuated by a sincere desire to benefit the public and to strengthen the administration of the law, carry out its purpose by threatening with criminal prosecution those who deal in maga-

zines which it regards as illegal; the effect being, as a
practical matter, to exclude such magazines from sale
through ordinary channels and thereby to inflict loss upon
their proprietors?

The injury to the persons affected does not flow from
any judgment of a court or public body; it is caused by the
defendants' notice which rests on the defendants' judgment. The result on the other person is the same whether
that judgment be right or wrong, *i.e.*, the sale of his magazine or book is seriously interfered with. Few dealers in
any trade will buy goods after notice that they will be
prosecuted if they resell them. Reputable dealers do not
care to take such a risk even when they believe that prosecution would prove unfounded. The defendants know this
and trade upon it. They secure their influence, not by
voluntary acquiescence in their opinions by the trade in
question, but by the coercion and intimidation of that trade
through the fear of prosecution if the defendants' views
are disregarded. [Cases cited.]

In my judgment this is clearly illegal. The defendants
have the right of every citizen to come to the courts with
complaints of crime; but they have no right to impose
their opinions on the book and magazine trade by threats
of prosecution if their views are not accepted. [Citing
cases.] The facts that the defendants are actuated by no
commercial motive and by no desire to injure the plaintiff
do not enlarge their rights in this respect, though it may
protect them under the Massachusetts General Laws, Chapter 265, Section 25.

Of course, the distributors have the right to take advice
as to whether publications which they sell violate the law,
and to act on such advice if they believe it to be sound.
The defendants have the right to express their views as to

the propriety or legality of a publication.   But the defendants have not the right to enforce their views by organized
threats—either open or covert—to the distributing trade
to prosecute persons who disagree with them.   The principles of law involved—which are interesting and might be
much elaborated—are analogous to those under which sec-
ondary boycotts are illegal [citing cases] and perhaps rest
ultimately on the reasons mentioned by Mr. Justice Holmes
in *Aikens v. Wisconsin,* 195 U. S. 194, at 204, and the decisions there referred to.

As to the April number of *The American Mercury,* the
injury, if any, to the plaintiffs by the acts of the defendants
Chase and the New England Watch and Ward Society have
been completed before the present bill was filed.   There
was no threat by any of the defendants of further illegal
acts as to that issue.   This being so, no case for equitable
relief as to it is shown; and it is unnecessary at present
to decide the question whether anything in it contravened
Massachusetts General Laws, Chapter 272, Section 28.

It follows that the motion to dismiss should be denied
and that a temporary injunction should issue in accordance
with the second and third prayers of the bill.

A new difficulty now beset us.   From all over the
country the Postmaster General had received complaints inspired by religious people whose real ground
of objection was that "Hatrack" was a vicious attack
upon revivalist meetings.   The stated ground was
obscenity.   The magazine had been passed by the Post
Office at Hammondton, New Jersey, prior to the distribution.   All copies had been distributed.   Yet on the
day following Judge Parmenter's decision that the
magazine did not violate the law, the Post Office De-

partment in Washington declared the issue unmailable as "obscene." We learned of this through the newspapers. We had had no notice. There was no hearing. During the month the usual group of more or less salacious periodicals had appeared. We had gathered a choice collection of titillating April magazines which aroused some question as to why the discrimination. True, a *Mercury* article, "Mr. Coolidge," by Frank R. Kent, had caused an uproar in Washington. It had not painted a noble figure, upholding the Coolidge fiction of greatness.

We wondered why action had been taken without a hearing. Quack medicines and fraudulent stock advertisements are accorded this privilege. Murderous cancer cures circulate, sometimes for months, before they are barred from the mails. But then, they are not obscene—merely fatal.

Off to Washington went Mencken, the publisher Alfred Knopf, and myself, to appear before Horace J. Donnelly, the Solicitor of the Post Office Department, and two assistants. The Coolidge type of mind is prevalent in Washington, but we scarcely expected to behold the Coolidge physiognomy on another than its eminent possessor. Yet Mr. Donnelly proudly exhibited a makeup not unlike that of his chief. In an Indian costume, with feathers, or a ten-gallon hat, the difference would not be noticeable. Besides, Donnelly was passive, immobile, with little enthusiasm and no humor.

One tribute must be paid our government officials. They listen patiently. We showed Judge Parmenter'ϲ

decision and argued the law. We regretted the necessity of presenting our case to a Judge, even though he
was called a Solicitor, who had already committed himself, acting *ex parte*. Nor were we encouraged by the
thought that he represented the Coolidge administration, toward which the attitude of the *Mercury* could
not be designated as gentle. Noting the calm manner
of our auditor, and recognizing that hot blood does not
characterize the Coolidge administration, we gently
asked these gentlemen whether they had got a "kick"
out of reading "Hatrack." They resented the imputation. But like most government officials, they felt that
others were of a somewhat coarser clay and were entitled to be saved.

A few days later Mr. Donnelly informed us that he,
Mr. Donnelly, had carefully considered whether or not
he, Mr. Donnelly, was right the first time and had come
to the conclusion that he, Mr. Donnelly, was.

We sued out an injunction against the Post Office
in the New York Federal District. In such a proceeding the legal issue is quite different from that in
a criminal court. There the question is as to whether
or not an article violates the law, and a defendant is entitled to acquittal unless violation appears
beyond a reasonable doubt. The Massachusetts
statute applied only when an article was "manifestly"
corrupting. On the other hand, a determination of the
Post Office Department is *prima-facie* correct and the
conclusion will be upheld if there is any basis for it
whatever. Or, to put it conversely, an injunction will
be denied unless the court feels that no reasonable man

could have come to the conclusion that the article
violated the law.

At the request of the Government, argument was
delayed and good fortune smiled on us when the motion
came on to be heard before Judge Julian Mack. His
Honor looked at the papers and said, "What is this
all about? I have read *The American Mercury*, I am
familiar with the article 'Hatrack.' No one but a
moron could be affected by it." When I later repeated
this observation in the higher court, Judge Learned
Hand made the query, "Isn't the moron the test, Mr.
Hays?" The preliminary statement of Judge Mack
though cheering was not wholly satisfactory, for naturally I had expected that an eloquent argument upon
the bureaucracy of government would contribute to a
more substantial fee. The Government attorneys
seemed somewhat nonplused at the breath of fresh
air which emanated from the direction of the Judge.
They suggested that in giving us a hearing they
had granted every right which the law accords. This
magnanimity was not so clear when they shifted
their position from the article "Hatrack" to "Clinical
Notes," for no question having been raised thereon,
this had not been the subject of the hearing. But
Judge Mack failed to be abashed even by the suggestion that sex was not as important as was ordinarily supposed. And then these high-minded protectors of American liberty and morality sprang a real
surprise. They pointed out that on page xxxiii of
the advertising section, appeared a notice of the Harry
F. Marks Bookshop, which referred to Brantome's

"Lives of Fair and Gallant Ladies." "This indeed,"
said they, "was violative of the law," for here was
an advertisement of an obscene publication. They
handed the volumes to the Judge with careful markings
drawing attention to pornographic passages. My attention was diverted as I contemplated what had happened to the morals of the unfortunate clerk who had
been obliged to go through the book looking for smutty
passages. No doubt his life was ruined, particularly if
he read French, for the spicier contributions appeared
in the original language.

I have often noted the exceptional interest aroused
in court by the objectionable passages of any book.
Ordinarily the police, accustomed to a more purifying
type of literature, thumb with avidity the corrupting
items. But Judge Mack seemed to be familiar with
Brantome. He had apparently arrived at his elevation in spite of his reading of the classics. He referred
to the familiar distinction between modern literature
and those classical survivals of centuries which, having
come to be looked on as our literary heritage, are not
ordinarily regarded as within the obscenity statutes.
The law wisely recognizes that no work lasts without
literary quality, and age itself proves some merit other
than obscenity. Even Mr. Justice Ford, one of our
most persistent vice-hunters, has said that no one
outside of a lunatic asylum would object to the Bible
or Shakespeare.

Mr. Donnelly's cohorts jumped in another direction.
Having argued their generosity in having given us the
opportunity to change Mr. Donnelly's mind, having

shifted from "Hatrack" to "Clinical Notes," and then to Brantome, all without success, they then argued that, since all copies of the magazine had been mailed, the question was a moot one and that therefore the court should not grant the injunction. We asked why, if the question was moot, they had prohibited distribution, unless the purpose was to be found in the ulterior direction of discrediting the reputation of the magazine. The Court interjected that the issue was not moot if there was one copy left which the publishers desired to mail. The injunction was granted—one more blow at hypocrisy.

Then, in spite of the fact that the Government attorneys had argued that the question was moot, they continued to spend the money of taxpayers by appealing the case to the Circuit Court of Appeals. That court concluded that the question was academic and vacated the injunction.[5]

But the "American Mercury" case had made the issue clear. Massachusetts became the Tennessee of the North. Massachusetts ("there she stands!"), once the literary center of America, was a byword for jeering comment. The police would not forgive Chase for having swallowed Mencken's bait, and the poor old fellow, with his Watch and Ward Society, was sadly discredited. Mencken took his scalp. Chase held on for a time, discouraged and unhappy, and then departed this life for a place, we may hope, where his soul will no longer be troubled by pornographic litera-

[5] The American Mercury vs. Kiely, Postmaster et al., 19 Fed. (2d) 295 (1927).

ture. I have felt that perhaps none of us did justice
to the Reverend Jason Franklin Chase. We had supposed that he was the most effective self-appointed custodian of Boston's morals. Yet a year after his death
we realized that perhaps he had exercised a certain
restraining influence.

Subsequent to the death of Chase, the Boston Police
Department took charge of the morals of the community and with the aid of the District Attorney,
made it its business to protect the delicate sexual
propensities of Boston's literary public. In February,
1927, nine books were suppressed by intimation from
the Police Department, for obviously these gentlemen
have no need to go into court. They need merely "tip
off" the booksellers. It is said that the books were
read by an Assistant District Attorney who was unac-
customed to modern or any other literature. Thus, at
the time this is written, the standard is set for Boston.
Those who take literature seriously are unable to scan
a volume at a book store and buy it. Those who are
looking for spicy material are in this indirect manner
advised by the Police Department what books to order
by mail. Some of the works then suppressed were
probably judged by their titles. "The Hard-Boiled
Virgin," by Frances Newman, published by Boni &
Liveright, hardly justified its alluring title. I wonder which is the obscene word, "hard-boiled" or "virgin." The book itself is too highbrow for the average
reader and is certainly not "spicy." The "Plastic
Age" was likewise banned, although it had been allowed to circulate during the milder days of J. Frank

Chase. Its crime was that it gave too much information to fathers and mothers. Then there was "The Ancient Hunger," a book which would naturally be condemned on its title. "The Beadle" was banned because "it clarifies rather than condemns seduction." "The Marriage Bed," according to the District Attorney, tries to "defend matrimony as an institution." It was bad because the author was frank "in spots."

In April, 1927, the authorities went wild. Complaint was made against Sinclair Lewis's "Elmer Gantry," a work of such moment and importance in sales value, that the booksellers themselves had read the book and approved it. Still timid, however, they applied to District Attorney Foley who informed Richard F. Fuller, head of the Booksellers' Committee, that in his opinion the book violated the law. Mr. Foley wrote: "Evidence that this book is sold or offered for sale within the confines of Suffolk County will be followed by prompt action by this office." Yet the authorities claim they are not censors! What censorship could be more effective than a threat from the District Attorney? Better a censor of literary training, as he would have to be, than a determination by district attorneys and their assistants whose natural political desire is to cater to the "good" people in the community.

A group of Boston publishers headed by Ellery Sedgwick, editor of the *Atlantic Monthly*, issued a protest:

"As citizens concerned with public decency and the maintenance of public sanity, as publishers associated during the active lifetime of all of us with books and magazines of honorable reputation, we wish publicly and seriously to protest against the high-handed, erratic and ill-advised interference of public officials with the sale and distribution of books, many of them of recognized standing and freely sold elsewhere throughout the United States. . . . It is difficult for many in self-respect to keep silence in the face of this violation of the *historic* traditions of Boston and New England."

Probably the letter referred to "historic traditions" some time back.

The Boston *Herald* urged the Police Department:

"Do not make us ridiculous. Do not imply to the world that those whom we elect to office have no comprehension of the intellectual freedom upon which civilizations of the world have been built. Do not broadcast the idea that we are children; do not conclude that somebody must tell us what we may see and read and hear and think. Do not revise our dictionaries by leaving out all bad words and all that might be proved to have unsavory connotations. Leave our dictionaries as they are and trust the human race to work out its own destiny in free play of individual freedom."

The Booksellers' Committee, long in the saddle, through coöperation with Chase, protested:

"We feel our opinion on what is bad or what is not in violation of the General Laws, Chapter 272, Section 78, is of no value. . . . We are, therefore, sending you for the opinion of your office, the books mentioned on the attached list."

Among these was practically every novel of any significance written in America or perhaps elsewhere in the last year. Among others: "The Private Life of Helen of Troy" and "Galahad," by John Erskine; "Revelry," by Samuel Hopkins Adams; "The Green Hat," by Michael Arlen; "Twilight," by Count Keyserling; "Revolt of Modern Youth," by Judge Lindsey and Wainwright Evans; "Nigger Heaven," by Carl Van Vechten; "Sorrell and Son," by Warwick Deeping; "Power," by Lion Feuchtwanger; "Sweepings," by Lester Cohen; "Manhattan Transfer," by John Dos Passos; "Ariane," by Claude Anet; "It's Not Done," by William C. Bullitt; "The World of William Clissold," by Wells; "The Sun Also Rises," by Ernest Hemingway; "Doomsday," by Warwick Deeping; "Dark Laughter," by Sherwood Anderson; "High Winds," by Arthur Train; "What I Believe," by Bertrand Russell; "Circus Parade," by Jim Tully; "Count Bruga," by Ben Hecht; "The Captive," by Bourdet; "Crazy Pavements," by Beverley Nichols.

Back came the package unopened. A letter from the District Attorney made clear that thereafter he would discountenance the gentlemen's agreement theretofore existing by which his opinion would be given in case of the submission of a book. He wrote:

"Whether or not a given publication is in violation of this section is a question to be settled not by my opinion or by the opinion of those engaged in the sale of books, but by a court and jury."

Very good! Why had not this been done? He added:

"I shall therefore expect your committee will hereafter prevent sale by its members of books or other publications

which violate the provisions of the statute by exercise of
your own sound common sense. If your committee does
not do this, I shall of course be compelled to take action
to enforce this provision of the law."

The committee then, is advised to exercise pressure and
this in spite of the opinion in the "American Mercury"
case. The suggestion that they use sound common
sense meets universal approval.

"An American Tragedy," by Theodore Dreiser, was
under official criticism and Captain George A. Patterson, head of the Vice Squad, reported that it contained
obscene language, an opinion endorsed by Superintendent Crowley. The suggestion was made that
thereafter the District Attorney's Office would ask
for jail sentences. With this in mind, booksellers and
others were invited to test the law. Donald Friede,
former vice-president of Boni & Liveright, Inc., appeared in Boston and arranged to sell a copy of the
book. An appointment was made at Police Headquarters. Superintendent Crowley was not cheered
by our visit. Captain Patterson asked Friede if he
had books to sell and the price. Friede sold "An
American Tragedy."

We then offered two other books: "Shakespeare's
Complete Works" and Hawthorne's "Scarlet Letter."
Captain Patterson was about to buy but Superintendent Crowley was canny. He looked over Shakespeare,
then over Hawthorne: "It is best to go slowly and
deliberately in this matter and I do not want to buy
more than one book." "Why?" we queried. "Why
make us go through this two or three times? Does

your refusal mean that you approve of these books?"
The answer came back, "I am not saying anything and
won't say anything about those two books. I have
refused to buy them and that is all." Shakespeare
and Hawthorne are apparently not wholly disapproved
by the Boston police.

Application was made by the police to Judge Murray for a warrant against Friede for having ventured
to sell "An American Tragedy." Passages were submitted. Judge Murray said these were not obscene.
Further investigation was necessary. It is said that
Judge Murray asked Captain Patterson if he thought
anything he read in this book would corrupt his morals.
The Captain replied that he was sure his own morals
would not be corrupted and he had the same confidence
in his assistant, Lieutenant Hines. Neither of these
literati had taken the trouble to read the entire book.
They returned later with new citations.

A warrant was issued and a date fixed for trial
before the Municipal Court. The case came before
Judge Devlin, who had in the meantime read the book.
Booksellers testified that the demand was by mature
people of the rare type who would be ready, willing
and able to pay $5 for two volumes. Evidence was
given of Dreiser's reputation, and it was shown that
the book was used in a course at Harvard University
on American literature. It seemed almost unthinkable
that any court would hold that this great work of
Dreiser's, acclaimed as the greatest American novel of
the day, based upon a true story, would be banned by
law. It was argued that it would be impossible to

write a story truly showing the gradual deterioration and disintegration of the principal character in Dreiser's book without depicting his relations with women. The point of the novel depended wholly upon that portrayal. In a two-volume book of many hundreds of pages, none but a curious kind of human animal would thumb it through to find the few particular passages that would arouse sex impulse. And no book is violative of a Massachusetts statute unless it is "manifestly corrupting to the morals of youth."

We were surprised that the court took the case seriously. But it did, as appeared when it solemnly pronounced judgment: "Guilty!" The case is not at an end.

Later, Upton Sinclair's book, "Oil," was brought into prominence by the literary activities of the Boston police. Sinclair has remarked that due to their efforts he is now for the first time "square with his publishers." "We authors," said he, "are using America as our sales territory, and Boston is our advertising department." Sinclair went to Boston and offered to sell the book to the police but could find no buyer. The authorities were satisfied with the one culprit they had, some obscure book clerk. Sinclair was later successful in selling one apparently genuine copy of "Oil." The police paid and inspected. Inside the cover was the Bible. The purchase price was not refunded. The picturesque author appeared on the Boston Common and in a public meeting said he would be inclined to offer a reward of $1,000 to any one arresting him were he not fearful that he might be charged with bribery.

Nothing happened. Sinclair then published an edition of his book where the passages to which there was objection were deleted and their places taken by fig-leaves. The edition, known as the "fig-leaf edition," was sold by sandwich men parading the streets of Boston. To an imaginative mind one can readily imagine the awful obscenity of these suggestive fig leaves.

On an occasion when the Government sought to "get" a Danish scientist, named Herman Moens, it had him indicted for publishing a work on anthropology containing pictures of men and women in the nude. He was found guilty. A new edition appeared with a strip of white across the "middle" parts of the pictures. Never have I seen anything more suggestively obscene.

Even J. Frank Chase would not have condemned three of the outstanding books of 1927, "Elmer Gantry," "An American Tragedy," and "Oil."

A Boston reporter remarked to me that in spite of criticism of the activities of the Watch and Ward Society and the police, one would be obliged to admit that literature in Boston has remained clean and the morals of the citizens high. I pointed out to him that any community whose sexual impulses were so repressed that these books excited libidinous thought, should look to its moral condition. Mayor Walker of New York once said: "No woman was ever ruined by a book." Possibly he was not referring to Boston.

Sinclair sells the "Fig Leaf Edition" and with Boston's
help, makes "Oil" a "best seller."

FREEDOM OF RESIDENCE

FREEDOM OF RESIDENCE

THE PEOPLE *vs.* OSSIAN H. SWEET *et al.* IN THE RE-
CORDER'S COURT OF DETROIT—THE NEGRO SEG-
REGATION PROBLEM

ON September 8, 1925, Dr. Ossian H. Sweet, a
colored physician of Detroit, moved into a small house
which he had purchased at the corner of Garland
Street and Charlevoix Avenue, in the City of Detroit.
The location was in a white neighborhood in a city
where racial antagonism runs high and Dr. Sweet,
anticipating trouble, had brought with him a sizable
quantity of guns, revolvers and ammunition. His family consisted of himself, wife and baby. The baby was
sent out of the house to a grandmother's. On the evening of September 9th there were gathered in the house
two brothers, seven friends, Dr. Sweet and his wife.
Policemen had been sent to the neighborhood ostensibly
(and perhaps actually) to protect the Sweet family.
At about 8:25 when, according to the police, all was
quiet and peaceful, shots blazed from various windows
of the second floor of the house, and from a porch in
the rear. One Leo Breiner, amiably smoking his pipe
across the way, was killed. Another was wounded.
Both happened to be whites. The eleven colored occupants of the Sweet house, including Mrs. Sweet, were
arrested, charged with first-degree murder.

Colored people regarded the case as one which raised the definite question of race segregation. Claim was made that the shots were fired in defense of the home. It was pointed out that in Detroit the negro population had vastly increased in numbers (much of this increase being due to the importation of non-union workers); that negro districts had become congested and were centers of filth and squalor; that it was almost impossible for a negro to obtain a decent home except in a white neighborhood; that the whites were always hostile and the colored man was ordinarily either compelled to move or to use force to protect himself.

The issue was clearly presented by the Sweet case. The National Association for the Advancement of Colored People undertook the defense. Three local colored lawyers, Messrs. Perry, Rowlette and Mahoney, were engaged by the defense as well as Mr. Walter Nelson, also of Detroit, Herbert J. Friedman of Chicago, and myself; all under the leadership of Clarence Darrow.

A conference with Darrow was held at my home in New York, where a committee from the National Association, consisting of Charles H. Studin and Arthur Spingarn, two members of the New York Bar, and Walter White and James Weldon Johnson, leaders of the colored race and officers of the Association, were present. Spingarn, a man with black hair and swarthy complexion, related the facts to Darrow. Darrow sympathetically suggested that he knew full well the difficulties faced by his race. Spingarn explained he was not a negro, whereupon Darrow turned to Charles Studin and said, "Well, you understand

"Home *Sweet* Home"

what I mean." Whereupon Studin stated that he
was not a colored man. Darrow turned to Walter
White: "I would not make that mistake with you."
White raised his blonde head, spoke through his blue
eyes and proudly said he was a negro.

We engaged in some discussion as to why people
with more white blood in their veins than negro (and
this applies to a large part of the race in this
country) should identify their lives with the more unfortunate class and thus subject themselves to prejudice. We learned then a fact which was emphasized
in our later associations in this case: that to negroes
there is no problem so vital as that of color; that
race consciousness and race pride have solidified our
colored citizens.

We were not surprised to learn that negroes move
into white districts from necessity rather than choice.
Some cities have passed ordinances limiting the area
of residence. The Supreme Court of the United States
has declared such laws unconstitutional,[1] yet many cities have adopted and continue to adopt them. Thus a
law of the Louisiana Legislature in 1924 enables the
City of New Orleans to enforce segregation by ordinance.[2] In other places covenants between property
owners not to sell property to negroes have become
the practice, and recently such covenants have been
held lawful.[3] But primarily segregation has been enforced by mob violence and terrorism. Where one

[1] Buchanan vs. Warley, 254 U. S. 60 (1917).
[2] Harmon vs. Tyler, 273 U. S. 668 (1927), where this law was
declared unconstitutional.
[3] Corrigan vs. Buckley, 271 U. S. 323 (1926).

negro tamely submits, the situation is made more difficult for others. In Detroit Ossian Sweet stood his ground. Thus the trial for murder.

Arrived in Detroit, we visited the defendants in jail. Only one, Mrs. Sweet, had been released on bail. Even this had aroused the fury of the community. Up two flights of steps, steel doors were unlocked to permit passage, and then closed. We were ushered into a small room, dimly lighted by a dirty window, furnished with a table and a few broken chairs. Our clients were summoned. They seemed cheered by our visit but not hopeful. They had spent sixty summer days in a dingy city jail; and negroes in Detroit involved in a killing have reason to be pessimistic. On the face of it, our case was not strong. It seemed clear that Breiner had been shot by the fusillade from that house. Ten men had gathered there with provisions to withstand a possible siege, with guns and ammunition. Shooting from various windows indicated a concerted plan. And there had been police protection. Besides this, the authorities had taken statements, so-called confessions, from all the defendants.

Our clients were **Dr.** Ossian Sweet, his wife Gladys Sweet, his brother Otis Sweet, a dentist, Henry Sweet, another brother from Wilberforce Academy, John Latting, a student friend of Henry Sweet, William E. Davis, a Federal narcotic officer, Joe Mack, chauffeur for Sweet, Morris Murray, a handy man helper, and Washington, Morris and Watson, all insurance men, friends of the doctor who had come to the Sweet home because trouble was expected.

We had concluded that the only defense lay in making a clean breast of the whole matter, and said so
flatly. But our clients seemed evasive. None was inclined to talk. We took their stories one by one and
they didn't wholly jibe. For some time Joe Mack
insisted that during the excitement he had locked himself in the bathroom and was taking a bath. That
seemed unlikely. Again, each claimed to have no knowledge of where any one else had been, or what he had
been doing. There were the statements made to the
police. Our clients had a very human desire to support their original and inept stories. Then they
seemed to feel that in spite of our expostulations, we
might be just as well pleased if we did not know too
much. There was one exception, but his attitude put
us in a worse predicament. He was rather proud of
the fracas—the whites had learned a lesson. They
couldn't tread on a negro with impunity.

The defense depended upon the attitude of mind of
the defendants at the time of the shooting. Did they
think they were in danger? Were they actually
scared? They had become heroes in the eyes of their
race—eleven million negroes scattered all over the
country. Darrow was there to defend them. Not all
of them cared to admit they had been scared.

But finally, little by little, we managed to impress
upon them that we actually wanted the truth, the whole
truth and nothing but the truth, and that there lay the
only hope of the defense.

The trial began before Judge Frank Murphy in the
Recorder's Court on October 30th. Selection of the

jury was slow and difficult. No juror would admit
prejudice if he knew he had it, and as a matter of fact,
consciousness of prejudice would go far to negative it.
The danger lay in the insidious effect of the usual attitude which is unconscious. Probably no man or woman
really thinks that his or her judgment in a murder
trial would be influenced by the color of the defendant.
Yet the newspapers of Detroit had for a long period
attributed lawless acts to negroes and the comment
in the press on the Sweet case seemed to indicate that
on the night of the shooting the Sweet home was well
protected by the police; that calm prevailed in the
neighborhood and that the killing was wanton and malicious. The atmosphere was, at the beginning, clearly
hostile to the defendants. The general theory has been
that as the negro advances in the world, prejudice will
dwindle; but probably in an industrial city like Detroit,
where the colored population increased from some 4,000
in 1900 to 6,000 in 1910, and to some 60,000 in 1925,
the labor competition has heightened the antagonism.

The difficulty of securing an impartial jury was
clearly evident when one asked how the talesman would
feel if property in his neighborhood was bought by a
negro. Without exception, the talesmen said they
recognized the negro's right of free residence as well
as his right of self-defense. But they seemed to question the wisdom of the exercise of such rights. Generally they seemed to agree with the philosophy later
expressed by the Prosecutor, that people have many
rights which they voluntarily waive. One has a right
to grab a seat in a street car before a woman gets to

it. One has a right to attend a dance (particularly if he is the host) in a bathing suit. One has the right to put his feet on the table, or take off his shoes in the parlor. But we don't do it. It doesn't conform to practice. The talesmen did not seem to realize, nor did the Prosecutor, that there are some rights which one cannot waive and remain free, such as the right to live, and the right to refuse to be intimidated, whatever the cost.

One juror was excused because he admitted he belonged to the Ku Klux Klan, though his particular phobia was directed against foreigners. One negro appeared on the panel. He was peremptorily dismissed, although under an honest interpretation of the provision coming from Magna Charta that one should be tried by his peers, he should have been the most acceptable. Finally, however, after interrogating about a hundred men and women, we were satisfied, or rather not dissatisfied, with the jury. It seemed about as good as we could get and there was always the danger that if we challenged one, the next might be worse. It afterwards transpired that some of those of whom we had been most fearful were our best friends.

The picture painted by the prosecution showed a warm summer evening in a quiet, neighborly community. The Sweet house stood on a corner. Diagonally across was the high school with a spacious yard. Opposite and along the street were small frame houses owned and occupied by simple, kindly people—the men mostly mechanics, the women housewives, dutifully caring for broods of children. People were sitting on

their porches enjoying the cool air after dusk, visiting and chatting. A few sauntered casually along the street. Some were on their way to a corner grocery. Here and there a car was parked. Of course, the fact that negroes had moved into the corner house was of interest, but peace and quiet was assured by half a dozen policemen who stood guard at various places, keeping people away from the sidewalk in front and on the side of the Sweet house. Suddenly, unexpectedly and without provocation, a fusillade of shots rang out from the rear, sides and front of the house, and Leo Breiner, chatting with a group on the porch of the Dove home opposite, was killed. His pipe was still in his mouth when he was carried away. Another man in the group was wounded. "Murder!" cried the Prosecutor. "Cold-blooded murder!" The newspapers echoed his cry: "Another murder by negroes. They are becoming a menace to the community!"

Before the taking of evidence the defense moved that the prosecution provide a bill of particulars. There were eleven defendants, including Mrs. Sweet. We knew there was no evidence as to who fired the shot, and we wished to limit the prosecution definitely to their only possible theory—that of conspiracy. We wished to compel the State to confine its testimony to proof of specific allegations rather than to permit it to determine its theory at the close of the trial. Such a bill was ordered. The theory set forth therein was that the defendants premeditatedly and with malice, armed themselves with the agreement that one or more of them would shoot to kill in the event of threatened or actual trespass on the property, or of real or threatened damage, however slight, to property, and that the deceased came to his death by a bullet fired by one of the defendants in pursuance of a common understanding.

The Sweet house stood in a quiet neighborhood. The Prosecutor sought to prove that on the night in question, there were few, other than police officers, around. Witness after witness testified that there was no excitement. Witness after witness happened to be there purely out of "curiosity." It soon developed, however, that when the people in the neighborhood learned that the Sweet family had bought the house, they had met together in a schoolhouse and formed what they called the "Water Works Improvement Association." One Eben E. Draper was asked when the association was started. He answered, "A long time ago." Asked when he first heard Sweet was going to move into the neighborhood, he replied, "That was a long time ago, too."

Q. Did that have anything to do with your joining that club?

A. Possibly.

Q. Did it?

A. Yes.

Q. You joined that club to aid in keeping that a white district?

A. Yes.

Q. At the meeting in the school was any reference made to keeping the district free from colored people?

A. Yes.

Q. How many people were present at that meeting?
A. Seven hundred.

The innocuous purposes of the association were expressed as follows:

"(1) To render constructive social and civic service; (2) to maintain a clean and healthy condition in streets and alleys; (3) to observe the spirit of the traffic ordinances for safety and protection of residents; (4) to coöperate with all city departments and all beneficial plans; (5) to coöperate with the police in the maintenance of law and order; and (6) to coöperate in the enforcement of existing property restrictions and to originate such other restrictions as would preserve and protect the locality as a respectable community."

The casual, quiet and adroit Darrow brought from each witness the admission that practically the only purpose of the association was to keep out Dr. Sweet and his family. One, Monet, testified:

Q. Did you join the organization as a property owner?
A. I did.
Q. What was your object?
A. To keep the neighborhood up to its existing high standard.
Q. Your interest was mainly in your property?
A. Yes.
Q. Your interest was in keeping out negroes to maintain the value of your property?
A. Yes.

Inspector Norton M. Schuknecht, in charge of the police who were guarding Dr. Sweet's house, testified that with him on the night of the riots were eight patrolmen, a sergeant and a lieutenant.

Q. There was no one there when you got there? The time of your arrival is about 7:30?

A. There were people on the street, but they were walking up and down and there was no congregating.

He instructed his officers:

"I told them Dr. Sweet could live there if we had to take every man in the police station to see that he did."

Q. Did you see any one armed with clubs or other weapons?

A. Not at any time.

Q. What happened at about 8:15?

A. Suddenly a volley of shots was fired from the windows of Dr. Sweet's home.

Q. What could you see?

A. I saw flashes of guns.

Q. How many shots?

A. About fifteen or twenty.

Dove, who owned the house across the way from the Doctor's, was put on the stand to testify to the shooting of Breiner. He said there were more women and children around the night of the shooting than men. Darrow cross-examined him:

Q. Did you ever make an estimate of the number of women and children in a crowd before?

A. No, I can't say that I have.

"As long as the question was asked by the State you thought you were safe in answering it the way you did?" (This aroused the Prosecutor, but the question stood.) "No, not exactly." The witness was reluctant. "Was there a crowd?" "No." "Was there any disturbance?" "No." He was asked if he belonged to any organization or club. No answer. "Have you any reason for not answering that question?" drawled Darrow. "When did you hear that Dr. Sweet had bought the place?" "Quite a while before he moved in I heard rumors from the neighbors." "Quite a discussion?" "Yes, I guess so." "How long before he moved in?" "Six weeks or two months." "You heard it from all the neighbors?" "Yes, two, three or four of them." "You discussed it with your wife?" "Yes." "You didn't want him there?" "I am not prejudiced against them but I don't believe in mixing whites and blacks." "So you did not want him there?" "No, I guess not." Of one thing he was certain: The crowd that wasn't there had shown no undue delay in dispersing when the shots were fired.

Officers testified to the protection accorded the Sweet house. On September 8th, the night before, at the request of a friend of Sweet, officers had been stationed before the house. A few people had gathered. Through the day of the 9th all was quiet. Two negro boys had been seen around the premises, on the porch or in the yard, but this had aroused no comment. In the evening in order to avoid any disturbance, the sidewalk around the premises had been kept clear and automobile traffic was diverted at near-by corners by several policemen. One had been stationed in the rear of the premises; in fact, he testified that from a point near the rear garage he had fired his revolver at two men on the rear porch after the shooting. One officer had taken a point of vantage on the roof of an apartment across the way. He testified that when the shooting started and he saw the blaze of the guns, he had ducked behind a parapet. When Darrow asked him how he could see what was going on, he responded that he had raised his head, upon which Darrow queried, "A head's rather an important part of the body for a policeman, isn't it?" It was an apt question because on cross-examination it was admitted that the police had not taken the trouble to inform Dr. Sweet of the measures taken for his protection.

After the firing, when Inspector Schuknecht had gone into the house, he merely inquired, "What the hell are you fellows shooting for?" He made no arrest until he learned that men had been hit. A search of the premises revealed guns and revolvers—ten firearms for eleven people—including Mrs. Sweet, and plenty of ammunition. The defendants had been taken to the police station by automobile, and a quantity of ammunition was later found on the floor of the car. The defendants were left alone for a while in a large room. In a cuspidor near Dr. Sweet's chair were found a number of bullets and also a key to Dr. Sweet's house, apparently inadvertently dropped there by the Doctor.

The arsenal of guns was displayed at the counsel table in front of the jury and the arms identified. It appeared that Mrs. Sweet had been cooking a ham for her visitors and that provisions had been brought to withstand a long siege. The shades had been drawn. Just before the shooting, a lookout had peered through the window of the first floor. According to the police, the house appeared to be an armed fortress. Evidence was introduced by photographs of the effect of the bullets, holes in the trees and windows across the way, in the plaster and woodwork inside the houses, in the walls next door. The women and children who lived in those houses were enumerated.

That the fatal shot was fired by one of the defendants from the second floor of the Sweet house admitted of little doubt, though the bullet had gone through the body of Breiner in a straight horizontal line which led to the suggestion that possibly the shot was fired by an officer from the yard in the rear of the house.

The claim of self-defense—shooting because of reasonable apprehension of danger from a mob—led to inquiry on cross-examination of the size, attitude and action of the mob, if there was a mob. The police fortunately had overstated the case: all was calm and quiet as the light breeze of the summer evening. The neighbors, admittedly interested, were on their verandas and a few, including women and children, were casually strolling about. The police were unable to explain why reserves had been called, why traffic had been stopped, why they ordered people to "move on," why they sent an officer to the apartment house roof across the way, or why all this activity had centered around the hour of 8:15 P.M. And as witness after witness under the guidance of the District Attorney testified that there was no crowd and no excitement, the cumulative effect (as well as little suggestive facts subtly drawn by Darrow) created the contrary impression. Darrow slouched in a chair, busily engaged in working out cross-word puzzles. The Prosecutor would examine the witness. Darrow would drawl a question: "What were you doing there?" "I live near by." "What brought you to that corner?" "Curiosity." "About what?" "Nothing in particular." "You knew that colored people had moved into that house?" "Yes." "Did that have anything to do with your curiosity?" "Maybe." "Many people there?" "No." "There were strangers there—people you didn't ordinarily see in the neighborhood?" "Some." "How many?" "Twenty-five or thirty." "Within what distance?" Then "Did you want the negroes there?" "Did you belong to the Water Works Improvement Association?" "Why?" "Did you attend meetings?" "How many were there?" "What was said?" "What were you talking about that evening?" One youngster gave the show away. "There was a great crowd—no, I won't say a great crowd, a large crowd—well, there were a few people there and the officers were keeping them moving." Darrow was on his feet. "Have you talked to any one about the case?" "Lieutenant Johnson" (the police detective). "And when you started to answer the question you forgot to say a few people, didn't you?" "Yes, sir."

Some of the witnesses had not gathered at the corner merely through curiosity. Many happened to be going to or coming from the grocery. The little shop did a big potential business, though few of the crowd carried bundles. "What did you buy at the grocery?" asked Darrow of a poor, befuddled individual. The answer came so suddenly that it was

obviously a happy inspiration. "A package of cigarettes." "No groceries?" "My wife took the groceries." "Why didn't you tell us your wife was with
you?" queried Darrow, diverting attention for a moment from the groceries. The witness fumbled. "What
groceries did your wife carry?" "A bottle of milk."

One witness was worried about his son who had failed
to return home on time; one was looking for her daughter; another paced up and down waiting for a perfectly
good and healthy wife to come along on the street car.
Why all the anxiety?

The prosecution called as a witness a man who ran
a gasoline station on a near-by corner. Confused as to
whether his place was on the northeast or the north-
west corner, he wilted as the Prosecutor, for no particular reason, pressed on this point. He gave the
usual testimony, however, that he saw no crowd that
evening. When released from direct examination he
seemed relieved. Darrow showed a friendly spirit.
"How old are you?" "How much of a family have
you?" "You work in the morning at the automobile
factory and in the afternoon you sell gasoline?"
"Pretty tough, isn't it?" "Pretty tired in the evening?" "Don't notice much what's going on?" "Just
collect money for gas?" "Did you sell more than usual
that evening?" "Why was that?" "Many cars?"
"Did you look on this, that or the other corner?"
The witness had found a friend at last. He opened
up satisfactorily.

Finally after about seventy had testified that few
people were about, there was little doubt that a fair-

sized crowd had gathered, moved by "curiosity" or something more sinister. And in Michigan such a gathering is designated by statute as a "mob."

And then it appeared that one witness had heard a number of rat-tat-tats, as though pebbles had been thrown against the house just before the firing, and a crash of window glass. The size of the pebbles? Perhaps two inches in diameter—like those on the table (referring to exhibits)—stones and lumps of cement picked from the roof and yard the next day. Darrow dropped one of the pebbles as he was about to hand it to the witness. It resounded loudly as it bumped along the floor. And two boys testified that a gang had been throwing stones. The police had been oblivious of all this.

Sufficient was elicited from the State's witnesses to lay a fair foundation for the plea of self-defense. We had been troubled about the statements given by the defendants to the police. They had been denied counsel. They had been browbeaten, intimidated and cajoled. They did not know that any one had been killed, and there had been a suggestion that if they told a clear story, they would be free of trouble. None of them had remembered clearly what had been said to the police and as it transpired, only one, Henry Sweet, had admitted firing. The defendants had tried to put the best possible complexion upon the situation. Each had loyally failed to remember anything about any one else. Mrs. Sweet had been pressed about what her husband was doing around the time of the shooting and where he was. Her recollection was at fault. She did not remember when he came home, when she had seen him, how often she had seen him, or where. When asked whether she was trying not to remember, she responded: "I don't remember because I don't remember." The examining attorney gave her up in disgust.

Henry Sweet, a college student, felt that if he took the responsibility, the others would be released. He had stated that he had shot from a front window, although I rather gathered the impression that he actually had been on the rear porch. At one place the minutes read that he had shot at the crowd; in another place, over the heads of the crowd. And it later appeared that the fatal bullet had not come from the gun which he used.

As stated, the charge as fixed by the bill of particulars was founded on conspiracy. Nothing that had been proved showed any agreement, either express or necessarily by implication. The occupancy of the house, the possession of firearms, the gathering at the house, and all other facts were quite consistent with a legal purpose, that of self-protection. There was nothing to show that the fatal bullet was not fired by some individual in a panic. The Prosecutor could not point to any one person.

The Prosecutor claimed to have shown facts from which a conspiracy might be inferred. Eleven people were in a house in no way fit for social entertainment, hospitality or comfort. There was a concerted and systematic shooting from different parts of the house indicating the participation of several individuals. There were enough weapons to arm each man, ammunition to supply each weapon. The assignment of defendants to firing stations was evidenced by the finding of mattresses, chairs, quilts, empty shells and cigar stubs at various windows. One defendant admitted having fired. In answer to the objection that all of this did not show that the defendants had agreed to shoot unnecessarily, the Prosecutor claimed that a number of weapons were hidden, that the lights in the house were kept out to prevent identification, that the defendants denied ownership of the guns, and that no one had attempted less violent means to prevent trouble.

In order to make his position clear, the Prosecutor suggested a parallel case:

"Suppose four persons were riding down Woodward Avenue in an automobile with the curtains drawn, a thing they could lawfully do. Suppose that they had been riding together in the car for at least three hours; suppose that suddenly volleys are fired from four sides of the car, one shot killing a bystander; suppose that on the car being stopped four weapons are found hidden under the cushions or in the pockets of the car; suppose that when arrested none of the four men said a word about the shots except that the driver stated that there would be no more shooting. If we put the Sweet house on wheels, we have exactly the same situation."

We argued the point strenuously. Every fact presented by the prosecution was consistent with innocence, and where evidence is circumstantial, defendants cannot be found guilty unless the facts admit of no

other conclusion. In the midst of the argument came
a baby's wail from the rear of the room. "Who
brought that child in here?" inquired the Judge.
"That is the Sweet baby," we answered. "We had her
brought here as an illustration. Had she been in that
house that night, she might well have been arrested
and tried and the evidence here would condemn her to
the same extent that it does the defendants." The
Prosecutor offered to dismiss as to Mrs. Sweet. She
protested. She refused to be favored. The motion to
dismiss was denied.

The position of the defense was clearly stated in the
opening.

"The defense in this case faces and admits facts which
are sometimes subject to equivocation and avoidance. We
are not ashamed of our clients and we shall not apologize
for them. We are American citizens; you men of the jury
are American citizens; they are American citizens. Each
juryman said that he conceded equal rights to all Americans. On the basis of the legal rights of the defendants
we make our defense. We say this with the full realization
of the sacredness of human life and having quite as much
sympathy for the bereaved family of the deceased as has
the prosecution.

"We shall first state our theory of the law and then state
the facts we intend to prove. The right of self-defense
in Anglo-Saxon history is centuries old and is well expressed in the old phraseology of Lord Chatham:

" 'The poorest man may in his cottage bid defiance to all
the forces of the Crown; it may be frail, its roof may shake,
the wind may blow through it; the storm may enter, the
rain may enter; but the King of England cannot enter;

all his forces dare not cross the threshold of that ruined tenement.'

"And did we not have this right of self-defense, were the use of arms never justified, we should all be subject to the terrible passions of man who would have no reason to fear man's retaliation. Self-defense is a necessary feature of organized society. It is the dearest right of a free man. Anything less than the right to use the fullest measure of protection when home and life are threatened would be contrary to human nature. No civilized society could survive without the right of self-defense. But, however valuable that right may be to a powerful man in the high classes of society, it is essential to the humble citizen and particularly to one who is subject to prejudice because he differs in race, creed or color from the ruling class in any community. I have said this in order to make clear that our defense is based upon a sacred ancient right, that of protection of home and life.

"But the right of self-defense cannot be an excuse for wantonly taking human life. To shoot to protect oneself is a right arising from the necessities of a particular situation as the facts appear to the person involved. You, gentlemen of the jury, have had told you a part of the story of September 9th, as it appeared from the outside, and it will be our duty and pleasure to show you the facts as they appeared from inside that little house on Garland Street and Charlevoix Avenue—the facts as they appeared to eleven people of the black race who had behind them a history, who were affected by knowledge of the appalling and almost uncivilized treatment of their race by those who should be their brothers and protectors. In other words, we shall show not only what happened in the house, but we shall attempt a far more difficult task—that of repro-

ducing in the cool atmosphere of a courtroom, a state of
mind—the state of mind of these defendants, worried, distrustful, tortured and apparently trapped—a state of mind
induced by what has happened to others of their race, not
only in the South where their ancestors were once slaves,
but even in the North in the States which once fought for
their freedom.

"We conceive the law to be this—that a man is not justified in shooting merely because he is fearful—but that a
man is justified if he has reasonable ground for fear. In
other words, one must put himself in a position of a reasonable man. But the reasonable man is not a fiction. He
is a man with a background, with a color, with the color
with which he has been endowed. The question is not what
a white man in a city of whites would do under certain
circumstances. The question is what a colored man, a reasonable colored man, with his knowledge of the prejudice
against him because of his color; with his knowledge that
people had threatened to bomb his home and kill him if he
moved into the neighborhood; with his knowledge that
there was a society of men (a so-called Improvement Association) formed for the purpose of ejecting him from his
home; with his knowledge of what mobs do and have done
to colored people when they have the power; with his
knowledge of history, his knowledge of psychology; with
his apprehension and fear from the facts as they appear
to him.

"Perhaps a good illustration of our theory of the law
would be to consider the situation of a white man in a
colored community, say Hayti. Assume that a white man,
through the course of years, has succeeded in acquiring an
education and accumulated a little capital; that he has
moved into a nice residential district; that he sees outside

his home what appears to him a mob of colored people; that his life has been threatened; that this white man had knowledge of other ferocious and unjustified attacks and knew the results of mob violence. Under those circumstances a white man charged with murder before a jury of colored men would be entitled to show how the situation appeared to him, whether such appearance arose from immediate facts, or from his knowledge of other incidents, his knowledge of psychology, his knowledge of history.

"In other words, our theory is self-defense and we claim the law to be that one is justified in defending himself when he apprehends that his life is in danger and when that apprehension is based upon reason.

"Doctor Ossian H. Sweet—Doctor, stand up so the jury can look you over—was born in Orlando, Florida, in October, 1895. His father was a minister and farmer. His grandfather was a slave. There were six children, of whom three are before you now. Defendant Doctor Otis Sweet, a dentist highly respected among his people in the City of Detroit, and Henry Sweet, who is now a college student. Henry and Otis, stand up. The other member of the Sweet family before you to-day is Mrs. Sweet, whose name was Mitchell before her marriage. Mrs. Sweet, stand up.

"These are four of the defendants and the first fact in our case of which we shall expect you gentlemen to take notice is that they do not look like murderers.

"The story of Dr. Sweet's life gives one pride in America, just as the story of this case makes one ashamed for America. Pride comes from watching this man, born on a farm of humble people, gradually rising through life to become, after years of work, study and earnest application, a member of an honored profession. As a boy, Dr.

Sweet learned from his grandfather the cruel stories of slavery in Alabama."

The story was continued. And, in conclusion, the jury heard the words of Joseph S. Cotter, Jr., the negro poet:

> "Brother, come!
> And let us go unto our God.
> And when we stand before Him
> I shall say—
> 'Lord, I do not hate,
> I am hated.
> I scourge no one,
> I am scourged.
> I covet no lands,
> My lands are coveted.
> I mock no people,
> My people are mocked.'
> And, brother, what shall you say?"

The defense adduced evidence to show the following: At the age of fourteen Dr. Sweet had left home to attend Wilberforce Academy in Ohio. He had been promised a scholarship but when he arrived at the school there were no funds for the purpose. He waited on tables, shoveled snow, fired the furnaces and did various kinds of menial work to get an education. In the summer he came to Detroit selling soft drinks and washing dishes at Boblo Island. For a time he was a bellhop on the lake-navigating steamers. Finally, after eight years he graduated from Wilberforce Academy and at about twenty-two years of age entered Howard

University, a medical school in Washington. He
worked his way again at college, chiefly by serving at
parties. Upon graduation he entered the Freedman's
Hospital of Washington and in 1921 came to Detroit
and started to practice medicine. In December, 1922,
he married Miss Mitchell, who had attended the public
schools of Detroit, Eastern High School and the Detroit Teachers' College. She also had taken a pre-
medical course at the Detroit Junior College. Dr.
Sweet and his wife lived with her mother, Mrs. Mitchell,
on Kearney Street, in small, cramped quarters. His
practice grew. In a short time having acquired a little
capital, he and his wife went abroad. He studied in
Vienna, specializing in gynecology and pediatrics. He
traveled through Italy and Egypt and the Mediter-
ranean. After six months in Vienna he took up the
study of radiology under Madame Curie, in France.
In Paris a child was born, the baby, be it noted, whom
Dr. Sweet did not dare to take to his new home. Dr.
Sweet had wished his wife confined in the American
Hospital in Paris. He had theretofore subscribed 300
francs, all he could afford, when the hospital had asked
Americans for funds, but his wife was refused admittance. This had been the only instance of race discrimination which he had suffered while abroad.

In the summer of 1924 Dr. Sweet and Mrs. Sweet,
with the baby, returned home. He soon reëstablished
his practice and started to save money for a home.
By the spring of 1925 he began to look around. He
was first offered a house through white agents who
advised him to buy in the name of some white friend

so that there would be no trouble. Dr. Sweet refused
to do this. Then in May he found the house at Garland and Charlevoix, a house owned by Mrs. Smith, a
white woman married to a colored man. The purchase
price was $18,500, of which $3,500 was paid in cash,
the balance payable at $150 a month. Mr. Smith was
present when the house was purchased. Dr. Sweet
asked Mrs. Smith about the neighbors, whether there
were Klansmen among them. He was reassured when
told that the people were mostly foreigners. It was
agreed that Mrs. Smith might remain in the house
until August first, and later Dr. Sweet consented that
she might stay a little longer.

During the summer a number of instances occurred
in the City of Detroit in which colored men were forced
out of their homes by mobs. One Dr. Turner, a highly
respected colored physician, bought a house on
Spokane Avenue. When he moved in, a mob surrounded the place. The police were on guard. Dr.
Sweet drove to the section and found the streets blocked
by masses of people. A man knocked on the door of
the Turner house and said, "I am a friend." Dr.
Turner opened the door. The mob broke in. They
raged and stampeded all over the house, smashed furniture, ruined the interior. A van was backed to the
door and the furniture was loaded. A scene that seared
itself on the mind of Dr. Sweet pictured the leader
and a few followers with one or two policemen in the
Turner sitting-room trying to prevail upon him to sell
his property and get out. Mrs. Turner refused to sign
the deed. The following night there were police in the

basement of the house and, with their consent, fifteen or twenty armed colored men held guard upstairs. Dr. Turner didn't stay in his new home.

About a week after this on Bangor Street, a mob surrounded a house bought by a colored man. Armed friends were inside. They fired and the mob dispersed. But the negro didn't stay there long.

On Scofield Street a negro, Fletcher, bought a home. Again a mob threatened. Two tons of coal for one of the neighbors had been dumped on the sidewalk. During the night it had all been thrown against the house and windows. There were armed men in the Fletcher house. One of them shot and a bystander was wounded. Fletcher was arrested. The matter was dropped, but Fletcher moved.

A colored man named Bristol had bought a lot in an unimproved section on American Avenue many years ago. He built a house, the handsomest on the block. He leased to white tenants but they did not pay the rent. Colored people were afraid to live there. He himself moved in. He asked for police protection which brought the inquiry from headquarters as to why he lived in a neighborhood where he was not wanted. He brought colored men to the house to protect him. About dusk a white woman mounted a box and called the men cowards for not attacking the property. She offered to lead the mob. Bristol had arranged with a number of colored men in a field across the way that if he needed help he would fire a gun. One block distant was a colored district. A policeman fired a shot. The negroes opened fire over the heads of the people.

Squads of police arrived with machine guns, and officers, without warrants, in violation of the Constitution of the United States and of the State of Michigan, searched the homes of the colored people in the neighborhood and took away their arms. Bristol didn't move, but lived under police guard and in constant fear.

On Merrill Street a colored woman with a baby of four or five weeks was compelled to fire on a mob to protect herself and her child. One Dr. Burton had bought a house and lot in North Detroit but threatening letters from the Ku Klux Klan kept him out of the house.

Forty or fifty colored people had been killed by the police in the City of Detroit during the prior year and little or no investigation had followed. Complaints were made. The Mayor wrote a letter to the Police Commissioner referring to the unwarranted killings and mistreatment of negroes. The newspapers constantly referred to lawlessness of negroes. Every unsolved crime was placed at their door.

It was during such a time that the Water Works Improvement Association was formed. Mrs. Smith told Dr. Sweet that she had received a telephone call that if Dr. Sweet carried out his contract, she would be killed, the Doctor would be killed and the house would be blown up. Mrs. Smith appeared in agonized anxiety on a second and third occasion. The neighbors had said it was a dirty trick to sell property to colored people. She said to Sweet, "My God, since the other doctor has allowed them to run him out, it looks

like they will run everybody out." During the summer
Sweet received messages that if he dared move into his
home, he would be shipped back to Antoine Street.

On Tuesday, September 8th, at about 10:30
o'clock in the morning, Dr. Sweet appeared with two
small vans containing furniture. He brought arms
and ammunition. Some of the weapons had been given
to him; he had bought three guns, using money which
he had saved to enable him to attend a medical convention.

At the time of moving, there came with Dr. Sweet
others who were going to live at the house. They were
John Latting and Henry Sweet. Both were seniors at
Wilberforce University; they had lived in the Mitchell
house. These boys expected to stay four or five days
with the Doctor, after which they would return to college. Both were in the Reserve Officers Training Corps.
There was also Morris Murray, who had done odd jobs
around the Doctor's house and painted his office. Joe
Mack who had been driving the Doctor's car, likewise
came. Another brother, Dr. O. O. Sweet, the dentist,
who had been staying at Mrs. Mitchell's, also intended
to live with the Doctor, and William Davis, a Federal
narcotic officer, had arranged for a room. Davis and
Dr. O. O. Sweet had been college mates at Howard University. Davis had fought in France as a captain in
the Argonne.

Some of these people came in the morning, some in
the afternoon. Joe Mack heard that the man in the
grocery store would not sell them food. When the
vans came up with the little furniture that Dr. Sweet

had—he had not needed much furniture at the home of his mother-in-law—the women of the neighborhood scurried from house to house. Through the day those in the house were subjects of covert scrutiny. The police were on guard and Officer McPherson, then in charge, kept in close touch with Sweet, assuring him of adequate protection. Through the day there were threats. Even little girls went around shouting "nigger." Toward evening crowds began to gather. Two girls had come to the house to help Mrs. Sweet with furnishings, to measure the size of the rooms. They wanted to leave but not daring to brave the mob stayed overnight. The mob continued to grow. Cars were passing in procession. Taxicabs made numerous trips, each time unloading passengers. At about three o'clock in the morning some one started throwing stones on the roof. At daylight there were perhaps fifty people left on the street. There was not much sleep in the Sweet house that night. Early the next day when Joe Mack and John Latting went out, some one said to them: "The crowd had a meeting last night in the confectionery store. You fellows better watch yourselves. They say they are going to get you out of here to-night."

On the morning of September 9th Dr. Sweet bought furniture. He attended to his practice through the day.

He returned home about five in the afternoon. Earlier he had met Watson, Washington and Morris, insurance agents, told them he expected trouble and asked that they come up to help protect him. They showed no hesitation. They gladly came. The issue concerned not only Dr. Sweet but their race.

"What did you do when you got home the evening of September 9th," Dr. Sweet was asked. "First thing I remember is of my wife telling me about a telephone conversation she had with Mrs. Butler, in which the latter told her of overhearing a conversation between the motorman of a street car and a woman passenger, to the effect that a negro family had moved into the neighborhood and they would be out before the next night." "When did you first observe anything outside?" "We were playing cards. It was about eight o'clock when something hit the roof of the house." "What happened after that?" "Somebody went to the window and I heard them remark, 'People, the people!'" "And then?" "I ran out to the kitchen where my wife was. There were several lights burning. I turned them out and opened the door. I heard some one yell, 'Go and raise hell in front; I am going back.' Frightened, and after getting a gun, I ran upstairs. Stones were hitting the house intermittently. I threw myself on the bed and lay there a short while—perhaps fifteen or twenty minutes—when a stone came through a window. Part of the glass hit me." "What happened next?" "Pandemonium—I guess that's the best way to describe it—broke loose. Every one was running from room to room. There was a general uproar. Somebody yelled, 'There's some one coming.' They said, 'That's your brother.' A car had pulled up to the curb. My brother and Mr. Davis got out. The mob yelled, 'Here's niggers, get them! Get them!'

As they rushed in, a mob surged forward, fifteen or twenty feet. It looked like a human sea. Stones kept coming faster. I was downstairs. Another window was smashed. Then one shot, then eight or ten from upstairs. Then it was all over." "What was your state of mind at the time of the shooting?" "When I opened the door and saw the mob, I realized I was facing the same mob that had hounded my people through its entire history. In my mind I was pretty confident of what I was up against. I had my back against the wall. I was filled with a peculiar fear, the fear of one who knows the history of my race. I knew what mobs had done to my people before."

And then Dr. Sweet told something of the negroes' tragic story, the lynchings, sometimes of innocent victims in various parts of the country, burnings at the stake by slow fire, of women mistreated by mobs, of negroes taken from policemen said to be guarding them, and killed, of the Washington riots, of East St. Louis, Tulsa, Chicago and Arkansas. Just two years before in a little town of Rosewood, near Orlando, eighteen negro homes and a negro church were burned and five negroes were shot to death in a series of outrages. Dr. Sweet himself had been in Washington at the time of the race riots and had seen men hunted through the streets. He had learned that the only thing which saved hundreds from extermination was that they were prepared to and did defend themselves. The race riots in Chicago had made a great impression upon him because Mrs. Sweet had had a number of cousins living in Chicago at the time. One of these cousins was a policeman who had shot in defense of his life. He was charged with murder. And the Arkansas trouble was vivid in his mind because there, four brothers—the Johnsons—one of them a fellow physician, one a dentist like Sweet's brother, one an influential business man, and the other a visitor from a neighboring state, had been taken from a train and had been murdered in cold blood. Tulsa was responsible for the death of Dr. A. C. Jackson, a colored physician who was said by the Mayo Brothers to have been the foremost colored surgeon in the country. He was defending his home. An officer of the law on guard had assured him that he would be protected if he surrendered. In the hands of the police he was killed in cold blood. In Texas one Henry Lowrie had surrendered under a promise of safe conduct from the government. He was taken from a train by a mob and burned at the stake. Dr. Sweet related how men had been taken from the streets, from their homes, from trains as well as from jails, and in one case even from a courtroom. He stated that almost three thousand colored people were lynched in the last generation. He made it clear that thoughts on these happenings were in the minds of these men on that dreadful day and night of September 8th and that fatal evening of September 9th. All this was admitted in evidence as bearing upon the psychology of the occupants of the Sweet house at the time of the shooting, and in order that the jury might determine whether reasonable men in their position would be fearful. All this gave a picture of what went on inside the house, and inside the minds of those inside the house.

Newspapers and reports of the National Association for the Advancement of Colored People were introduced, not to prove the facts, but to show the material which went to make up the psychology of the colored men. Dr. Sweet had testified that from reports he had read, white lynchers had never been prosecuted. The Prosecutor pointed out (referring to the report of the National Association for the Advancement of Colored People) that five men had been jailed in one case, but on careful perusal it appeared that in that riot, a white child had been killed. When Walter White testified concerning the National Association, the last question to him was, "Are you a negro?" and the answer "Yes" brought home to the jury that one might be a negro and still be white.

But defense witnesses differed with the Prosecutor as to what had occurred outside the house. Crowds of people had surged backward and forward, centering at Garland Street and Charlevoix Avenue. Three negroes, not related but all of them named Smith, testified that they were driving near the corner at about eight o'clock that evening and that the mob had threatened to lynch them, throwing missiles at the car. One of them seemed to resent the cross-examination as a species of impertinence. He was asked where he had had dinner, how long he had been driving, whom he had seen. Finally in a burst of impatience the old colored gentleman exclaimed, "I eats where I please, goes where I please and I pays my bills." Shortly after the shooting another colored man who was driving through the district was met by shouts of "There's a nigger; lynch him!"

Evidence is not permitted as to the character of defendants but is limited to reputation. Witnesses were called on this point. As to Mrs. Sweet, one remarked that he had never heard any one say anything about her reputation. The Prosecutor moved his testimony be stricken out. The interjection of the defense that that was one way of proving a woman's reputation aroused considerable amusement. Comments such as this occurred frequently. Darrow lost no opportunity to keep the jury in a light humor. "We'll never get a verdict of guilty," remarked the Prosecutor to his assistant, "unless we keep the case serious."

The defense witnesses, most of them colored, were people of a distinctly higher type than the whites who testified for the prosecution. Surely Sweet was moving to a neighborhood of his inferiors. Lies, evasion, prejudice and stupidity characterized their expression. Physically they were low-browed, mean and unintelligent looking, ugly. On the other hand, the colored witnesses were largely professional men and women, of clear features, good looks and unusual intelligence. At no point did the Nordics show to advantage.

In his address to the jury, Darrow showed his master hand. The ordinary lawyer collates facts, analyzes evidence and makes his appeal. There are few who use history, psychology and philosophy in order to show the real, underlying facts. Darrow said to those men on the jury that if he had merely to appeal to reason, he would have little doubt of the result, but that the

difficulty lay deeper.   It arose from a prejudice which
white men take in with their mother's milk.   The feeling
is typified by a poem of Countee Cullen, which was read
to the jury:

> "Once riding in old Baltimore,
>   Heart full, head full of glee,
> I saw a Baltimorean
>   Stand gazing there at me.
>
> "Now, I was eight and very small,
>   And he was no whit bigger,
> And so I smiled, but he stuck out
>   His tongue and called me 'nigger.'
>
> "I saw the whole of Baltimore
>   From April till December,
> Of all the things that I saw there
>   That's all that I remember."

Darrow questioned whether it was possible for twelve
white men (however they might try) to give a fair trial
to a negro.

"The Sweets spent their first night in their first home
afraid to go to bed.   The next night they spent in jail.
Now the State wants them to spend the rest of their lives
in the penitentiary.   The State claims there was no mob
there that night.   Gentlemen, the State has put on enough
witnesses who said they were there, to make a mob.

"There are persons in the North and the South who say
a black man is inferior to the white and should be controlled by the whites.   There are also those who recognize
his rights and say he should enjoy them.   To me this case

is a cross-section of human history. It involves the future, and the hope of some of us that the future shall be better than the past."

A fair and impartial judiciary has never been better represented than by Judge Frank Murphy at this trial. We were bitterly disappointed when he failed to grant the motion to dismiss. But in his charge to the jury Judge Murphy left no word unsaid to indicate clearly that a man's home is his castle and that no one has a right to assail or invade it. He left no question of the right to shoot when one has reasonable ground to fear that his life or property is in danger. In spite of the general attitude of the community, he made it clear that these rights belong to negroes as well as to white men.

The jury filed out, followed by the anxious eyes of the defendants, boxed in at the left of the courtroom. The crowd outside, mostly colored, waited quietly and with patience, pathetically doubtful of justice in a white man's court. Upon the verdict would depend the right of negroes to defend their homes and their lives against the rage of a white mob. Dr. Sweet had committed the unpardonable crime of purchasing a home in a white section of Detroit and of trying to live in that home. He had had the presumption not to be intimidated by threats against his life. He had moved there in spite of an expression of vigorous dissent from the community.

The jurors were closeted close to the courtroom and occasionally one would hear voices in angry debate and sometimes words. We heard the words, "What's the use of arguing with these fellows?" Again, "Two of you had these fellows convicted before you came here," and on another occasion, and this was encouraging, "I'll stay here twenty years, if necessary, and I am younger than any of you."

Time passed and the jury continued their deliberations. Late each night they were taken to a hotel. We spent the days and nights lolling around the courthouse, playing cards, going over to the jail trying to cheer up the defendants. Finally, when there was no further chance of agreement, after forty-six hours of deliberation, the jury was discharged.

It was clear that they were ready to acquit most of the defendants but some of them felt that there should be a penalty paid by some one. A white man had been killed.

Immediately we made a motion that the defendants be released on bail and insisted that if there were further trials each defendant should be tried separately. We knew full well that there were several who would never be tried again and that the feeling in the community had to some extent abated.

In April and May, 1926, Henry Sweet was again placed on trial. He was represented by Thomas Chawk and Julian Perry, in addition to Darrow. A few words of Darrow's summation are worth recording:

"I am the last one to come here to stir up race hatred, or any other hatred. I do not believe in the law of hate. I may not be true to my ideals always, but I believe in the law of love, and I believe you can do nothing with hatred. I would like to see a time when man loves his fellowman, and forgets his color or his creed. We will never be civilized until that time comes. I know the Negro race has a long road to go. I believe the life of the Negro race has been a life of tragedy, of injustice, of oppression. The law has made him equal, but man has not. And, after all, the last analysis is, what has man done?—and not what has the law done? I know there is a long road ahead of him, before he can take the place which I believe he should take. I know that before him there are suffering, sorrow, tribulation and death among the blacks, and perhaps the whites. I am sorry. I would do what I could to avert it. I would advise patience; I would advise toleration; I would advise understanding; I would advise all of those things which are necessary for men who live together."

Henry Sweet was acquitted and on July 21, 1927, the charges against the other defendants were dismissed.

At the corner of Garland Street and Charlevoix Avenue stands a little frame house. The wind does not blow through open spaces in the walls; the rain does not pour through the roof. It is not shattered. It is not dilapidated. It is not even uninhabitable. There is no gruesome story that ghosts have taken possession. The shutters are closed; the doors are nailed. It is unoccupied. It was a house bought by a negro, Dr. Sweet. He has no other property; he has no other home. Since the trial the baby has died so perhaps a home is not so important. But residence in Detroit is not free so long as that house stands idle.

FREEDOM OF THE STAGE

FREEDOM OF THE STAGE

The "Captive" Case in New York—Liveright vs.
Banton—Liveright vs. Waldorf Theatres
Corporation

Every once in a while a moral spasm shakes the city
of New York, and the stage is accused of the corruption of youth. Up and down Broadway the tremors
upset the theatrical profession, and there are worried
queries of where the dreaded blow will fall. Theater
owners, managers, and producers, chorus girls, ac-
tresses and stage hands, authors, librettists and mu-
sicians, knowing that accusation is condemnation, and
that in this vague field a legal adviser is merely a
"guesser," tremble for their livelihood. Since general
suppression would cause a public uproar, the hand of
discrimination must pick, choose and strike.

In the year 1927, excitement and indignation, not
so much of the public as of the vigilantes, knew no
bounds. Broadway presented musical shows in which
the ladies of the chorus were not uncomfortably robed.
It provided many variations on the love or sex problem.
There was "The Shanghai Gesture," which taught to
the uninitiated the intricate details of a Chinese house
of prostitution; there was "Lulu Belle," showing the
demoralization of a perfectly good and pious negro,

brought about by the amorous charms of a fascinating siren; there was "The Constant Wife," which suggested circumstances under which married women, for rational reasons, might go off "on their own"; there was "An American Tragedy," a dramatization of Dreiser's novel, which was suppressed in Boston, and in which a poor devil, depicted in the toils of two charming girls, attempted to solve the problem by disposing of the one who had lost her charm, after having first lost her virtue. Besides these, there were "Sex," "The Virgin Man," and "The Captive."

The attack on "The Captive" brought an entirely new theory into the law of repression. The existing New York statute prohibited "any obscene, indecent, immoral or impure play . . . which would tend to the corruption of the morals of youth or others." It has always been held that the statute refers to plays which would excite sexual or lecherous desire. The condemnation did not concern the taste of the District Attorney or any other individual, nor did it prevent the portrayal of any theme or subject matter, unless it excited lust. Early court records show an attempt to charge obscenity in a scurrilous publication which attacked a body of Christian clergymen. The court held that the statute was not directed against such material,[1] and, as an indication that the tendency of the article in question was not to excite "impure" desire, pointed out the fact that a dissenting opinion quoted the article in full. Some time ago the courts had occasion to consider the book "Madeleine," the

[1] People vs. Eastman, 188 N. Y. 478 (1917).

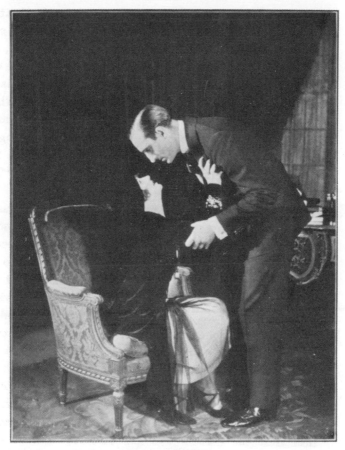

Helen Menken and Basil Rathbone in a scene from
"The Captive."

autobiography of a prostitute, a narrative containing revolting details of houses of ill fame. In spite of the theme, the book was not held violative of the law.[2] A well-known Federal case found nothing obscene in a pamphlet which discussed "Sexual Debility, Its Cause and Cure." [3]

The play "The Captive," by Edouard Bourdet, an eminent French author, portrays the consequences which arise from a well-known psychological condition, namely, the attraction of one woman for another. Irene de Montcel, not wishing to leave Paris with her family, refuses to tell her father the reason. She leads him to believe that the cause is her love for Jacques Dirieu, a suitor favored by the father. Jacques, informed of the real trouble, nevertheless marries Irene. In spite of her earnest efforts she cannot give herself whole-heartedly to him. As she says, "It's like . . . a prison to which I must return captive, despite myself." She promises Jacques that she will not see the other woman without informing him. Fearing her own impulses, Irene begs Jacques to take her away. He refuses. He gives the reason:

"You want to know why? Look at yourself; you are breathless—your eyes are dazed, your hands are trembling—because you have seen her again; that's why. For a year I have been living with a statue, and that woman had only to reappear for the statue to come to life, to have become a human being capable of suffering and trembling. Well, I give up, Irene, you understand, I give up. You should not have said that you could love me."

2 People *vs.* Brainard, 192 (N. Y.) A. D. 816 (1920).
3 Hansen *vs.* United States, 157 Fed. 749 (1907).

Irene: "How did . . . I know? I tried my best to love you. You always speak of what you have done; what about me? What about me? What about my feelings— did you ever know anything about them?"

Jacques goes out. Violets come for Irene. Jacques returns. Irene has gone.

The woman who attracts Irene at no time appears. The subject is handled in a delicate, artistic, subtle and unoffending manner. There is not an offensive or vulgar line in the play, nor any obscene situation.

In fact, the District Attorney is reported to have said:

"While 'Sex' and 'The Virgin Man' appeal to morons, 'The Captive' will capture anybody. It is not the lines and not the acting, *but the theme*. The other two are indecent and vulgar, but this one is thoroughly bad."

But if the objection is to the theme, then the only ground on which complaint can be made is that people should be kept in ignorance of actual facts of psychological and emotional reactions that occur in human life. This is the contention of the District Attorney— "that there is no necessity in life or logic for the average normal young man or woman to ever know the facts concerning that phase of human existence." [4]

So in Tennessee, where they claim that there is no necessity in life or logic for the average normal young man or woman ever to know of certain phases of science! After all, evolution relates to the far past. The descent of man is merely of abstract significance.

On the other hand, the question of perversion pre-

[4] Quoted from affidavit filed in Court.

sents a serious social problem. Its extent cannot be
determined, for it concerns facts which the average
individual would hesitate to reveal.   Katherine B.
Davis, formerly Commissioner of Correction in New
York, made some inquiry into the subject, sending letters to various women, the larger percentage of the
academic class. From about a thousand replies it appeared that in that group nineteen per cent found
greater physical attraction in other women than in
men, and in more than half of these instances the
emotion had physical expression. Yet this is a subject of which some would keep people in ignorance!

Foreign countries, notably Germany, are beginning
to face the facts and legislate accordingly. Anglo-
Saxons are horrified at unusual emotions. To them
they seem unnatural. They draw a fixed line between
the male and the female. Nature doesn't. They hold
human beings responsible, and condemn freaks of nature. They blast those whom they should pity—for
the germ plasm and its development are not of one's
making. And no doubt the imagination and creative
energy caused by romantic love are not affected by the
sex of the object, for emotions are subjective after all.
Oscar Wilde was sent to jail but his contribution to
mankind was perhaps inspired by the very emotions
which led to his downfall.

Types such as Irene exist. The play holds a mirror
to a phase of human life. Lack of knowledge and understanding emphasize life's tragedy. Unless we feel
that there is knowledge which in itself is indecent and
obscene, we should not condemn a play because its theme

deals with an unusual, though true, personality. It is not surprising that women educators, deans of women's colleges and heads of girls' finishing schools wrote to the management in great numbers to the effect that they strongly approved of the play because they were concerned with the necessity of impressing the girls in their charge with the dangers of an attachment by one woman for another. Women educators know that so-called "crushes" in girls' colleges are not unusual and to them the presentation of a strong, though delicate, argument showing the possible tragedy of such a relationship has real value. Habit formation may play some part in perverse development. Recent experiments on male mice have sought to find the resistance that animals will overcome to satisfy hunger for the female. A tread in the bottom of the cage conducts electricity. If the difficulty and hurt of satisfying sex hunger is too great, the animal turns to a male, and after a time will not go near the female. It is of importance for the human being to recognize the danger and tragedy of habits which may wreck a normal life—and perhaps even more important that parents should not be left in ignorance.

In connection with "The Captive," District Attorney Banton was faced with a difficult problem. Those who have no objection to stage realism are not vociferous. Others make complaint. For some unknown reason, those who complain that their sensibilities are affected, are supposed to be the "good" people of the community, and political acumen always favors the good people. But obviously Mr. Banton could not bar

all plays on Broadway except "Abie's Irish Rose."
"Pollyanna" was not on the boards.

Various plans were suggested by which the District
Attorney might rid himself of some of his responsi-
bilities. A play jury was formed, composed of intelligent men, with literary background, and with confidence
in the decency of their fellowmen. After attending a
performance, they sanctioned the continuance of "The
Captive." There was little hope for the vice-hunters
in such a wanton jury.

Suggestions were made that the law provide for
some form of censorship. Popular opinion opposed
this, fearing as usual the shadow of the word "censor,"
rather than the substance of what a censor represents.
Where the spirit of the community is one of repression,
so that pressure is exercised upon public officials, the
proper kind of "censor"—if there is any such animal—
might be a protection. Censorship is obnoxious to me,
yet even this is better than a situation where an elec-
tive District Attorney can by crooking his finger suppress any play because of the fear his action inspires.

"The Captive," after successful runs in Paris and
other European capitals, opened in New York on September 26, 1926, with a brilliant cast, headed by Basil
Rathbone and Helen Menken. It was received with
almost unanimous commendatory press criticism, and
from some of the papers which later joined in the hue
and cry against it.

The New York *Sun* said:

" 'The Captive' is a thoroughly absorbing, admirable
and, incidentally, respectable play. Go of your own accord

and see as brave and wise and feelingful a play as you have every human and moral right to enjoy."

The New York *American* said:

"Edouard Bourdet has dealt with his subject splendidly, reverently and without the least ribaldry. There is not one risqué line in the entire drama. Intense and marvelously sympathetic."

The *New York Times* said:

"Expertly written and admirably played. 'The Captive' is a genuine achievement . . . sincere and cleanly finished."

The New York *Herald-Tribune* said:

" 'The Captive' is a good play excellently done. It is decent, and that is more than can be said of many current exhibitions whose frivolous transgressions go unindicted by the authorities."

The New York *World* said:

"Bourdet has written 'The Captive' with infinite tact and reticence. It calls to all pitying hearts the world 'round."

The New York *Evening Post* said:

" 'The Captive' promises to do no violence even to the most sensitive. Audiences of normal men and women will find the play simply and frankly absorbing."

Students of Princeton and Columbia voted "The Captive" the most important play of the season.

The pulpit joined in the laudation; physicians and scientists were enthusiastic at its high moral and social value. Said William A. White, Superintendent of the

St. Elizabeth Hospital of Washington, D. C., and one
of America's foremost psychiatrists:

"While criticism of Bourdet's play should consider it
first and foremost as a play, a work of art, a tragic drama,
it must needs also take into consideration the comment
which has arisen in many quarters relegating it to the
pornographic and salacious, thus classifying it with that
group of presentations that are bringing the stage into
disrepute.   The stupidity and injustice of this attitude
need special consideration to the end that a real work of
art shall not be misjudged and lost as the result of a
passing misapprehension."

The success of the play was instantaneous and continued.   Here was a thought-provoking and serious
drama!

In February, 1927, attachés of the District Attorney's office held inconspicuous place in the audience.
Officers of the New York Police Department scanned
the spectators, to determine their ages, escorts,
social background and emotional reactions.   Lieutenant
McCoy contemplatively chewed his pencil.   The play
opened.   The characters appeared.   All were modestly
dressed; the background was a sitting-room.   The bed-
rooms, thought he correctly, must be behind the drop
curtain.   No vulgar lines offended his delicate ear.
The developing plot, however, shook his complacency
early in the second act.   Have his ears deceived him?
No, it was said again.   "*She* loves *her*," wrote he in
bold, broad strokes of his pencil!

On February 15th, the authorities decided that the
author, translator, producers, actors, and stage hands

had, since the prior September, engaged nightly, and on Wednesday and Saturday afternoons, in the commission of crime—to wit, corrupting the morals of the community. They were ingloriously herded into Jefferson Market Court, and together with drunks, prostitutes, gunmen and other criminals, released on bail. But these hardened malefactors were not ashamed of their crime. One and all stated that they were proud to appear in the play—that it was one of the masterpieces of the stage.

A day was set for hearing. As the intervening days passed, the enthusiasm of the actors waned. They foresaw a trial by jury, and a jury trial is dangerous under such circumstances.

The Frohman Company, the producer of "The Captive," not only had a conservative and respectable history, but, in addition, it was (and is) controlled by The Paramount Famous Lasky Corporation, which, as every one knows, produces motion pictures, not only in what Mr. Mencken is pleased to call civilized metropolises, but in the sticks and for the hicks. It is said that from these latter the larger profits from the fillums accrue. So an untarnished reputation was essential for the Frohman Company. Like Cæsar's wife, it must be above suspicion. True, it had produced "The Captive" for some months and had garnered the emoluments thereof. But some gentlemen hesitate to take responsibility for their acts when a Deal can be arranged. If the Frohman Company would close the play, the authorities would forget that it had corrupted the community from September until February.

Horace Liveright then appeared upon the scene—tactless perhaps, because he had already had several tilts with The Society for the Suppression of Vice, and even the higher authorities, because of his publication of "radical" books of all sorts, social or economic. Had he not practically single-handed defeated Justice Ford's so-called Clean Books Bill in the Albany Legislature? Had he not successfully debated the question of censorship throughout the country to the annoyance of those in high places?

On the evening before the day set for the hearing, Mr. Liveright had been requested by a spokesman for the cast of "The Captive" to appear in court. Intensely interested in the case, having endeavored, originally, to buy the production rights of the play, and, having lost by a matter of hours, the publication of the book to Brentano's (who, by the way, still freely circulate it throughout the country), Mr. Liveright lent a willing ear. Realizing that he was not legally involved in the proceedings, Mr. Liveright went to the Jefferson Market Police Court the next day without benefit of lawyer or clergy. Elbowing his way through the crowded courtroom, to the jostling knot of actors, lawyers, and officials who stood behind the railing around the Magistrate's desk, he waited until the Court demanded of the actors their promise never to appear in the production again should the case against the Frohman Company be dismissed. Before Ann Trevor, the pretty blonde English actress, could reply to the Magistrate's question, Mr. Liveright suggested to the court that he himself would be interested in producing the play; and that he wanted the members of the cast to realize that he was behind them with what resources he possessed, should they decide to challenge this attempt to prevent them from earning an honest living. The Magistrate was not favorably impressed. Those who run counter to the authorities have little judicial favor. He declared the intruder out of order and the sergeant-of-arms emphasized the ruling by throwing Liveright out of the sanctified enclosure. In earlier days when an Indian tried to lasso a locomotive, some one remarked that he admired the Indian's courage but could not commend his judgment.

Helen Menken and three other members of the cast, having firmly and dramatically promised never again to act in "The Captive," were released. The Frohman Company was likewise discharged. Ann Trevor, Basil Rathbone, and others, who declined to make promises which they regarded as degrading, were held for further hearing.

For the next half hour the lobbies of the court building were gay with congratulations, denunciations and interviews with newspaper reporters, to the generous accompaniment of camera clicks and offers from vaudeville managements. When the smoke of battle had somewhat lifted, the members of the cast taxied to Mr. Liveright's apartment on Fifty-seventh Street to consider the situation. During the discussion Mr. Liveright remembered that at the opening night of "The Captive" he had talked between the second and third acts of the play with his friend, James J. Walker, who before becoming Mayor of New York had made an impassioned speech of congratulation at a dinner given in Mr. Liveright's honor at the Hotel Brevoort after the so-called Clean Books Bill had been defeated. His Honor had highly commended "The Captive." According to an official of the Frohman Company who was present at the meeting in Mr. Liveright's apartment, he had stopped for a minute at the conclusion of the play at the office of William Harris, the Treasurer of the Frohman Company, and had said to him: "I don't see anything wrong with this, it seems like a good play to me."

Surely the first step to take was to get in touch with Mayor Walker, to obtain his support. But how was one to get him on the telephone? The home number was not in the official directory. Appeals to other city officials failed to elicit the coveted information. During all this time, Mr. Liveright's Japanese servant had been passing tea and other contraband refreshment; quietly but suddenly Sutsuma glided into the room and nonchalantly presented a slip of paper on which was written, "Walker 6766 (Resident of Major)." But, alas, Oriental diplomacy and skill proved of no assistance. His Honor was not at home and three imploring messages that he come to the rescue were either ignored or never delivered to him.

Nevertheless, Mr. Liveright had acquired the production rights of the play from the author, and the members of the group at his apartment, earnestly resentful of the condemnation of their play, and for the moment imbued with a sense of the dignity of American citizenship, carried away by the argument that it was somewhat cowardly to expect only the mean and lowly to fight against oppression, all signed this statement which was issued by Mr. Liveright:

"We, the undersigned, members of 'The Captive' company, feel that the principle involved in the attempted suppression of 'The Captive' is more important than our personal interests. The play has been acclaimed by the intelligent public as a masterpiece of dramatic literature. Critics all over the world have paid tribute to the author. Far from feeling that we have been engaged in the commission of a crime for the past six months, we feel that we have been privileged in using our talents in a play of the highest literary merit and social value. Commendation has come from people in all walks of life, including the ministry; and the play jury, which considered the play at the request of the District Attorney, found in it nothing objectionable.

"Our counsel advises us that we are violating no law. We owe it to ourselves, our profession, and to our public to refuse to be intimidated. We expect to receive the protection of the courts against unjust prosecution.

HELEN MENKEN,	MINNA PHILLIPS,
BASIL RATHBONE,	JOHN MILTERN,
ARTHUR WONTNER,	ARTHUR LEWIS,
GAIL KANE,	PERCY SHOSTAC,

ANN TREVOR."

Acting Mayor McKee responded nobly, "We will meet that challenge. If Mr. Liveright attempts to put on that play, he and every member of the cast will be placed under arrest."

In the meantime public interest was likewise engaged

in the plays, "Sex" and "The Virgin Man," both of which had obtained Supreme Court injunctions to prevent police interference until a final court determination was made on the question of their obscenity. Never having seen either of these plays, I have no opinion of them. The general thought was that they were fashioned after "The Captive," but with a purpose of exploiting perversion, and that the presentation was made in a manner to excite sexual thrills. It was said that the producers had added extra parts in rehearsal in order to give a real "kick." After the successful production of "The Captive" in Paris, others there attempted to ape the theme, but the result was so inartistic that such other plays failed to catch the public. In a civilized community a poor play falls of its own weight. This very likely would have been the fate of both "Sex" and "The Virgin Man" had the activity of the District Attorney not whetted the appetite of an eager public. One not looking for pornography may still be interested in learning—and seeing—what the fuss is all about. Be that as it may, long after "The Captive" was closed by the Frohman Company, at a cost of the return of some $80,000, which represented advance sales, and with a total loss of between $150,000 and $300,000 (including prospective profits), these other two plays were continued.[5]

Gilbert Miller, the former producer, and among the ablest and most artistic of to-day, sounded the valedictory. After stating that the reception of "The

[5] Eventually they were condemned after jury-trial, where the actors and producers were found guilty.

Captive" seemed fully to justify his judgment, he added:

"The entire press resounded with the most lavish praise a play had received for at least a decade. Special emphasis was laid upon the author's wholly delicate and wholly inoffensive treatment of a subject which though new to our stage was not for that reason forbidden. . . . I am therefore strongly of the belief that it was grossly unfair under the circumstances for the authorities to have classed 'The Captive' by their recent action with plays . . . which present an entirely different problem."

The Frohman Company refused to sell Liveright the sets. Magistrate Renault, who was still to hear the cases of the remaining defendants, stated that "the attitude of the management of this play is most commendable."

It was apparent that Liveright could not produce the play unless some relief were had from the Court by way of injunction. When the defendants again appeared in the Magistrate's Court they, with one exception, gave their promise not to appear again in "The Captive" until some competent court should decide that the play was not violative of the law. Percy Shostac, the stage manager, refused to make any concession. "I refuse," said he, "not because I want to make this a test case . . . but because I think it is morally degrading to have to give such a promise in connection with a great work of art."

We were ready to proceed with the case. Here was an opportunity for a direct test of the alleged "obscenity," but Mr. James Wallace, Assistant District

Attorney, seemed to discover, so he said, an "Ethiopian
in the woodpile." Although the case had been set peremptorily, the prosecution declared itself not ready to
proceed, and Mr. Wallace later scotched the Ethiopian,
and successfully prevented a legal test, by dismissing
the case against Shostac with the approval of the
Court.

Liveright had neither scenery, cast, nor theater.
He lacked everything but determination. Action was
brought against the authorities. Contention was made
that the District Attorney and the police were sup-
pressing "The Captive" by illegal interference and
threats, that their action showed a determination to
prohibit presentation, whether or not there was ground
for complaint. Had there been a crime they should
have proceeded against the Frohman Company and
those in the cast. There is nothing in the law which
gave either them or the magistrate a right to release
this company if it withdrew the play or the individual
defendants on condition that they should promise not
to appear again. A crime had or had not been committed. The refusal to proceed against Shostac showed
the purpose of the authorities.

We admitted that one cannot ordinarily enjoin the
authorities from enforcing the criminal law, though
we made that admission grudgingly. When one fights
official suppression, and invokes the aid of a Court of
Equity, he is always met by this argument—and this
even though he is trying to prevent illegal acts of the
police. Sometimes keepers of houses of prostitution
and gamblers have succeeded in obtaining injunctive

relief against trespass, but such cases seem to meet with more favor. They only indirectly involve questions of liberty of the citizen. We were not trying here to enjoin the authorities from making arrest for crime. If the court should find that the play "The Captive" was not violative of the law, then the whole intimidating action of the District Attorney, with its direct and implied threats, was in violation of valuable property rights. The officials had declared that the City accepted Mr. Liveright's challenge, which indicated the disposition of the authorities to threaten, intimidate and to suppress the play without legal determination of its propriety.

The District Attorney, in argument before Mr. Justice Jeremiah F. Mahoney, not only contended that the play was obscene, but pointed out the provocative conduct of any one who would attempt to produce a play of which the authorities disapproved. It appeared that James L. Coy, Acting Lieutenant of the Police Department, James B. Sinnott, the Police Secretary, and Charles Kane, First Grade Detective, were the literary censors. The policemen were shocked by a play which "unlawfully endeavored to make it appear that perverted sexual relations are more alluring and attractive than natural marital cohabitation." And, said they, "the male characters are weaklings compared to the females described in the play." How shocking are these thoughts to police lieutenants and detectives! "The vast majority of people go to the theater for amusement." Isn't it too bad that some find an interest in problem plays? Finally, stated one of the police officers:

"Seventy per cent of the audience attending the performance on the day I was there were under twenty-five years of age, and sixty per cent of the audience were women. The majority of them came unescorted, either two or three girls together. This was particularly true of those sitting in the balcony or gallery. Men also came in pairs. They were mostly young men. Where a gentleman was accompanied by a lady they were usually over thirty-five years of age."

This is appalling! Imagine women going to the theater unescorted and men arriving in "pairs"! One queries whether the officers did not see what they were looking for. They failed to remark that they had come in triplets.

Liveright, determined to go ahead, had difficulty in obtaining a playhouse. After discouraging rebuffs, he finally acquired a lease of the Waldorf Theatre, the agreement providing that it was subject to cancelation in the event that the play was violative of the law, or that any Court should so find.

The Waldorf Theatre Company then notified Liveright that the District Attorney had advised that the play was obscene and in violation of the Penal Law. Therefore it gave notice that it would not permit public presentation. The receipt of this notice was not wholly unexpected nor unwelcome. A Court decision was essential. Liveright could not get together a cast until the question of obscenity was decided. The former actors had specifically pledged themselves in this respect, and no other actor of note would take part in a performance, with the likelihood of arrest, trial and possible imprisonment, in the event that it should transpire that the authorities had "guessed" right and Liveright and his legal advisers had "guessed" wrong, the right or wrong to be determined by the sensitiveness of the moral natures of twelve good men and true.

Jurors are influenced by somewhat the same considerations as judges, district attorneys and church people. An acquittal suggests loose morals. A condemnation assumes virtue. "Would this play arouse sexual passion?" would be the legal question set before them by the Judge's charge. The normal man would be emotionally much more interested in an affair between a man and a woman. But the jury would set for themselves the question: "Do we think a play dealing with an abnormal psychosis should be presented?" More specifically, the juryman would ask himself, "Do I like this kind of a play or do I want my wife to think I like this kind of a play?" One could hardly blame an actor who refused to hazard not only his time and salary, but likewise his liberty, on a chance like this.

Even people of artistic standing and educational background objected to "The Captive." They asked the usual question, "What good does it do?" as though the test of a play had to do with whether or not it would in their opinion do "good"—a matter on which almost all people differ.

Knowing that the courts are not prone to hold against the authorities or to buck a public opinion which seemed to feel that something should be done about the stage, we were not confident that the injunction against the authorities would be maintained. The case might be thrown out without any consideration of the real question involved.

On the other hand, having received notice that the Waldorf Theatre refused to permit us to enter on the ground that the play was obscene, we felt there was no possible way for the courts to avoid passing upon the main issue, thus presented. We, therefore, brought an injunction proceeding against the Theatre on the basis of the lease, which excused the defendant only in case the play was obscene under the law. We alleged that the play was not violative of the law; that the Waldorf Theatre refused to permit us to enter the premises; that Liveright had a large financial interest in the production and that his rights would be destroyed unless an injunction were granted. I may add that the lease specifically released both parties from any claim for money damages. The Waldorf Theatre Company relied upon the position taken by the authorities. The important question concerned the Judge who was to be vested with power to make the decision. Carefully we scanned the law journals to determine what judges were sitting. Carefully we considered the background, training and former decisions of each. The law is the law, but— Daily a call from Liveright would ask for an opinion, to which we answered that we did not regard the play as in any sense obscene, and that we thought we had raised the question in a manner to compel the Court to pass on it. We appeared before Judge John L. Walsh but later learned that he was disinclined to consider the case. With his permission we withdrew our motion and asked Mr. Justice Mahoney to pass upon this injunction, together with that against the police.

Some days later, the Court denied both injunctions,[6] stating that under ordinary circumstances any Judge passes upon the question of obscenity with considerable diffidence "because it must be conceded that in view of our mixed population such a question can better be passed upon by a jury drawn from those of varied experiences and engaged in different occupations." He quoted from an earlier case in which the propriety of the book "Mademoiselle de Maupin" had been upheld:[7]

"The conflict among the members of this court itself points a finger at the dangers of a censorship entrusted to men of one profession, of like education and similar surroundings."

He added that the nature of the proceeding compelled him to determine whether or not "The Captive" violated the law. He stated that a reading of the play justified the claim that it possessed extraordinary literary merit which one would expect from an author of Bourdet's reputation. He discounted the fact that the play had succeeded in other lands "because other people might have different customs and views," a suggestion which implies that obscenity is a matter of tradition and confirms the thought that if one's views are narrow enough, anything is obscene. He referred to

[6] *New York Law Journal*, March 9, 1927, Vol. 76, p. 2592.
[7] Halsey *vs.* New York Society for the Suppression of Vice, 234 N. Y. 1 (1922).

the fact that the views of critics are inadmissible as evidence, as "they frequently look with a single eye to purity of construction, vividness of phrase and skill in implanting ideas in luminous expression." He considered the contention that if the play was condemned it would be solely because of the theme, but concluded that the question was whether the tendency of the play is to "deprave or corrupt those whose minds are open to such immoral influences and who might come in contact with it," that the statute looks to the protection not of the mature and intelligent, but "to those who are young, ignorant and sensually inclined." If this is the test, few serious plays have a chance before a court.

After all, intelligent people should have some rights. If they are not permitted to view any production which might have an adverse effect on the immature, the vicious and the morally degraded, the field of the playwright and producer is limited to innocuous palaver. Hardly any serious portrayal of life on the stage will escape the condemnation of those who fear, not for themselves, but for others whose morality is endangered by facing facts.

The opinion arouses the fear that the question of whether or not one could produce a play would depend largely upon the discriminatory will of the District Attorney. This indeed is a fact. It suggests the danger underlying any law of this kind, unless construed narrowly to apply to those plays about which there can be little difference of opinion. One need do no "guessing" as to what is a dirty and filthy play.

Construed from this point of view, obscenity laws are reasonably definite. We have already adverted to this in considering the "American Mercury" case.

It is curious how in the domain of business, the law requires definite and explicit laws, so that one is in no danger of "guessing" himself into jail. Any "criminal statute to be valid must be so clearly and definitely expressed that an ordinary man can determine in advance whether his contemplated act is within or without the law, and if deviation from a standard is prohibited, the standard must be definitely fixed." [8] The quotation has been approved by the Supreme Court of the United States. The courts do not seem to have applied this reasoning when the standard concerns morality, emotion, freedom of expression and matters of like kind. Indefinite laws are prohibited by the Fourteenth Amendment to the Federal Constitution. They come within the old maxim, "where the law is uncertain there is no law." They come within the objection that any criminal statute offends "due process" unless it is general, uniform, fixed and certain. They are equivalent to the Chinese code which prescribes a punishment for those guilty of "improper conduct." They violate the *ex post facto* provisions of the Constitution because until after trial no one can tell what the law is. They upset the general principle of our Government which is supposed to be one of law and not of men, for with indefinite statutes the Government is necessarily of men rather than of law. Tyranny has always found its simplest pressure in measures which would enable

[8] United States *vs.* Armstrong, 265 Fed. 683 (1920).

power to discriminate. When a Government wants to "get" a man, the course is easy if the law is indefinite.

The Court commended the District Attorney for his action and did not fail to point out that the inference might be drawn that Liveright had purchased the play in the hope of "increased financial returns due to the notoriety and publicity this play has received." Rarely has any one sought to assert his rights without this aspersion. Yet Liveright, as a matter of fact, had sought to obtain the play long before it had been produced by the Frohman Company.

Having found that the play was violative of the law, the Court denied the injunction asked for against the police as well as that against the Waldorf Theatre. The decision at least cleared the atmosphere. Judge Mahoney had not refused to face the issue. He apparently realized that the test by jury trial after production would mean absolute determination by a District Attorney. Whatever may be the theoretical standpoint, practically, if a play is charged with immorality and the cast threatened with jail, the play is at an end. The only relief from intimidation is by injunctive process.

We appealed to the Appellate Division. The defendant was not averse to a decision in our favor, for of course it meant the rental of his theater for a play which had been successfully produced. The defendant's attorney presented what was obviously a weak argument in opposition. When the presiding Judge inquired whether he was anxious to lose the case, he evaded the question. I saw no reason why we should not frankly admit that our interests were the same and that we were both anxious to have a decision on the law. But somehow the thought is that the courts are better satisfied if the issue is one on which the parties differ.

It seems rather stupid in a civilized community to compel a fight in order to get a decision. There is a procedure by which questions can sometimes be submitted to court for what are called "declaratory judgments" on points of law. The court still has discretion, however, to refuse to give judgment. In a case like this, the issue would no doubt be avoided. In the ordinary civil case the parties may agree upon a statement of facts and thus get a determination. Theodore Dreiser and his publishers once tried this procedure in connection with "The Genius." The Court held that the question of whether or not a book was obscene, was *the* question of fact to be determined. Therefore, the issue could not be presented in that way.[9] One must take a chance of jail in order to determine the law.

The Appellate Court affirmed the judgment,[10] suggesting that while its judgment would not be binding on the police authorities, yet in effect, if they should pass on the question of obscenity, the decision might interfere with police activity. Why not? The Court said:

"It cannot be said dogmatically that the morals of youth, or even of adults, would not be affected by presenting a

9 Dreiser *vs.* John Lane Co., 183 (N. Y.) A. D. 773 (1918).
10 220 (N. Y.) A. D. 182; 220 (N. Y.) A. D. 836 (1927).

theme of the character here exhibited with the action and dialogue which accompany it.

"The action might give to some minds a lecherous swing causing a corruption of the moral tone of the susceptible members of the audience."

But, primarily the Court refused "to countenance the procedure resorted to" in the application, which would

"ultimately constitute the civil arm of the courts as censors of the drama and its allied arts of literature, of painting and of sculpture.   One need but have the contractual duty imposed to produce, publish or install a play, book or work of art and upon refusal of performance demand that the arm of the court be raised to compel the execution of the compact. . . . The regulation of dramatic productions by compulsion or interposition of the injunctive process has no analogy or parallel in the realm of equitable jurisdiction hitherto entertained.   We are not prone so to widen its sphere as to embrace it."

The Court suggested that if Liveright had any remedy against the Waldorf Theatre by reason of loss of profits, he might sue and the damages would be assessed by jury, if he could convince the jury that "*no immoral suggestion or lewd or lecherous instinct may be aroused as a result of performing the play.*"

Of course, such a decision makes the District Attorney the censor and prevents any recourse to the court, for relief is denied through any process which is immediately available.   In any case involving a question of property in which a moral issue is not involved, equity will interfere.   The court did not seem to realize that its fear of assuming the functions of a censor merely passed such functions on to a prosecuting officer. The courts have often acted as censors. On appeal from a judgment, the Appellate Courts determine questions of obscenity not, it is true, as to whether a book or a play is obscene, but rather as to whether reasonable men could conclude that it was obscene. The question may become one of law rather than of fact.

But we were not through yet. The District Attorney had contended under the law "The Captive" could not be produced, but in spite of the assurance with which he banned the play, an amendment to the New York statute was suggested so as to make it a misdemeanor to present not only "an obscene, indecent, immoral or impure play, exhibition, show or entertainment," but likewise "any obscene, indecent, immoral, impure scene, tableau, incident, part or portion" of any of the above and likewise condemning any play, scene or tableau "depicting or dealing with the subject of sex degeneracy or sex perversion." [11] This raises the interesting question as to what is sex degeneracy or sex perversion. Are Ibsen's "Ghosts," and Brieux's "Damaged Goods" included in the category? The condemnation of a play, any part or incident of which is obscene, presents another interesting consideration. Heretofore, with plays as with books, the whole counted. This law is censorship or suppression gone wild. Shakespeare, Sophocles, and the "Nibelungenlied" should be banned under this test. Of course they would not

[11] Section 1140-a New York Penal Code, April 5, 1927.

be, but this is because such power is exercised not without, but with, discrimination.

But this wasn't enough. The proposed law provided that on conviction the license of the theater owner might be taken away and the theater might be closed for a period of one year. This gives complete power to any District Attorney.

Since a producer of a play will never know whether or not a jury will declare it obscene until after trial, the law will always operate *ex post facto*. An analogy was suggested to the padlock procedure for liquor prohibition violations, but the parallel is not sound. The manager of a hotel knows whether he is selling liquor. The owner of a theater may be heavily penalized for housing a performance which both he and the majority of his patrons sincerely believe to be both elevating and beautiful. Many District Attorneys all over the country objected, sometimes under pressure, to "Desire Under The Elms." A manager who dared to present a large part of Eugene O'Neill's work might do it under threat of very serious consequences.

The bill passed the legislature and was signed by Governor Smith. True, he indicated that such powers should be reasonably exercised. Yet the difference between tyranny and liberty lies not in the will of an individual but in the law; lies not in the exercise of the power, but in its possession.

The new attitude is far worse than censorship. Make a law inclusive enough, and the penalty severe enough, and a censor would be far preferable. At least then one knows what he can do. Not only the

author and the manager, but even the owner of the
theater is constituted a censor who is bound to be
more fearful, timid and unintelligent than any public
authority could be. This would be so if the law were
enforced. As a matter of fact, the law won't be enforced except in specific instances, and thus again we
add to the vast number of unenforcible laws, the effect
of which is to weaken respect for law (which may be
an evil) and to make every individual subject to discrimination, which is certainly an evil.

The amendment ended the possibility of producing
"The Captive."

Horace B. Liveright is also a publisher. Some years
ago a book by Maxwell Bodenheim, "Replenishing Jessica," published by him, displeased John S. Sumner, of
the Society for the Suppression of Vice. An indictment
followed. The case lay dormant for some time. After
the indictment a bookseller was arrested for selling the
book and discharged in a Magistrate's Court. But
after Liveright had had the audacity to fight the District Attorney in the endeavor to produce "The Captive," the old indictment was called for trial in March,
1928.* The District Attorney is an honorable man,
but citizens who endeavor to assert their rights feel the
hand of power.

The demand for a clean stage is not a new phenomenon. One can imagine the Athenians objecting
to the plays of Sophocles with a particular drive at
the "Œdipus Rex." In Elizabethan times a large part

* After a five-day trial, it took the jury less than fifteen
minutes to conclude that the book was not obscene.

of the community condemned Shakespeare and Beaumont and Fletcher. Obscenity depends upon the customs of the time, upon whether the portrayal is usual or novel. The character of the audience is important. In London is a private theater with which the censor does not interfere. A play produced there is no different than if produced elsewhere, yet there is a basis for different consideration. No doubt our "little" theaters of an experimental type might produce plays which the authorities would find objectionable if presented on Broadway. It is less likely, however, that the District Attorney will receive complaint, and ordinarily he is not anxious to act unless persuaded by what he thinks is a public demand. If he used intelligence—although this is a good deal to ask from a public official—he would find a basis for distinction. Such discrimination might suggest to him the indefiniteness of these laws.

After all, a theater is, in a sense, the most democratic institution on the face of the earth. No one is compelled to attend a performance. The box-office receipts show what people want to see. With their purchases they cast the vote. Conceivably a nude statue, an indecent advertisement or a suggestive painting might be seen by chance, but ordinarily when one goes to a theater, particularly in view of the high prices that prevail, he knows fairly well what will be portrayed. Some twenty years ago Anthony Comstock attacked Shaw's "Mrs. Warren's Profession." His activity proved a great advertisement. Although manners and customs did not then permit of the liberality which is

accepted to-day, the Court of Special Sessions released
the defendants, holding that the play did not violate the
law.   Comstock designated Shaw as "that Irish smut-
hound," to which Shaw replied that he admitted that
his play might affect "weak-minded or ignorant people."

Whether or not any one play should be produced
is of relatively minor importance.   The state of the
law and the power held by authority present a grave
issue.   "The Captive" is significant because it shows
that we are beginning to condemn plays because of
their theme.   We object to thought on certain subjects.
Precedents of suppression are dangerous.   "Revelry"
was a play which was said to reflect rather unfavorably
upon President Harding, though it showed him to be a
human being whose chief fault lay in his faith in his
advisers and friends.   It met opposition from the
authorities in Philadelphia.

Consider the productions on Broadway to-day.   They
are not very different from last year.   Laws may come
and laws may go, yet public taste determines the character of the performances.

Year after year the annual reports of the New York
Society for the Suppression of Vice deplore the de-
moralizing indecency of the stage.   Quoting from an
unnamed Brooklyn judge in the report of 1924, they
say:

"The modern [motion] picture is sensual and nothing
demoralizes more than sensuality—   At the movies the
young see things they never should be allowed even to hear
or think about.   Under such conditions the downfall of
young girls is not remote.   [Sic.]   Similarly, the spoken

drama of the present day on the New York stage outrivals Paris for indecency."

In 1925 the report admits that the "sex impulse is important and necessary" but the report objects to what is called "its artificial stimulation" and to "that class of public show of recent growth which commercializes feminine nudity and caters to the animal side of nature."

But they fail to solve the important problem. What is artificial stimulation? Who is to be the judge?

Year after year in these reports the Society itself suggests the solution. In a concluding paragraph the report says:

"We believe that the parents should so educate their children in sex matters, seriously and reverently, that within a reasonable time many of those things which are now by judicial ruling indecent, will lose their quality of indecency."

This suggests education, not repression. Any other method means that the opinion of one man, if he happens to be in an official position, will control the stage, and since that one man is just an ordinary individual, his action will be affected by his particular training, his background and his emotions, to say nothing of political influences, friendship and the vast variety of motives that influence human beings—even when clothed with authority.

Again the authorities rattle the saber. Nobody knows whose head will be chopped off. One thing is certain—that a call from the District Attorney's office will close any play in New York, whatever the manager may think to be his rights. He knows it will be stopped, that he and his cast may be arrested and held for trial; that there is no possible injunctive relief; that the owner of the theater may have his license taken away. A wise producer will pander to The Authorities. He will not lack generosity in contributing to both campaign funds. He will accept privileges instead of demanding rights. For discrimination by officials, not laws by legislatures, will determine his fortunes. No district attorney can stop all plays which offend the sensibilities of Dr. Straton and his followers, but a show of activity on his part may be necessary. What plays shall he choose? Public officials in their inner circle are just ordinary human beings. "Jim is a good fellow. I'll drop him a tip to tone down that bedroom scene—he needs the money—we don't want to hurt him." Says another confrère: "We'll have the Church down on us if we attack Jones. Anyhow his play isn't so bad." "How about the Highlights Theater," suggests a young attaché of the office. "We've been after that guy for a long time. Ain't he the fellow who put on that play ridiculing Tammany? We'll show 'em." "Go and take a look at it," says his superior.

James G. Wallace, of the District Attorney's Office, saw the play "Maya," produced in a Shubert theater in February, 1928. Off went "Maya." James G. Wallace is the Lord Chancellor in "Iolanthe":

> *The law is the true embodiment*
> *Of everything that's excellent.*
> *It has no kind of fault or flaw,*
> *And I, my Lords, embody the law.*

Can the manager avoid the peril by clothing Venus in woolens, or by robing the chaste Diana? Possibly. Can he avoid it by changing a line or a scene of a successful play? Possibly. But assuredly he cannot tell, nor can he go to court with any practical method of combating power. "The answer is simple," say the vice-hunters; "put on clean shows." "But," says the manager, "what is a clean show?" The public is interested in social problems, in domestic difficulties caused by emotional disturbances in which sometimes a third person is involved, in relations between husband and wife in which sex unfortunately plays a part (or if not, it's worse), in romance of all kinds, in social intrigue, in questions actually affecting people's lives. And the public is interested in grace and beauty and form, which is not always displayed either to the best advantage, or in the cleanest manner, with superfluity of costume. If the stage is limited to those things which please morons, children and degenerates, the theaters might just as well close and leave entertainment to the motion pictures.

No article on the stage would be complete without reference to motion pictures. Under the law of New York State a commission is created, the commissioners to have "qualifications by education and experience for the duties of office." They shall grant a license to a film "unless such film, or a part thereof, is indecent, obscene, immoral, inhuman, sacrilegious or is of such a character that its exhibition would tend to corrupt morals or incite to crime." If the commission fails to license any film, they must furnish a written report of

the reasons for refusal, and a description of each re-
jected part. This is, of course, censorship, but it implies none of the power now held by the authorities over
the stage, for presumably the commission's findings are
subject to court review. Such is the effect of a hated
label, the word, "censorship," that Governor Smith,
who approved the absurd amendment to the Penal Law
which made a part or scene of a play the test of obscenity and which included padlock provisions against
the theater, favors the abolition of this board. Yet the
law itself, as well as laws of like character in other
States, may be responsible for the monotonous and
boresome character of the ordinary motion picture film.

We see films of innocuous and nauseous simplicity
and sentimental flapdoodle. Every picture represents
a wish fulfillment. Every hero is one's self. Ordinarily
at marriage, life is ended in an aura of success; or if
perchance life continues, all is serene unless one or the
other does "wrong." Men and women are faithful or
vicious. One perceives definitely whether the husband's
derelictions are due to the wife's nagging or whether
the wife's nagging is due to the husband's derelictions—
usually the latter. All is simple and clear cut. Lack
of convention (and atheism) always bring merited and
condign punishment. Virtue brings her own, as well
as other, rewards. Vice leads to the gutter and suicide.
The hero's actions are never influenced by hope of
reward (except honor) or fear of punishment (except
from his conscience) and the villain never otherwise.
The hero is sweet-tempered and tolerant except against
evil—and there he is a veritable tiger. Since he at-

tends Church (and has since he was a child), he has no problems. Wars are crusades fought for righteous, idealistic and selfless causes, where the enemy is always cruel, and therefore gets licked. The immigrant welcomed to America, the place of sure opportunity, loves this land of justice and liberty. People and actions are good or bad. Life is a success or a failure. There are no tones, no shades or shadows. And the moral effect is said to be certain. There is no portrayal of reality, yet it is thought that these lies will affect life. They do.

What is sacrilegious? What is inhuman? A year or two ago in Berlin I saw one of the most thrilling presentations that has ever been screened, the Russian revolutionary play, "Potemkin." There was considerable question as to whether production here would be permitted. Some scenes were ordered eliminated; among others a series of pictures depicting the miserable conditions under which the Russian sailors lived. How much more was cut I do not know. Suffice it to say that the picture as presented in America had nothing like the appeal of the original.

Since no one State is a large enough field for regimentation, demand was made not long ago for a Federal Commission to govern the industry. Pictures were to be prohibited which contained anything "obscene, immoral, inhuman, sacrilegious, or offensive to the sentiment of religious reverence"; anything which would tend to "impair health, effect [sic] morals, incite to crime, cause moral laxity, disturb public peace or friendly relations with foreign powers." Pictures were to be banned which should "hold up to scorn any race, nation, sect or religion" or which should "exploit or depict persons notorious for some crime or public scandal." Likewise, the commission was to prohibit films which should "aim to assist the election or defeat of any political candidate," or which should show "any cockfight, bull fight or prize fight." Individuals are to decide this for you and for me. All the above concern matters of opinion where there is no fixed standard —where men differ. There may be some subjects left for portrayal, but the future is long. There is little outside the kindergarten which would not have a deleterious effect on some people.

"The Callahans and the Murphys" cause public excitement. We must pass a law. Bigotry and intolerance must be legislated out of existence. On to the City Hall! Hail to the Irishman, who stalked from the movie palace with the audible comment: "If there are Irish here with Irish spunk, they'll follow me out."

The point is not that any commission of reasonable men is likely to exercise tyrannical power very strictly, any more than the Commission in New York makes use of its power in a notably repressive fashion. The demand for the legislation shows the desire to control morals by law and to save people from themselves; to make the judgment of one individual binding upon another. The new tendency is to prepare the path of life, rather than to prepare youth to overcome the evils which are bound to cross the path. I would draw a distinct line between ignorance and virtue. They are too often confused. I would be so frank in dealing with the problems of life that not even youth would be shocked and thrilled by the unexpected.

The crusaders would set up a howl if any one suggested that a law be passed compelling them to see something they disapprove, but they actually exercise this power on others. They fail to realize that to prohibit portrayal of what one likes is to compel him to see what he does not like, or to see nothing at all.

Private conversation is not censored and it probably would be no better if it were. Good taste has a good deal to do with what people talk about, and probably with the plays and pictures they see. "The Ten Commandments," "The Covered Wagon," and "The Big Parade" owe their attraction to natural, decent, human sentiment, and brilliant production.

In this, as in other lines, I should chance the dangers of freedom, with confidence that knowledge is safer than ignorance and in the faith of Abraham Lincoln: "Throw the people on their own resources and then this Republic, the last possible hope of the earth, will never perish from this world."

FREEDOM OF OPINION

FREEDOM OF OPINION

Commonwealth of Massachusetts *vs.* Nicola Sacco and Bartolomeo Vanzetti

"If it had not been for these thing, I might have live out my life, talking at street corners to scorning men. I might have die, unmarked, unknown, a failure. Now we are not a failure. This is our career and our triumph. Never in our full life can we hope to do such work for tolerance, for joostice, for man's onderstanding of man, as now we do by an accident. Our words—our lives—our pains—nothing! The taking of our lives—lives of a good shoemaker and a poor fish peddler—all! That last moment belong to us—that agony is our triumph."

—Vanzetti to Judge Webster Thayer

"We killed murderers," says the State of Massachusetts.

"You killed anarchists," responds the public opinion of the world.

Answers the State: "These men were duly tried, convicted and sentenced. For seven years, the case was pending in the Courts. Extraordinary legal protection was accorded these two Italian workers. Appeal was taken from the original judgment; motions for new trials were heard; appeals were taken from decision on these. The Governor made a special investigation, even appointing a committee of elderly and learned men to advise him. Recourse was had to the Judges of the Supreme Court of the United States."

Says the public opinion of mankind: "The case was tried before a weak, vindictive judge. All motions, even one to remove this judge for prejudice, were determined by him. Appeals merely raised the question of whether he had made errors of law, and a wrong exercise of discretion or injustice is not an error of law in Massachusetts. The Governor and his committee merely upheld the Courts and in their conclusions insulted the intelligence of mankind. For seven years of torture, these men were accorded the forms of law. Because of their opinions, they were denied justice."

Bartolomeo Vanzetti plied his trade as a fish peddler in Plymouth, Massachusetts, living with his friends, the Brini family. Nicola Sacco edged shoe-soles in a factory at Stoughton, where he lived with his wife Rosina, and his baby, Dante. They were Italian immigrants. They had the thought that human nature was good enough, or strong enough, or unselfish enough that some day we might have an idealistic society free of violence, that would not rest on law enforced by power, a society free of hate and exploitation, a society of love. They called this anarchism. Some call it Christianity. But they were atheists. They were radicals. They didn't believe in war—or in *The* War—and went to Mexico to avoid the draft. They had gathered money to feed the starving workers of Lawrence during the textile strike, in which some 30,000 men, women and children mill workers protested against pay of six to eight dollars for from 54 to 58 hours

A poor fish peddler—and a good shoemaker—Vanzetti and Sacco.

weekly work.   Sacco had assisted in 1913 in a three months' strike of workers of the Draper Mill in Hopedale; he had been arrested in 1916 for participating in a demonstration of sympathy for workers on strike on the Mesaba Iron Range in Minnesota.   Vanzetti had been active in the 1916 strike in Plymouth when workers in the cordage factory, mostly Italians turning sisal hemp into binder twine, living in hovels, on an average wage of $12 a week, spontaneously struck against unendurable conditions.   Sacco and Vanzetti were "goddam agitators."

Massachusetts forgot the words blazoned on the statute of Wendell Phillips.

"When the Muse of time shall be asked to name the greatest of them all, she shall dip her pen into the sunlight and write across the clear blue sky—*Agitator.*"

But Wendell Phillips is dead.   Those men were living.   A dead agitator may be a hero.   A living agitator is a nuisance, and these men were foreigners, workingmen, atheists, pacifists, radicals, anarchists.   They were simple, law abiding, hard-working men, but it was their misfortune to have ideals and, worse, to label those ideals by unpopular names.   "Are you an anarchist?" queried Judge Anderson of a poor foreigner held before him for deportation.   "Yes."   "What do you mean by anarchy?"   "I dunno."   "Why do you say you're an anarchist?"   "The policeman who arrested me told me so," said the defendant.

The sleepy Massachusetts town of South Braintree

was the scene of tragedy early on the afternoon of April 15, 1920.   Parmenter, the paymaster of the Slater & Morrel shoe factory, and Berardelli, his assistant, were, while carrying the company's pay roll of $15,776.51 from the office building to the factory, set upon and killed by a gang of bandits who got away with the pay roll.   In the words of Governor Alvan T. Fuller, "The crime was particularly brutal.   The murder of the paymaster and the guard was not necessary to the robbery.   The murders were accomplished first, the robbery afterward.   The first shot laid Berardelli low in the roadway and after Parmenter was shot, he dropped the money box in the road and ran across the street.   The money could then have been taken, but the murderers pursued Parmenter across the road and shot him again and then returned and fired three more shots into Berardelli, four in all, leaving his lifeless form in the roadway.   The plan was evidently to kill the witnesses and terrorize the bystanders.   The murderers escaped in an automobile driven by one of their confederates, the automobile being afterward located in the woods at Bridgewater, eighteen miles distant."

This was one of a series of violent crimes which had disturbed the peace of towns in that vicinity.   The usual crime wave was awash.   There had been bank robberies and hold-ups.   On the 24th of the previous December at Bridgewater, four men had made an unsuccessful attempt to rob a pay-roll truck of the L. Q. White Shoe Company.

The "man hunt" for "reds" was also frightening and

enthralling the country.   The nervous Mitchell Palmer, with the aid of William J. Flynn, described by him as "the greatest anarchist expert in the United States," sought to stir up and suppress an imminent "revolution" of dangerous aliens.   The "deportation delirium" was under way.   Said Louis F. Post, Assistant Secretary of Labor, "The whole red crusade seems to have been saturated with the 'labor-spy' interests—the interests, that is, of private detective agencies, which, in the secret service of masterful corporations, were engaged in generating and intensifying suspicions and hatreds."

Boston bankers were paying for full page newspaper advertisements warning the country of its danger.   On one night in January, 1920, over two thousand people were arrested without warrant on suspicions aroused by *agents provocateur*.   As Charles E. Hughes said, "Very recently information has been laid by responsible citizens at the bar of public opinion of violations of personal rights which savor of the worst practices of tyranny."   These "responsible citizens," twelve well-known lawyers, among them Felix Frankfurter, who played an important part in this case, and Francis Fisher Kane and Frank P. Walsh, who were swept in by the momentum of the last few weeks before the executions of the two Italians, had published a documented report exposing Palmer's "frenzied activities."

They said:

"Wholesale arrests both of aliens and citizens have been made without warrant or any process of law; men and women have been jailed and held incommunicado without access of friends or counsel; homes have been entered without search warrants and property seized and removed; other property has been wantonly destroyed; workingmen and working women suspected of radical views have been shamefully abused and maltreated."

The Attorney General's office constituted itself a huge propaganda agency to stir up hate and fear of "radicals." Hysteria was rampant. The alien was a hunted beast, threatened with arrest, separation from his family, third-degree inquisition, and deportation.

In May, 1919, sixteen deadly bombs were found in the New York Post Office. In June, there were explosions in Philadelphia, Pittsburgh, Paterson, Cleveland and New York. One bomb was set off in front of Attorney General Palmer's home in Washington, and in the wreckage the police claim to have found a leaflet entitled "Plain Words." Andrea Salsedo and Robert Elia, anarchist printers in New York, were alleged to have had to do with printing this circular and early in 1920 were taken into custody and held incommunicado in the hands of agents of the Department of Justice in New York. All anarchists were under suspicion. Sacco and Vanzetti were on the Government list as belonging to the Galleani group with headquarters at Lynn, Massachusetts.

Vanzetti went to New York to see what could be done for his comrades. He consulted Walter Nelles of the American Civil Liberties Union. He was advised to collect and conceal radical literature, and to raise

funds for the defense of Elia and Salsedo. He returned
home on May 2nd. Two days later, the newspapers
reported that Salsedo's body had been found, crushed
to a pulp, on the pavement below the Park Row Building in New York City. The Department of Justice
denied the imputation that he had been thrown out
of the window, insisting that the man had been driven
insane by weeks of secret imprisonment, and had committed suicide. His companion, Elia, was never prosecuted for complicity in the bombings but was hurriedly
deported.

A protest meeting was arranged for May 9th at
Brockton, Mass., with Vanzetti as the chief speaker.
A friend, one Mike Boda, owned a dilapidated Over-
land car. On the evening of May 5th, Sacco and
Vanzetti called for the car to use it to collect the
"dangerous" literature in their friends' possession.
Boda's car was under suspicion. Sacco and Vanzetti,
informed that the license plates were irregular, took a
street car. They were arrested on the street car and
in Sacco's pocket was found an announcement of the
forthcoming meeting, addressed to "Fellow Workers,"
who had "fought all the wars," who "had worked for
the capitalists," but who had not found a piece of land
where they could "live like a human being and die like
a human being."

Bartolomeo Vanzetti, the Italian fish peddler, this
simple dreamer from the hills of Piedmont in Northern
Italy, was to have explained and solved the economic
difficulties of the world on May 9th in consideration of

small contributions for the benefit of Salsedo's family and to start a fund for the audacious undertaking of starting suit against the Honorable A. Mitchell Palmer, the powerful Attorney General of the United States, for damages for having caused the death of his friend, Salsedo.

But the trap shut on May 5, 1920. Sacco and Vanzetti never left jail until they were burned to death in the electric chair on August 22, 1927.

Thus it appears that Sacco and Vanzetti were arrested as anarchists, not as murderers; for opinion, not for crime. Any one who suggested their complicity in a brutal murder on April 15th would have had difficulty in answering obvious questions. Would they have been publicly active in radical circles had they committed murder? Would Vanzetti have intervened in Salsedo's behalf? Would they have arranged a public meeting in the vicinity at which Vanzetti was to speak? What became of the booty of over $15,000? If they had stolen the money would they be seeking small contributions from a handful of Italian radicals? Would they have come for Boda's car—a small second-hand Overland? These questions are still unanswered.

No wonder that Lawrence Letherman, for over twenty-five years in the employ of the Government, and Fred J. Weyand, then in the employ of the Department of Justice, later made affidavit that in the opinion of the agents of the Department "these men had nothing to do with the South Braintree murders." Letherman said:

"The Department of Justice in Boston was anxious to

get sufficient evidence against Sacco and Vanzetti to deport
them, but never succeeded in getting the kind and amount
of evidence required for that purpose. It was the opinion
of the Department Agents here that a conviction of Sacco
and Vanzetti for murder would be one way of disposing
of these two men."

When arrested, Sacco and Vanzetti were carrying
revolvers. When taken to the police station, they
failed to open their hearts to the police—in fact, they
deliberately lied. They tried to conceal their movements, they tried to protect their friends. This is
particularly important because the Court later left it
to the jury to determine whether the calling for the
car, the departure without getting it and the misstatements to the police, were evidence of "consciousness of
guilt" of the murder. Preposterous as it may seem,
this seems to have been regarded as the strongest evidence in the case, for in denying a later motion for a
new trial based on affidavits which completely discredited alleged eyewitnesses, the Court said:

"These verdicts did not rest, in my judgment, upon the
testimony of the eyewitnesses. . . . The evidence that convicted these defendants was circumstantial and was evidence that is known in law as 'consciousness of guilt.' "

Of course, when men lie to the police, they do so to
avoid what they think is the charge against them.
Sacco and Vanzetti were told they were held as "sus-
picious characters"; they thought they were held as
"radicals." Later, Katzmann, the Prosecutor, in ridiculing this as a cause for fear, asked, "What is deportation but a joyride to Italy?" But these baited,

hunted men had in mind the third-degree inquisition of Salsedo and Elia, the deportation of their friend Coacci from Ellis Island on April 16th, his wife and baby girl having been left behind to shift for themselves; the fate of Marucco from Latrobe, Pennsylvania, who died mysteriously on shipboard, and a picture of the crushed body of Salsedo on a New York pavement in a pool of blood. Yes, these men were fearful. From the examination of Sacco we have:

Q. (To Sacco) Any one time you mentioned that you were afraid, what did you mean by that?

A. I mean that I was afraid, for I know that my friends there in New York have jumped down from the jail in the street and killed himself. The papers say that he jump down, but we don't know. (Record, page 881.)

The authorities knew that the misstatements were due to the thought that they were wanted as radicals, for the questions put during the trial emphasized that thought.

Q. (To Vanzetti) Tell us all you recall that Stewart, the chief, asked you?

A. He asked me why we were in Bridgewater, how long I know Sacco, if I am a radical, if I am an anarchist or communist, and he ask me if I believe in the Government of the United States.

Q. What did you understand . . . you were being detained for at the Brockton police station?

A. I understand they arrested me for a political matter. (Record, pages 883-884.)

Q. (To Sacco) What did you think was . . . the crime that you were arrested for . . . ?

A. I never think anything else than radical.

.   .   .   .

Q. What occurred with Mr. Stewart that made you think you were being held for radical activities?

A. Well, because the first thing they asked me if I was an anarchist, a communist or socialist. (Record, page 1016.)

This was a murder case. Men may be convicted because of their opinions, but the law requires a framework. Orciani, an associate, had also been arrested. The three men were grilled about their movements on December 24, 1919, the day of the Bridgewater attempted hold-up, and on April 15, 1920, the day of the South Braintree crime. The bandits had been described as foreigners. The prisoners were brought before witnesses—not in a line-up with others of the same general type—but separately. The whole procedure was illegal, but the men were without counsel. They were ordered to pose so as to suggest the bandits. Even then, the witnesses were doubtful. "I might be mistaken," said one. "I am not positive," said another. "I couldn't see very well," said a third.

Orciani's factory record proved an alibi on both days. He was released. Sacco's factory record proved an alibi for one day—December 24th. He was charged with the crime of April 15th. Vanzetti was a fish peddler; he had no factory record for either day. He was charged with both crimes. Orciani, none. Sacco, one. Vanzetti, two.

Before the indictment in the South Braintree case, Vanzetti was tried in Plymouth charged with an "at-

tempt to rob" and an "attempt to kill" in the hold-up
at Bridgewater. The evidence was farcical. On the
one hand were absurd "identifications"; on the other
Italian housewives and uncouth laborers who testified
they had bought eels from Vanzetti on the day in question. A Mrs. Brooks noticed one man of four, who
"seemed some kind of a foreigner." "That man I should
judge was the defendant." She saw the attempted
hold-up from a railroad depot, although there were
buildings between, which shut off the view. A fourteen-
year-old boy saw the bandit for a moment from a distance of 145 feet.

> A. I could tell he was a foreigner by the way he ran.
> Q. What sort of a foreigner?
> A. Either Italian or Russian.
> Q. Does an Italian or a Russian run differently from
> a Swede or a Norwegian?
> A. Yes.
> Q. What is the difference?
> A. Unsteady.

Of course, there were other witnesses. Even their
testimony differed from that given by them at the
preliminary hearing and from identifications they had
given to detectives.

Evidence other than that of identification was trivial.
For instance, it was claimed that several shells found
on Vanzetti at the time of his arrest months later were
of a type similar to those found at the scene of the
Bridgewater crime.

Some twenty alibi witnesses for Vanzetti remembered
the date because of the purchase of eels on the day

before Christmas, a custom equivalent to our Thanksgiving turkeys. A baker testified that Vanzetti had wanted to borrow his delivery wagon and was in his shop at the very time of the crime.

Vanzetti was defended by John Vahey, who later became a partner of Prosecutor Katzmann. Vanzetti has since charged that Vahey betrayed him. Very likely (and this is the most charitable construction) the defense was carelessly optimistic.

The jury convicted Vanzetti with such enthusiasm that, disregarding the charge of the Court that there was no evidence to sustain the second count of the indictment, they found the defendant guilty on both counts, and Judge Webster Thayer gave Vanzetti the maximum, sentence—fifteen years. But worse, Vanzetti was given a criminal record.

One feature of the trial is peculiarly important: Vahey had not called witnesses who were available; he had taken no exceptions; it is said that he had advised Vanzetti not to take the witness stand, a fact afterwards deemed so significant by Governor Fuller that he laid great stress upon it. Vanzetti said of Vahey in an address to the Court:

"My first lawyer has been a partner of Mr. Katzmann as he is still now. The first lawyer of the defense, Mr. Vahey, has not defended me, has sold me for thirty golden money like Judas sold Jesus Christ."

Governor Fuller's report states that "investigating this case, I talked to the counsel of Vanzetti. . . ." One cannot help speculating on what Vahey told the Governor.

In sentencing the prisoner, Judge Thayer, afterwards to try the murder case, said (according to a statement made by Vanzetti):

"The defendants' ideals are cognate with the crime."

In the meantime Sacco had been held in jail—with what warrant I know not, for the indictment for murder was not handed down until September 11, 1920. The trial was set for February, 1921, but at the request of the defense, which needed time for preparation, was not begun till May 31st.

The court setting was appropriate for a trial of men holding unpopular views. Dedham, the seat of Norfolk County, is ordinarily a quiet, peaceful town, but fear of the "Reds" awakened it from its complacency. State troopers and city police were ostentatiously in evidence. In the courtroom, Sacco and Vanzetti sat in a steel cage, watched by alert deputies. Visitors were searched for concealed weapons. From the beginning, Judge Webster Thayer sounded the note of patriotism.

I shall not attempt to analyze the evidence. Those interested should read Felix Frankfurter's booklet, "The Case of Sacco and Vanzetti," or "The Life and Death of Sacco and Vanzetti" by Eugene Lyons. The prosecution was based on three lines—"consciousness of guilt," to which I have heretofore adverted, identification testimony, and evidence concerning the fatal bullet.

The identifications were wholly unsatisfactory. Witnesses, at first doubtful, became certain in the course of time. Some of them later recanted. Some testified to observation which was demonstrably impossible. Among those whom Governor Fuller later designated as "clear-eyed witnesses unafraid to tell the truth" with whom he was "proud to be associated" was a woman whose reputation was no longer doubtful, and one Carlos E. Goodridge, a horse thief, bigamist and a fugitive from justice, who was indebted to Katzmann for the "filing" of a case of larceny to which he had pleaded guilty.

There was also evidence to the effect that the fatal bullet came from Sacco's revolver. This was contradicted by defense witnesses and it later appeared that by prearrangement one Captain Proctor had merely testified that, in his opinion "it is consistent with being fired through that pistol" (Record 472), a statement understood by the defense and accepted by the Court as direct evidence of the fact.

As against this, witnesses who were present at the scene testified that Sacco and Vanzetti were not there— and each defendant proved his whereabouts on April 15th; Sacco had gone to Boston to arrange for a passport to Italy, Vanzetti was attending to his trade, according to witnesses who had been his customers on that day.

Sacco and Vanzetti were obliged to take the stand in order to explain their misstatements to the police. The crux of the case is found there. Interesting it is to note the justification for the vicious, prejudicial and unwarranted cross-examination. The Lowell Committee said:

"The cross-examination by Mr. Katzmann of the defendant Sacco on the subject of his political and social views seems at first unnecessarily harsh and designed rather to prejudice the jury against him than for the legitimate purpose of testing the sincerity of the defendants, but it must be remembered that the position at that time was very different from what it is now.

"We have already remarked that at the present moment their views on this subject are well known, but they were not so clear at the time.

"Except the call for a meeting found in his pocket there was no evidence that Sacco . . . was an anarchist.

"At that time of abnormal fear and credulity on the subject, little evidence was required to prove that any one was a dangerous radical. Harmless professors and students in our colleges were accused of dangerous opinions, and it was almost inevitable that any one who declared himself a radical possessed of inflammable literature would be instantly believed.

"For these reasons Mr. Katzmann was justified in subjecting Mr. Sacco to a rigorous cross-examination, to determine whether his confession that he and his friends were radicals liable to deportation, was true, or was merely assumed for the purpose of the defense."

This is specious. Katzmann admitted to that committee that he knew from the beginning that the defendants were radicals. Information in the files of the Department of Justice—as yet not open to the public —showed, according to the report of A. Mitchell Palmer to a Congressional committee, that these men belonged to the Galleani group of anarchists. Agents

of the Department were, at the time of arrest, seeking
to deport Sacco and Vanzetti. There was no justification for bringing the opinions of these men before the
Dedham jury. Those who claim that this was a fair
trial and that it was a trial for murder and not for
opinion, will have to answer the question raised by this
issue, unless they naïvely take the position that in the
reign of terror of the time, in the hysteria and delirium of 1920, the defendants' views did not affect
the jury.

One can imagine the bored jury of middle class business men, after listening to an array of pallid, doubtful
witnesses, suddenly called to attention by the clarion
call of patriotism. The opening question on cross-
examination of Vanzetti sounded the note:

Q. (By Mr. Katzmann) So you left Plymouth, Mr.
Vanzetti, in May, 1917, to dodge the draft, did you?

A. Yes, sir. . . .

Q. When this country was at war, you ran away, so
you would not have to fight as a soldier?

A. Yes. (Record 842-3.)

Q. You were going to advise in a public meeting men
who had gone to war? Are you that man?

A. Yes, sir, I am that man, not the man you want me,
but I am that man. (Record 865-6.)

And then to Sacco:

Q. (By Mr. Katzmann) Did you say yesterday you love
a free country?

A. Yes, sir.

Q. Did you love this country in the month of May,
1917?

A. I did not say—I don't want to say I did not love this country.

Q. Did you love this country in that month of 1917?

A. If you can, Mr. Katzmann, if you give me that—I could explain—

Q. Do you understand that question?

A. Yes.

Q. Then will you please answer it?

A. I can't answer• in one word.

Q. You can't say whether you loved the United States of America one week before the day you enlisted for the first draft?

A. I can't say in one word, Mr. Katzmann. (Record 919.)

Q. Did you love this country in the last week of May, 1917?

A. That is pretty hard for me to say in one word, Mr. Katzmann.

Q. There are two words you can use, Mr. Sacco, yes or no. Which one is it?

A. Yes.

Q. And in order to show your love for this United States of America when she was about to call upon you to become a soldier you ran away to Mexico? (R. 919.)

Q. Did you go to Mexico to avoid being a soldier for this country that you loved?

A. Yes. (Record 920.)

Q. And would it be your idea of showing your love for your wife that when she needed you, you ran away from her?

A. I did not run away from her.

Mr. Moore: I object.

The Witness: I was going to come after if I need her.

The Court: He may answer. Simply on the question of credibility, that is all.

Q. Would it be your idea of love for your wife that you were to run from her when she needed you?

Mr. Jeremiah McAnarney: Pardon me. I ask for an exception on that.

The Court: Excluded. One may not run away. He had not admitted he ran away.

Q. Then I will ask you, didn't you run away from Milford so as to avoid being a soldier for the United States?

A. I did not run away.

Q. You mean you walked away?

A. Yes.

Q. You don't understand me when I say "run away," do you?

A. That is vulgar.

Q. That is vulgar?

A. You can say a little intelligent, Mr. Katzmann.

Q. Dor't you think going away from your country is a vulgar thing to do when she needs you?

A. I don't believe in war.

Q. You don't believe in war?

A. No, sir.

Q. Do you think it is a cowardly thing to do what you did?

A. No, sir.

Q. Do you think it is a brave thing to do what you did?

A. Yes, sir.

Q. Do you think it would be a brave thing to go away from your own wife?

A. No.

Q. Whcn she needed you?

A. No. (Record 920-1.)

Q. Why didn't you stay there, down there in that free country, and work with a pick and shovel?

A. I don't think I did sacrifice to learn a job to go to pick and shovel in Mexico.

Q. Is it because—is your love for the United States of America commensurate with the amount of money you can get in this country per week?

A. Better conditions, yes.

Q. Better country to make money, isn't it?

A. Yes. . . .

Q. Is your love for this country measured by the amount of money you can earn here? . . .

A. I never loved money. (Record 921-2.)

Q. Is standing by a country when she needs a soldier evidence of love of country?

.   .   .   .

(After objection.)

The Court: I will let you inquire further first as to what he meant by the expression. (Record 926-7.)

Q. What did you mean when you said yesterday you loved a free country?

A. Give me a chance to explain.

Q. I am asking you to explain now.

A. . . . I came in this country. When I been started work here very hard and been work thirteen years, hard worker, I could not been afford much a family the way I did have the idea before. I could not put any money in the bank; I could no push my boy some to go to school and other things. I teach over here men who is with me. The free idea gives any man a chance to profess his own idea, not the supreme idea, not to give any person, not to be like Spain in position, yes, about twenty centuries ago, but to give a chance to print and education, literature, free

speech, that I see it was all wrong. I could see the best
men, intelligent, education, they been arrested and sent to
prison and died in prison for years and years without
getting them out, and Debs, one of the great men in his
country, he is in prison, still away in prison, because he
is a Socialist. He wanted the laboring class to have better
conditions and better living, more education, give a push
his son if he could have a chance some day, but they put
him in prison. Why? Because the capitalist class, they
know, they are against that, because the capitalist class,
they don't want our child to go to high school or college
or Harvard College.   There would be no chance, there
would not be no—they don't want the working class edu-
cationed; they want the working class to be a low all the
times, be underfoot, and not to be up with the head. . . .
I want to ask him who is going to Harvard College? What
benefit the working class they will get by those million
dollars they give by Rockefeller, D. Rockefellers. . . .
I like men to get everything that nature will give best, because they belong,—we are not the friend of any other
place, but we are belong to nations. So that is why my idea
has been changed. So that is why I love people who labor
and work and see better conditions every day develop,
makes no more war. We no want fight by the gun, and
we don't want to destroy young men. . . . *What right we
have to kill each other?* I been work for the Irish.
I have been working with the German fellow, with the
French, many other peoples. I love them people just as
I could love my wife, and my people for that did receive
me. Why should I go kill them men? What he done to
me? He never done anything, so I don't believe in no
war. I want to destroy those guns.

.   .   .   .

Q. The question is this: As far as you understood Fruzetti's views, were yours the same? (Objection overruled.)

Q. Answer, please.

A. (Through the interpreter) I cannot say yes or no.

Q. Is it because you can't or because you don't want to?

A. (Through the interpreter) Because it is a very delicate question.

Q. It is very delicate, isn't it, because he was deported for his views? (Record 939.)

Q. Do you know why Fruzetti was deported?

A. (Through the interpreter) Yes.

Q. Was it because he was of anarchistic opinions?

The Interpreter: He says he understands it now.

Q. Was it because Fruzetti entertained anarchistic opinions?

A. One reason, he was an anarchist. Another reason, Fruzetti been writing all the time on the newspapers, and I am not sure why the reason he been deported. . . .

Q. Was Fruzetti, before deportation, a subscriber to the same papers that you had in your house on May 5th?

A. Probably he is. (Objection.) . . .

Q. And the books which you intended to collect were books relating to anarchy, weren't they?

A. Not all of them.

Q. How many of them?

A. Well, all together. We are Socialists, democratic, any other socialistic information, Socialists, Syndicalists, Anarchists, any paper.

Q. Bolshevist?

A. I do not know what Bolshevism means.

Q. Soviet?

A. I do not know what Soviet means.

Q. Communism?

A. Yes, I got some on astronomy, too. (Record 941.)

. . . .

Q. After the time had gone by, were you going to bring them out, going to distribute the knowledge contained in them?

A. Certainly, because they are educational for book, educational.

Q. An education in anarchy, wasn't it?

A. Why, certainly. Anarchistic is not criminals.

Q. I didn't ask you if they are criminals or not. Nor are you to pass upon that, sir. Was it equally true as to the books and papers and periodicals that you expected to pick up at your friends' houses, that they were not to be destroyed?

A. Just to keep them, hide them.

Q. And then bring them forth afterwards when the time was over?

A. I suppose so. (Record 941-2.)

Q. And you are a man who tells this jury that the United States of America is a disappointment to you?

. . . .

Q. Well, you told us about how disappointed you were, and what you did not find and what you expected to find. Are you that man?

A. Yes. (Record 972-3.)

This was constantly interrupted by objections. The Court not only overruled these, but emphasized the testimony by his remarks. On one occasion Judge Thayer asked Mr. McAnarney, counsel for the defense, "Are you going to claim that what the defendant did was in the interest of the United States?"

The Massachusetts Bill of Rights, written by John Adams, provides:

"It is the right of every citizen to be tried by judges as free, impartial and independent as the lot of humanity will admit."

"Did you see what I did to those Anarchist bastards?" is a statement said to have been made by Judge Thayer during the progress of the trial.

The Lowell Committee reported:

"From all that has come to us, we are forced to conclude that the judge was indiscreet in conversations with outsiders during the trial," . . . and that he was guilty of a "grave breach of official decorum."

More than half of the Court's charge consisted of moral exhortations. The first words were:

"The Commonwealth of Massachusetts called upon you to render a most important service. Although you knew that such service would be arduous, painful and tiresome, yet you, like the true soldier, responded to that call in the spirit of supreme American loyalty. There is no better word in the English language than loyalty."

The last words of Katzmann in his fervent peroration were an appeal to patriotism:

"Gentlemen of the jury, do your duty! Do it like men! Stand together, you men of Norfolk!"

After five hours the jury on July 14, 1921, returned a verdict of guilty of murder in the first degree—The electric chair!

"Sono innocente," shouted Sacco from his cage.

"They kill innocent men," said Vanzetti quietly.

There had been little, if any, evidence against Vanzetti. This is clear from the report of the Lowell commission, which after garbling the testimony against Sacco, concluded that "on the whole, we are of opinion that Vanzetti also was guilty." But Vanzetti had refused to permit a closing argument which would seem to favor him. Said Fred H. Moore, trial counsel for the Italians:

"I thought there was a fighting chance the jury would disagree as to the two, but if they acquitted one, I knew enough of juries to feel sure they would soak the other. So I put it up to Vanzetti, 'What shall I do?' and he answered, 'Save Nick, he has the woman and child.' "

A motion for a new trial was made before Judge Thayer on October 19, 1921. It was denied, on Christmas Eve. Vanzetti said, "I think you have done that, to hand down your decision on the Eve of Christmas, to poison the heart of our family and of our beloved."

A great mass of new evidence was discovered by the defense. Gradually it was unearthed, and all was made subject to a motion or to motions, for a new trial on October 1, 1923. This was necessarily argued before Judge Thayer. This occasion marked the advent into the case of William G. Thompson, a conservative, powerful figure, steeped in the traditions of the Massachusetts Bar—a man so convinced of the innocence of the clients that he risked an honored name and a sound law practice in their behalf. And it was a real risk in Massachusetts. Herbert B. Ehrman was also associated in the defense. Those who defend men of radical views take the chance of the interpretation that they are defending the philosophies, as well as the persons, of the defendants.

There was evidence (a) that the foreman of the jury, one Ripley, had carried in his pocket and to the jury room, cartridges which were not in evidence; (b) that a few days before the trial he had said to a friend, "Damn them, they ought to hang anyway"; (c) that microscopic examinations of the fatal bullet proved that it could not have come from Sacco's pistol; (d) that one Gould, who was within five feet of the bandit car, had notified the police—but had not been called on to testify—that he was certain that Sacco and Vanzetti were not the men; (e) that the Proctor testimony as to the fatal bullet was deliberately framed to give a false impression. Proctor so averred by affidavit.

A year elapsed. The motion for a new trial was denied.

In May, 1926, the Supreme Judicial Court of Massachusetts found "no error" in the rulings of Judge Thayer and the verdicts were allowed to stand.[1] The questions upon which the trial judge passed were within his "discretion." According to earlier judicial definition, a judge exercises sound discretion when his attitude displays an "overwhelming passion to do that which is just."

There was still hope. Some one had committed the murders. Could the defendants point out the guilty, it was reasonable to expect that a new trial would be

[1] 255 Mass. 369.

granted. Confined in prison with Sacco was a young
Portuguese under sentence of death. In 1925 while
an appeal from his case was pending in the Supreme
Court (an appeal which was successful) he sent a note
to Sacco:

"I hear by confess to being in the South Braintree Shoe
Company crime and Sacco and Vanzetti was not in said
crime.
                    "CELESTINO F. MADEIROS."

Governor Fuller later stated in reference to this:
"It is popularly supposed he confessed to committing
this crime." It is.

Mr. Thompson was too astute a lawyer to accept
such a confession without thorough investigation.
Madeiros said he made the statement because:

"I seen Sacco's wife come up here with the kids and I
felt sorry for the kids."

Thompson notified the Prosecutor. Madeiros was
examined and cross-examined. He made a deposition
of a hundred pages, stating the facts with convincing
circumstantiality of detail. In answer to the thought
that the confession was made because he was a doomed
man, it appeared that he had told the story on many
occasions and before his conviction to a man named
Weeks, then under life sentence in another jail and
this was confirmed by Weeks. Not only this but he
had told others "that he would like to save Sacco and
Vanzetti because he knew they were perfectly innocent."

The Madeiros confession clearly pointed to a well-known band of professional criminals, known as the Morelli gang, most of whom were then in jail. They had long engaged in robbing freight cars in Providence, and, at the very time of the South Braintree murders, some of them were actually under indictment for stealing consignments from the Slater & Morrill factory in South Braintree. Description of members of this gang satisfied testimony at the trial, and one of the gang resembled Sacco. There were many corroborative details in the Madeiros statement. Every member of the murder party was accounted for, as well as the booty, of which Madeiros' share was $2,800, shown to have been in his possession.

Again a motion for a new trial was made—again before Judge Thayer. The decision would be upon the question of whether this new material would influence a jury so that on a retrial, a different conclusion *might* be reached. And in addition to the Madeiros confession were the affidavits of Weyand and Letherman to the effect that agents of the Department of Justice regarded the crime as the work of professionals, and that Sacco and Vanzetti had had nothing to do with it. But the Prosecutor called Letherman and Weyand "disloyal" because they disclosed Government secrets. "What are the secrets which they admit?" thundered Thompson. "A government which has come to value its own secrets more than it does the lives of its citizens has become a tyranny. Secrets, secrets! . . . There are, then, secrets to be admitted."

The motion for a new trial was denied by Judge Thayer in a long opinion devoted largely to exonerating the Morelli gang, to justifying his own position with the false statement oft repeated, that the Supreme Court had passed upon the verdict, and to condemning the lawyers for the defense. Bias, prejudice, and the art of the advocate, could write no stronger brief. He could not believe that the Federal Government could have "stooped so low" as "to enter into a fraudulent conspiracy with the government of Massachusetts to send two men to the electric chair, not because they were murderers, but because they were radicals." What are these governments anyhow? What is government? It is no abstract thing. It is just an individual or individuals, clothed with power. Has Judge Thayer forgotten Mitchell Palmer? Did he ever hear of the "reign of terror"?

An appeal was taken from the denial of the motion. On April 4, 1927, the decision was affirmed.[2]

On April 9th the defendants were called for sentence. History has no parallel to the scene in the Dedham Court House on this day. On the bench was Judge Thayer, a weak, shrinking figure representing authority. Before him were two convicted men, brave and unafraid, outcasts!

Clerk Worthington: Nicola Sacco, have you anything to say why sentence of death should not be passed upon you?
"Yes, sir." . . . And Sacco went on:

[2] 156 N. E. (Mass.) 57.

"I never knew, never heard, even read in history anything so cruel as this Court. After seven years prosecuting they still consider us guilty. And these gentle people here are arrayed with us in this court to-day.

"I know the sentence will be between two classes, the oppressed class and the rich class, and there will be always collision between one and the other. We fraternize the people with the books, with the literature. You persecute the people, tyrannize them and kill them. We try the education of people always. You try to put a path between us and some other nationality that hates each other. That is why I am here to-day on this bench, for having been of the oppressed class. Well, you are the oppressor.

.   .   .   .

"I forget one thing which my comrade remember me. As I said before, Judge Thayer know all my life, and he know that I am never been guilty, never—not yesterday, nor to-day, nor forever."

Clerk Worthington: Bartolomeo Vanzetti, have you anything to say why sentence of death should not be passed upon you?

"Yes. What I say is that I am innocent, not only of the Braintree crime, but also of the Bridgewater crime. That I am not only innocent of these two crimes, but in all my life I have never stolen and I have never killed and I have never spilled blood. That is what I want to say. And it is not all. Not only am I innocent of these two crimes, not only in all my life I have never stolen, never killed, never spilled blood, but I have struggled all my life, since I began to reason, to eliminate crime from the earth.

"Everybody that knows these two arms knows very well that I did not need to go into the streets and kill a man or try to take money. I can live by my two hands and

live well. But besides that, I can live even without work
with my hands for other people. I have had plenty of
chance to live independently and to live what the world
conceives to be a higher life than to gain our bread with
the sweat of our brow.

"My father in Italy is in a good condition. I could have
come back in Italy and he would have welcomed me every
time with open arms. Even if I come back there with not
a cent in my pocket, my father could have give me a position, not to work but to make business, or to oversee upon
the land that he owns. He has wrote me many letters in
that sense, and as another well-to-do relative has wrote me
letters in that sense that I can produce.

. . . .

"I have refused myself of what are considered the com-
modity and glories of life, the prides of a life of a good
position, because in my consideration it is not right to
exploit man. I have refused to go in business because I
understand that business is a speculation on profit upon
certain people that must depend upon the business man,
and I do not consider that that is right and therefore I
refuse to do that.

. . . .

"They have given a new trial to Madeiros for the reason
that the Judge had either forgot or omitted to tell the jury
that they should consider the man innocent until found
guilty in the court, or something of that sort. That man
has confessed. The man was tried on his confession and
was found guilty, and the Supreme Court gave him another
trial. We have proved that there could not have been
another Judge on the face of the earth more prejudiced,
more cruel and more hostile than you have been against us.
We have proven that. Still they refuse the new trial. We

know, and you know in your heart, that you have been against us from the very beginning, before you see us. Before you see us you already know that we were radicals, that we were underdogs, that we were the enemy of the institutions that you can believe in good faith in their goodness—I don't want to discuss that—and that it was easy at the time of the first trial to get a verdict of guiltiness.

"We know that you have spoken yourself, and have spoke your hostility against us, and your despisement against us with friends of yours on the train, at the University Club of Boston, at the Golf Club of Worcester. I am sure that if the people who know all what you say against us have the civil courage to take the stand, maybe, your Honor— I am sorry to say this because you are an old man, and I have an old father—but maybe you would be beside us in good justice at this time.

.   .   .   .

"We were tried during a time whose character has now passed into history. I mean by that, a time when there was a hysteria of resentment and hate against the people of our principles, against the foreigner, against slackers, and it seems to me—rather, I am positive of it, that both you and Mr. Katzmann have done all what it were in your power in order to work out, in order to agitate still more the passion of the juror, the prejudice of the juror, against us.

.   .   .   .

"The jury were hating us because we were against the war, and the jury don't know that it makes any difference between a man that is against the war because he believes that the war is unjust, because he hate no country, because he is a cosmopolitan, and a man that is against the war because he is in favor of the other country that fights

against the country in which he is, and therefore a spy, an
enemy, and he commits any crime in the country in which
he is in behalf of the other country in order to serve the
other country. We are not men of that kind. Nobody
can say that we are German spies or spies of any kind.
Katzmann knows very well that. Katzmann knows that
we were against the war because we did not believe in the
purpose for which they say that the war was fought. We
believed that the war is wrong, and we believe this more
now after ten years that we studied and observed and
understood it day by day—the consequences and the result
of the after war. We believe more now than ever that the
war was wrong, an̄ we are against war more now than
ever, and I am glad to be on the doomed scaffold if I can
say to mankind, 'Look out; you are in a catacomb of the
flower of mankind. For what? All that they say to you,
all that they have promised to you—it was a lie, it was an
illusion, it was a cheat, it was a fraud, it was a crime.
They promised you liberty. Where is liberty? They promised you prosperity. Where is prosperity? They have
promised you elevation. Where is the elevation?'

.   .   .   .

"In the best of my recollection and of my good faith,
during the trial Katzmann has told to the jury that a
certain Coacci has brought in Italy the money that, according to the State theory, I and Sacco have stolen in
Braintree. We never stole that money. But Katzmann,
when he told that to the jury, he knew already that that
was not true He knew already that that man was deported in Italy by the Federal police soon after our arrest.
I remember well that I was told that the Federal policeman
had him in their possession—that the Federal policeman
had taken away the trunks from the very ship where he

was, and brought the trunks back over here and look them over and found not a single money.

"Now, I call that murder, to tell to the jury that a friend or comrade or a relative or acquaintance of the charged man, of the indicted man, has carried the money to Italy, when he knows it was not true. I can call that nothing else but murder, a plain murder.

．　　　．　　　．　　　．　　　．　　　．　　　．

"Well, I have already say that I not only am not guilty of these two crimes, but I never committed a crime in my life,—I have never stolen and I have never killed and I have never spilt blood, and I have fought against crime, and I have fought and I have sacrificed myself even to eliminate the crimes that the law and the church legitimate and sanctify.

"This is what I say: I would not wish to a dog or to a snake, to the most low and misfortune creature of the earth—I would not wish to any of them what I have had to suffer for things that I am not guilty of. But my conviction is that I am suffering for things I am guilty of. I am suffering because I am a radical and indeed I am a radical; I have suffered because I was an Italian, and indeed I am an Italian; I have suffered more for my family and for my beloved than for myself; but I am so convinced to be right that you could execute me two times, and if I could be reborn two other times, I would live again to do what I have done already."

．　　　．　　　．　　　．　　　．　　　．　　　．

The Court: Under the law of Massachusetts the jury says whether a defendant is guilty or innocent. The Court has absolutely nothing to do with that question. The law of Massachusetts provides that a judge cannot deal in any

way with the facts. As far as he can go under our law is
to state the evidence.

.   .   .   .

First the Court pronounced sentence upon Nicola
Sacco:

*"It is considered and ordered by the Court that you,
Nicola Sacco, suffer the punishment of death by the passage of a current of electricity through your body within
the week beginning on Sunday, the tenth day of July, in
the Year of our Lord one thousand nine hundred and
twenty-seven. This is the sentence of the law."*

Then upon Vanzetti:

*"It is considered and ordered by the Court that you,
Bartolomeo Vanzetti . . ."*

Mr. Vanzetti: Wait a minute, please, your Honor. May
I speak for a minute with my lawyer, Mr. Thompson?

Mr. Thompson: I do not know what he has to say.

The Court: I think I should pronounce the sentence.
. . . *Bartolomeo Vanzetti, suffer the punishment of
death . . .*

Mr. Sacco: You know I am innocent. Those are the
same words I pronounced seven years ago. You condemn
two innocent men.

The Court: . . . *by the passage of a current of electricity through your body within the week beginning on
Sunday, the tenth day of July, in the year of our Lord
one thousand nine hundred and twenty-seven. This is the
sentence of the law.*

"A decent respect for the opinions of mankind,"
vociferously expressed throughout the world, demanded

that a new investigation be made. And here is perhaps the saddest part of the story. Governor Alvan T. Fuller agreed to investigate—

Heywood Broun, newspaper columnist, said in his column in *The World:*

"Governor Alvan T. Fuller never had any intention in all his investigations but to put a new and higher polish upon the proceedings. The justice of the business was not his concern. He hoped to make it respectable. He called old men from high places to stand behind his chair so that he might seem to speak with all the authority of a high priest or a Pilate."

This was before Broun lost his job on *The World.*

Governor Alvan T. Fuller, as a Congressman, had expressed his views of the "Red Scum of Europe" and "the wolves of anarchy." In connection with the expulsion of Berger from the House of Representatives he had said:

"Berger characterized the action of the House as a crucifixion, and in a manner of speaking it is. It is the crucifixion of the disloyal, the nailing of sedition to the cross of free government, where the whole brood of anarchists, Bolshevists, I.W.W.'s and revolutionaries may see and read a solemn warning. It is the same sort of crucifixion which sent Debs and Big Bill Haywood behind the bars, which suppressed Berkman and Emma Goldman and which has brought the hand of the law down upon a host of Reds."

But this, as well as Fuller's anti-union activities, was forgotten and hope ran high in the thought of his geniality, his election as an independent candidate and

the assurance that none, however biased, could look
into the mass of evidence and conclude either that the
trial had been fair or that the defendants were guilty.
On June 1, 1927, he appointed an advisory commission consisting of President A. Lawrence Lowell of
Harvard University, President Samuel W. Stratton of
the Massachusetts Institute of Technology and an ex-
judge of the probate courts, Robert Grant. These men
were elderly and respectable. Their reputations
seemed to assure that testimony would be weighed by
their reasons, not by their emotions. Even the fact that
Judge Grant was reported to have repeatedly condemned Sacco and Vanzetti, and to have refused to
resign when this became known, did not disturb the
optimism of liberals. As to the committee, Heywood
Broun later had this to say:

"What more can these immigrants from Italy expect?
It is not every prisoner who has a president of Harvard
University throw on the switch for him. And Robert
Grant is not only a former Judge, but one of the most
popular dinner guests in Boston. If this is a lynching, at
least the fish peddler and his friend, the factory hand, may
take unction to their souls that they will die at the hands
of men in dinner coats or academic gowns, according to
the conventionalities required by the hour of execution. . . ."

Sacco refused to sign a petition for pardon. Vanzetti made the appeal, not in dry, technical form, but
in a sincere, noble demand, not for mercy, but for
justice:

"On principle," Vanzetti declared, "we abhor violence,

deeming it the worst form of coercion and authority. We are with Garibaldi: *'Only the slaves have the right to violence to free themselves; only the violence that frees is legitimate and holy.'* We lived in this country twelve years before our arrest, and industriously, honestly, and without any act of violence. The only violence that has been committed is the violence practiced against us and not by us."

Sacco and Vanzetti were realists. They were not deluded. To most of us, the trial was a farce; the result an atrocious miscarriage of justice. To them, it was a logical outcome. They recognized that they were tried for opinion, convicted for opinion, and that society intended to kill them for their opinions. They were victims in a class war. Unthinkable to us—until we saw the ruthless progress of the machine. Sacco wrote to his friend Van Valkenburgh:

"As I wrote you before I repeat again to-day, only an international clamor—a protest—can free us. And yet, while we are so near the tomb, your letter amazes me with its unwarranted optimism, saying, 'You must not despair, dear Nicola, for though the suffering be long and weary, it is soon to end in freedom.'

"How you are deluded! This is not even common sense, coming from you. I would say nothing if such talk came from a man in the moon, but from you, who are also in the struggle for liberty, this is too much. Do you not know the ends to which the defenders of this decrepit old society will go? Under the circumstances it pains me to see such blind optimism in a comrade. Are you waiting to see them kill us first so that you can build us a monument?"

A joint letter to Celia Polisuk, who organized a students' committee, said:

" . . . please don't be too optimistic. The forces of darkness are exceedingly malicious, steadfast and implacable."

The first disquieting feeling arose from the fact that the Governor's inquiry was secret—that he was conducting a Star Chamber proceeding. Witnesses for the defense, browbeaten and indignant, gave the first hint. An ex-convict appeared before the Governor to confess participation in the Bridgewater crime and to exonerate Vanzetti. He was referred to, and ignored by, the police.

The Governor's Committee, while giving more leeway, refused to permit the presence of defense counsel at certain points in its hearing. They were merely rehearsing the hodgepodge of contradictory testimony.

Sacco and Vanzetti went on a hunger strike. The executions were postponed till August 10th.

The Governor and his Committee agreed with the judicial findings. Death to Sacco and Vanzetti!

The investigation was a wise political move. The plausible reports of the Governor and his Committee answered the doubts of multitudes of conscientious citizens, who knew little about the case.

To those familiar with the facts, however, the opinions were misleading, trivial and insulting to human intelligence. Bias and prejudice were written in every line. Contentions of the defense were cavalierly dismissed. The investigators chose not to believe wit-

nesses whose statements were embarrassing. Even testimony from the records of the case was misstated and
misinterpreted. The furor aroused by the convictions
was intensified when the weakness of the argument
against these men became apparent from the opinions,
which read like the briefs of advocates, not the conclusions of judges. Had they whitewashed Massachusetts?
They sustained the verdict as sound and the trial as
fair, while conceding that the Judge was nervous, un-
stable, and guilty of a "grave breach of official
decorum."

Resentment and indignation became an immense
roar of protest from all over the world. Thousands
of workers, meeting in Hyde Park, London, set up
a replica of the electric chair and damned America.
Tens of thousands gathered on the streets of Paris to
salute Vanzetti's sister, Luigia, hastening here to embrace her brother before his death. Luigia, a Catholic,
Bartolomeo, an atheist, but brother and sister! Parades and meetings of demonstration were held, not
only in every city of the United States but in every
capital of the world—from Madrid to Berlin—from
Berlin to Moscow—from Moscow to Tokio—from
Tokio to Buenos Aires—in Uruguay, Mexico, South
Africa. Workers' strikes were called in protest.
Eminent voices cabled their anguished prayers to Gov-
ernor Fuller—Romain Rolland, George Bernard
Shaw, Albert Einstein. Alfred Dreyfus, the victim of
French injustice, emerged from his obscurity to shock
the memory of a country that once appealed for him.
The rising wave of indignant anger broke upon the

rocks of Plymouth. The Puritan spirit, not to be moved from its obligation to "duty," gathered religious exaltation from the immensity of the opposing opinion. Boston remained calm, but with an ominous tensity.

Nathaniel Hawthorne in the early days, referring to an execution, described a New England state of mind:

"He was one of the martyrs to that terrible delusion which should teach us, among its other morals, that the influential classes, and those who take it upon themselves to be leaders of the people, are fully liable to all the pas· sionate error that has ever characterized the maddest mob. Clergymen, judges, statesmen—wisest, calmest, holiest persons of their day—stood in the inner circle round about the gallows, loudest to applaud the work of blood, latest to confess themselves miserably deceived."

The reference, of course, was not to the 1927 hys- teria in Massachusetts. Hawthorne was describing the situation when one Matthew Maule, early in New Eng- land's history, was executed on a charge of witchcraft.

Another motion for a new trial was made, based upon further evidence—a new eyewitness of the crime, an admission from the chief of police that a tear in the cap found at the murder scene was made by him, whereas at the trial it was made to appear that it was caused by Sacco hanging the cap on a hook in the factory. Affidavits revealing Thayer's animus, which was alleged as a ground for relief, or at least for re- moving him from the case, were filed. Against the protest of Arthur D. Hill (who had succeeded Thomp- son and Ehrman on their retirement from the case),

Judge Thayer even heard this motion. His denial led to an appeal.

The day of execution arrived. There were still steps pending in the legal pantomime. Hour after hour passed—pickets wearing mourning bands held death watch before the State House. At 11:24 P.M., after even the trousers of the condemned men had been slit for the electrodes, came a reprieve until August 22nd. Again the men were removed from the death house. The cruel torture, the horrible barbarity of it all! And the legalism, for the killing was postponed "to afford the courts an opportunity to complete the consideration of the proceedings now pending."

The clamor of opposition gathered momentum. Sacco and Vanzetti were symbols of injustice. But the opposition was allowed no voice in Boston. Halls were closed to protest on hint of the police. Picketers were arrested as fast as they appeared. Powers Hapgood, a young coal miner, Harvard graduate and nephew of Norman Hapgood, former Ambassador, was arrested for speaking on the Common without a permit. He was found guilty. A new and more serious charge was then laid against him arising out of the same offense—that of rioting. He was found guilty.

The lawyers argued the appeal from Judge Thayer's latest ruling before the full bench. A few days later the appeal was denied on the ground that it was too late—whatever the evidence—to move for a new trial, and that Judge Thayer and all other judges were without jurisdiction to determine whether Judge Thayer had been prejudiced.[3]

A new defense committee, formed by Robert Morss Lovett, and supported by Jessica Henderson, had taken headquarters at the Hotel Bellevue in Boston. It derived its support, not from so-called radicals, but from conservatives and liberals who still believed it inconceivable that men could be put to death while available evidence was still uncovered, while Government files were still unopened, while doubt remained. At the rooms of the Sacco-Vanzetti Defense Committee was a great air of hubbub and excitement. Volunteers from various places, chiefly New York, were pounding typewriters, getting out publicity material. We learned that early that morning, the home of MacHardy, a juror who had sat in the case, had been bombed, and that this was attributed to Sacco and Vanzetti sympathizers. One group was anxious to point out to the newspapers that the last persons in the world who would engage in such an undertaking were those who were anxious to help Sacco and Vanzetti and this was emphasized by a letter from Governor Fuller to MacHardy practically charging every sympathizer of the Italians with contributing to the crime:

"It would be well for those who through ignorance or malice or sentimentality contribute to such dire results to be held jointly responsible. It is a painful admission I have to make, but one that is apparent—that here and active in our community are elements which would threaten and coerce government and court officials."

[3] 158 N. E. (Mass.) 167 (1927).

This new committee was determined upon one last effort to open the files of the Federal Government. Former agents had sworn that the government had investigated anarchist activities and, in connection with them, the South Braintree case; that those agents had concluded that the crime was the work of professional criminals, that, nevertheless, the Government had cooperated in framing Sacco and Vanzetti as one way of "disposing of these men." Not tracing the booty to the defendants, the prosecution had contended that Sacco and Vanzetti had committed murder and robbery to get money, which they gave to the anarchist cause. It was thought the Government files would show that this was untrue. Some claimed that the records would show that Sacco and Vanzetti, as members of the Galleani group, had been under surveillance prior to, and at the time of, the crime and that an inspection of the files would prove their innocence. Irrespective of all this, however, one thing was certain—that the files would show that these were hunted men, who had reason to fear, which would explain their misstatements to the police attributed to a "consciousness of guilt." The records would also show that Katzmann knew that these men were anarchists, which would blast any justification for the vicious cross-examination through which he had paraded the unpopular views of the defendants before the jury. These files would expose his legal trickery.

With Francis Fisher Kane of Philadelphia, I set off for Ludlow, Vermont, to see Attorney General Sargent. Walter Frank and Robert Morss Lovett were to seek the coöperation of Senator Butler of Massachusetts. We stopped off at Bellows Falls for the night and by automobile made the trip through the quiet Vermont hills to the home of the Attorney General. A guard met us at the door: "Your business?" he inquired. "The Sacco-Vanzetti case." He expressed doubt as to an audience. I wrote on a card:

"MY DEAR MR. ATTORNEY GENERAL:

"The right of petition is older than this government itself. Have Americans lost that right or is it denied them by the present administration?"

Use of this was not necessary, however, as the Attorney General appeared, motioned us to seats in the garden and asked our mission. We told him of the Government files and their importance in this case. He referred to the fact that Mr. Thompson had once made that inquiry and that it was his impression that Mr. Thompson had refused the files when offered. We showed him copies of Mr. Thompson's affidavit to the contrary.

Mr. Sargent was a shrewd lawyer. He finally turned to me and said: "Just what is your complaint? I understand that these men admitted that they were anarchists as an excuse for their misstatements. Now you claim that the District Attorney merely confirmed the fact that they were anarchists; that his cross-examination did not break them down, but, on the contrary, confirmed their statements. Why do you object to this?" We answered that Katzmann's ostensible purpose was not his real purpose. That his sole interest had been to get before the jury the ideas of these men, with the expectation that this would arouse prejudice. That the issue of opinion had thus been brought into the case, and that it was idle to argue, in a case of such obvious weakness, that this did not affect the jury. The men were convicted for their opinions, not for murder.

We were encouraged by the courtesy, patience and geniality of the Attorney General, although to us, immersed in the impending tragedy, his attitude seemed casual. We were referred to George R. Farnum, Assistant Attorney General in Washington.

Off to Washington. A note to Frank Walsh asked him to join us. In the morning he was there. We sent telegrams to Charles E. Hughes, who, we later found, was abroad, and to President Coolidge, who was not abroad but might have been so far as any effect on him was concerned.

We sent the President this telegram:

"To CALVIN COOLIDGE,
    "*President of the United States:*
"As counsel for Sacco and Vanzetti we request that government files relating to this case be opened before the men are executed. It seems to us that the honor of our country would be irretrievably sullied if these men were put to death when millions of people sincerely believe that important evidence is kept secret by the Government. To-day we conferred at Ludlow with Attorney General Sargent, who directed us to see Acting Attorney General Farnum, with whom we confer Sunday morning. We are

volunteers, but are acting with Mr. Arthur Hill, counsel
for defendants.

"ARTHUR GARFIELD HAYS,
"FRANCIS FISHER KANE."

In spite of the public excitement and resentment, in
spite of the indignation of all countries in the world
arousing ill-will toward America, in spite of the obvious connection, at the beginning, of the Federal Government with this case, in spite of world-wide propaganda by the Government to the effect that these men
were properly convicted as murderers, in spite of the
precedent of the Tom Mooney case, the silent man of
the White House remained silent.

When Walsh, Kane and I called at the Department
of Justice, we found Acting Attorney General George
R. Farnum awaiting us. We knew he would be there.
Farnum has a record for conscientious service. Sunday sacrifices are not important when duty calls. We
found Farnum just as patient and courteous as the
Attorney General, but we soon recognized the type.
When men go into Government service they tend to
become machine-like. The impression made on Farnum's sense of justice or his emotions, reacted to
strengthen the machine, which, as a cog in the Government, regards precedent and policy as of more importance than life or death of individuals.

We showed him how the files would help the defense. We repeated the statement of Attorney Thompson: "A government which has come to value its own
secrets more than the lives of its citizens is a tyranny,

call it by what name you will." We limited ourselves
to a request that the files be opened to three lawyers,
one appointed by the Department of Justice; that they
should not be made public but should be used in such
manner as the ends of justice demanded.

We felt we were making some impression. But when
Mr. Farnum said that he would give his decision before we left the room, we feared that the matter had
been predetermined. Finally, after three hours, the
Assistant Attorney General announced his decision.
He said that he was informed that there was no material evidence in the Government files as to the guilt
or innocence of Sacco and Vanzetti. He refused to
commit himself on the question of whether the files contained their names prior to their arrest or whether
there were references therein to members of the Galleani group of anarchists or the connection of these
men with that group. He stated he did not regard
that as material, and further, that he was not prepared to state what position he would have taken if
he had thought this was material. We told him his
statement was at variance with the affidavits of two
former officials of the Department of Justice. We
questioned the fact that what he admitted was not
material. We asked him whether he personally had
examined the files, to which he replied in the negative.

We narrowed our request to an investigation by one
lawyer together with a representative of the Department, their research to be limited to a period beginning
sixty days before the arrest and ending ninety days
after the conclusion of the trial, with the understand-

ing that none of the report be made public. This was likewise refused. Finally, however, Mr. Farnum dictated a statement to the effect that while he did not authorize us to convey any message, yet he would say that if a request were received from Governor Fuller, the Attorney General of Massachusetts or the Lowell Commission for access to the files, it would be immediately granted. This was helpful. It seemed to us inconceivable that any one would take the responsibility of having these men put to death where there was at hand evidence which might throw some light on the case. We could not help feeling that no individual could be so implacable, no governmental machine so relentless, no Christian so cruel, as not to be relieved at even an excuse to postpone an execution in a case like this.

We arrived in Boston the morning of August 22nd. The execution was scheduled for midnight. We had telegraphed from Washington to the Governor and to A. Lawrence Lowell. The latter had left his home —"whereabouts unknown."

We called the Governor's secretary at half hour intervals in an attempt to obtain an audience. Finally, at about 12:30, we went to the State House. Herman A. McDonald, His Excellency's hard-boiled secretary, was apparently not cheered by our visit, yet we were encouraged that Governor Fuller was willing to spend this last day in the harrowing task of hearing appeals —appeals for mercy from some, for justice from others, and from others appeals for time that the matter might be further investigated (and then appeals from patriotic citizens belonging to the American Legion and the Key Men of America, and from other eminently respectable gentlemen, that he should remain stiff-necked and not be influenced by the horror with which "bad" men regarded the contemplated execution).

While we waited, a committee of such "bad" men, headed by Paul Kellogg, editor of the *Survey Magazine*, consisting of Owen Lovejoy and others, trooped out of the Governor's office. A labor delegation from New York, led by Judge Jacob Panken, awaited an audience.

Mr. McDonald assured us that we would have "to make it snappy." We were ushered into the presence of the Governor, clothed on that day, August 22, 1927, with the power of a God—the power of life and death.

We explained our mission—that we were for the moment interested in just the one phase of the case of Sacco and Vanzetti—that relating to the Government files, which the Federal officials had offered to open. Disclaiming any contention that the files showed a frame-up or improper collusion between departments of Government, we pointed out that on the basis of affidavits of former Government agents, the evidence therein contained was material to the case. We pleaded that the men should not be put to death while these files remained secret. What answer would there be to a large and sincere public opinion which felt that this secrecy in itself was evidence of connivance by the Federal Government?

"Do you think these men are innocent?" inquired the Governor.

"We wouldn't be here if we didn't."

"Have you interviewed the witnesses? Don't you think I know more about this case than you do?"

We refrained from pointing out that he had believed one set of witnesses rather than another, and that in view of his background and his attitude expressed in Congress toward radicals, his choice of where to place his confidence was natural. Instead, we answered that the report of the Lowell Committee, appointed by him, had effectively contributed to the "doubts" and, in admitting the "grave breach of official decorum" and the "indiscretions" of Judge Thayer, had made clear that the trial had not been before an "impartial" judge as guaranteed by the Massachusetts Bill of Rights. Later, Frank Walsh made the query: Did the Lowell Committee believe the witnesses who testified that Judge Thayer had called these men "anarchist bastards" and other vile names; did Thayer confess, or on the other hand had he denied the accusations, the committee regarding his denial as a lie? An important question, for one or the other must have happened in view of the committee's report! Did Judge Thayer confess or did he lie? The Governor ignored the question.

"If the Lowell Committee report made the strongest possible case against these men," we continued, "it is not surprising that there should be doubt."

"Who said it made the strongest case?" said the Governor.

"They owed it to the public to state all the facts

that led to their conclusion, so presumably they did."

"Why did Vanzetti fail to take the stand in the Plymouth case?"

Apparently this had great significance to the Governor. He had referred to it in his report. It seemed a controlling circumstance, for the question, so I am informed, was put to many who conferred with him that day.

"Presumably he was advised not to take the stand."

"Perhaps he refused to take the stand." (Did the Governor have private information of conferences between Vanzetti and his former counsel? If so, where did he get it? We knew merely that Vanzetti had for years claimed that counsel in the Plymouth case had betrayed his interests at the trial and had advised him not to testify.) "Isn't it your experience that an innocent man insists upon taking the stand?" asked the Governor.

"There may be many reasons, Governor, why a man should not take the stand. Advice against it is often sound, particularly with the defendant a foreigner and holding unpopular views. See what happened to them in the other case when they did. They seem to be damned if they don't and damned if they do."

The philosophy of protecting a defendant who fails to testify is so apparent that, under the law, no man is required to take the stand, and the jury is instructed that failure to testify may not even be considered as an indication of guilt.

"But, Governor," we asserted, "we are entitled to rely on the Lowell report. We wish to refer to just

one statement in that report. One of the alleged facts
on which the committee came to its conclusion was
that the cap found at the scene of the murder fitted
Sacco. The Defense Committee denies this. On this
point there were three witnesses at the trial. First,
Sacco, who testified it was not his cap. When it was
tried on, it was apparently far too small, sitting on
the back of his head, as is shown by newspaper car-
toons at the time. Secondly, Mrs. Sacco, who said it
was not her husband's cap; and then the superintendent of the factory, who said he thought it was of the
color of Sacco's cap, but refused to identify it. Governor, this question can be factually determined. Before you kill Sacco, try on the cap! What answer
can there be to this? Have you read the editorial of
the New York *World*, analyzing the report and quoting
the evidence on this?"

"Who wrote that editorial?" asked the Governor.
We gave our opinion that presumably the writer was
Walter Lippmann, but we knew that the Governor
attributed it to Felix Frankfurter, though we wondered why this should affect the soundness of the argument.

Contempt for former officials who would relate
"secrets" in the files of the government; an assurance
that the United States Government, even in the days of
A. Mitchell Palmer, could do no wrong; reliance upon
the failure of Vanzetti to take the stand as an indication of guilt, leaving an inference that there was a
sinister attack by innuendo on the part of Vanzetti's
former lawyer; and animus toward Felix Frankfurter,

as one whose fight for these men in his book—"Sacco
and Vanzetti"—had caused the public excitement, all
were apparently working in the Governor's subcon-
sciousness. And then, some time before, Fuller had refused to interfere with the execution of the "car-barn"
bandits—three gay and rather popular youngsters of
the Catholic faith—and this in spite of a petition
signed by thousands of Boston citizens.

The point of our conference had been diverted but
as we left we again made our appeal that the government files be opened. Then our last thought to the
Governor: "Only an infallible judge should fix an im-
mutable sentence."

As the day wore on and the Governor had not called
together his Advisory Committee, we gradually lost
hope.

Numbers of people were joining parades, five, ten,
fifteen at a time. These pickets walked in front of
the State House bearing placards:

"Try it on. The Lowell Commission reported that
the cap found at the murder scene fit Sacco. Try
it on."

"Why do you refuse to believe our witnesses?"

"If Sacco and Vanzetti are executed, justice is dead
in Massachusetts."

I watched one of these picket lines forming outside
the Bellevue Hotel, with Edna St. Vincent Millay, the
distinguished poet, at the head, followed by Katherine
Huntington, Margaret Hatfield, John Dos Passos,
John Howard Lawson, and others. Like a funeral
cortège, they walked slowly near the curb in single

file past the State House. Across the street outside
of Boston Common were crowds of spectators. Seven
minutes were allowed before arrest. The picketers
were then taken by the police. As they passed through
the streets there was occasional handclapping. At
the police station were swarms of others who had been
on earlier picket lines, who were still arranging for
bail.

About 5:30 there appeared Miss Ellen Hayes,
seventy-six years of age, formerly a professor of
mathematics in Wellesley, who had come to join the
picketers. Quiet, dignified, determined, trudging along
in square-toed boots, she led the last line of the day,
bearing a banner on which was written: "Hail Sacco
and Vanzetti. The élite of the world greet you as
heroes." After seven minutes she was grabbed by the
police.

Sacco-Vanzetti headquarters at the Hotel Bellevue
seethed with excitement. Up in Room 712 were gathered a number of lawyers unable to restrain themselves
from taking part—Finnerty of Washington, Spellman
and Palmer of New York. All night they had worked
on a new set of papers in the hope that on some new
theory, a Federal judge would allow a writ of habeas
corpus. Mr. Hill and his staff of attorneys had
sought a writ from Mr. Justice Holmes of the Supreme Court. Denied there, they sought Mr. Justice
Brandeis. He refused to intervene as members of his
family were interested in the case. No one questioned
that Susan Brandeis, the judge's daughter, or Mrs.
Brandeis, his wife, friends of Mrs. Glendower Evans,

who had given of time and fortune, were sympathetic, and appalled at the great injustice of it all. Yet, because of this very feeling at his own hearth, Judge Brandeis refused to consider the case. The attorneys had then sought Judge Harlan Stone, but there came back word that he likewise refused. A request to Judge Taft in Canada met with the answer that his jurisdiction could not be exercised in a foreign country.

All of these appeals had been made on the theory that the prejudice of the one judge who had sat on the case meant that the defense had not had the "due process of law" guaranteed by the Fourteenth Amendment to the Federal Constitution. The precedent relied upon had come from the Leo Frank case, where Mr. Justice Holmes, in a dissenting opinion, had presented the view that a Federal Court might intervene where a trial was practically influenced or directed by a mob.[4] Following this had come the Arkansas case of *Dempsey vs. Moore*,[5] where a number of negroes were railroaded toward execution through the mere form of a trial. The good citizens of the town had agreed not to lynch the negroes if justice would only heedlessly rush these men to death. The court had there held that the question could be determined on a motion for a writ of habeas corpus. Yet both of these cases, as Mr. Justice Holmes is said to have pointed out, concern, not the attitude of the judge, but the effect of outside influences. Where the matter involved the judge himself, the jury or internal court procedure, the granting of a writ

[4] Frank *vs.* Mangum, 237 U. S. 309, 345 (1914).
[5] 261 U. S. 86 (1922).

might set an unfortunate precedent which would involve
the United States Courts in every State murder case.

Undiscouraged by this attitude of the Federal
Judges, the new lawyers prepared their papers, basing
their theory upon the proposition, not merely that
Judge Thayer had been prejudiced, but that the whole
procedure was a frame-up, participated in by the Department of Justice and the prosecuting attorney.
That in order to "get" these "radicals," whether or not
they were guilty, witnesses had been suborned or their
testimony perverted, and the testimony of others had
been suppressed. The papers claimed that the whole
case was the result of a conspiracy to aid injustice.

Again the Bench was assiduous that the men be
denied no "form of law." The hearing was set by
Federal Judge Lowell, who ordered the clerk's office
kept open for late filing of papers and who remained
after hours to hear the application. Judge Lowell
listened patiently to the argument. A sufficient answer
seemed to him to be indicated by his question, "Do you
men know anything about a Norfolk County Jury?"
He held that he had no jurisdiction. The lawyers hurried off to Mr. Justice Holmes on this new application.

In the meantime efforts had been made to locate Federal Judge George A. Anderson. Here was a man, we
felt, who might grant the writ if he thought that injustice was done, for no one in the United States is
more familiar with the "red scare" and the hysteria
of 1920 than this same judge. It was he who had,
on a trial for deportation before him, condemned the
Department of Justice in no unmeasured terms, who

had pointed out that *agents provocateur*, arrests without warrant, and other tactics of Mitchell Palmer's Department were the very antithesis of the principles underlying our institutions.

Judge Anderson was in Williamstown, Massachusetts. A call was made to an airport for a plane. It was found the nearest landing field was at Albany, and from there the lawyers would have to go by automobile to Williamstown. Another difficulty appeared when we were informed from the flying field that the pilot had never before flown at night. We did not tell this to the lawyers who contemplated the trip.

Mr. Justice Holmes refused to issue a writ. The lawyers started from Beverly, the Judge's home, for the air field. In the meantime we had communicated with the Governor's secretary and the Attorney General, begging that the execution be held up at least for a few hours until Judge Anderson had passed on the application.

We had heard rumors that the police had made off with Powers Hapgood. Where he was no one was certain. But into our room came a young man from the Psychopathic Hospital, who, agitated by the Sacco-Vanzetti case, was willing to risk his job to give us information. "They have Hapgood there," he told us. We telephoned to a physician, asked him to get two others, and immediately left for the hospital. I asked to see the order of commitment. That, said the doctor in charge, was a private document. Completely forgetting that this was the State of Massachusetts, I insisted that no American citizen could be deprived of his liberty without an order of court. I pleaded and stormed. Ten days for observation! This at any rate was an obvious frame-up. The doctors were immovable.

The evening wore on. In the room at the Bellevue Hotel were Tom O'Connor, Art Shields and Don Levine of the Sacco-Vanzetti Committee, Walter Frank, Eugene Boissevain and Edna St. Vincent Millay. Perhaps the pen of a poet could accomplish more than verbal appeals. Miss Millay had conferred with the Governor during the day. She had not sought to argue the evidence. She had related to the Governor a story she had heard as a child, of the reason for the abolition of capital punishment in the State of Maine. Two men had been charged with murder. The only witness for the defense was a poor fisherman. His story was not believed. The defendants were found guilty and executed. Years afterward the murderer confessed.

Edna St. Vincent Millay retired to the next room to write a letter and at twenty minutes to twelve brought in the following:

"YOUR EXCELLENCY:

"During my interview with you this afternoon, I called to your attention a distressing instance of the miscarriage of justice in a neighboring state. I suggested that, for all of your careful weighing of the evidence, for all your courage in the face of threats and violent words, for all your honest conviction that these men are guilty, you, no less than the Governor of Maine in my story, who was so tragically mistaken, are but human flesh and spirit, and that it is human to err.

"To-night, with the world in doubt, with this Commonwealth drawing into its lungs with every breath the difficult air of doubt, with the eyes of Europe turned westward upon Massachusetts and upon the whole United States in distress and harrowing doubt—are you still so sure? For, indeed, your spirit, however strong, is but the frail spirit of a man. Have you no need, in this hour, of a spirit greater than your own?

"Think back. Think back a long time. Which way would He have turned, this Jesus of your faith? Oh, not the way in which your feet are set!

"You promised me, and I believed you truly, that you would think of what I said. I exact of you this promise now. Be for a moment alone with yourself. Look inward upon yourself for a moment. Which way would He have turned, this Jesus of your faith?

"I cry to you with a million voices; answer our doubt! Exert the clemency which your high office affords!

"There is need in Massachusetts of a great man to-night. It is not yet too late for you to be that man.

"EDNA ST. VINCENT MILLAY."

We hurried to the State House. Guards were at the entrance. One of them offered to take the letter to the Governor. We were told the letter was delivered.

At the entrance we met Francis Fisher Kane, who, undiscouraged, had spent hours during the evening in the Governor's office waiting for a chance to make a final appeal, that before these men be executed the Government's files be opened. He was trembling with emotion.

During the evening Mrs. Sacco and Vanzetti's sister had visited the Governor. No hope had been given to either. Then had come Thompson and Ehrmann, former attorneys for the doomed men. Convinced of the innocence of their clients, they had again argued the case which the Governor felt had been proved beyond reasonable doubt. Kane had been allowed two minutes but he took ten. He had made the last effort.

Despondently we left the State House and quietly returned to the hotel rooms. A call came in from the lawyers who had arrived at the airport near Boston. "Should they continue on their way? Would the execution be held off for even a few hours? Could we not prevail upon the Warden, who was not compelled to execute sentence immediately, to wait for just a little while?" They rang off. The telephone bell again rang. O'Connor listened, turned to us, and said: "Nick's gone." A few minutes in silence. The telephone again, "It's all over with Bart."

We did not know until the next day how bravely these men had died. Sacco had gone to the chair, self-reliant and erect. His last words were:

"Long live anarchism!"
"Farewell, my wife and child, and all my friends."
"Good evening, gentlemen!"
"Farewell, mother!"

Vanzetti had been no less composed. With a simple, rather naïve kindliness, he shook hands with the guards before he took his fatal seat. Then he said:

"I wish to tell you that I am innocent. I never committed any crime, some sin.

"I thank you for everything you have done for me.

"I am innocent of all crime, not only of this one, but of all. I am an innocent man.

"I must forgive some people for what they are now doing to me."

Sacco and Vanzetti were dead. Strange as it may seem our spirits were quiescent in the morning. We had, of course, early called for the papers. Convinced that these men were innocent, certain that they had been done to death for their opinions, we were proud of the way they died. In the committee room and hotel lobby, some talked gently, some shed quiet tears. Most of the people around there were rather silent and solemn with grief, the inevitability of death having replaced to a slight extent the outraged indignation with which we had gone on our way for the past few days.

If the radical movement needed martyrs, Massachusetts has supplied the need. To those who had striven in the defense was sent a small slip of paper with this memento—

This Day

August 23, 1927

NICOLA SACCO

and

BARTOLOMEO VANZETTI

workingmen, and dreamers of the brotherhood of man, who hoped it might be found in America, were done to a cruel death by the children of those who fled, long ago, to this land for freedom.

*   *   *

Their voices are gone into all the earth, and they will be remembered in gratitude and tears, when the names of those who murdered them—

Judges—Governors—Scholars

—have gone down into everlasting shame.

FREEDOM OF OPINION

FREEDOM OF OPINION

SACCO AND VANZETTI—TWO INNOCENT MEN—THE
REAL CRIMINALS IN THE BRIDGEWATER AND SOUTH
BRAINTREE CASES

"THEIR voices are gone into all the earth, and they
will be remembered. . . ."

Sacco and Vanzetti were dead, but the case would not
die. Five large volumes were published containing all
the testimony, as well as the evidence presented to the
Lowell Committee. All across America people were
reading the poignant letters of Sacco and Vanzetti.
Around these men, who had become symbols, rose a vast
literature of protest and exposure. Little by little, the
facts were brought to the consciousness of the public
still interested in the tragedy. So distrustful was public opinion of the justice of Governor Fuller's course,
that his ambition to become Ambassador to France was
squelched. He was once mentioned as a possible Vice-
Presidential nominee, but even the Republican party
realized that that was impossible.

In fictional form Upton Sinclair's book "Boston" [1]
told the story of the case to a world-wide audience.
The legal aspects of the case were masterfully surveyed

[1] "Boston", in two volumes, by Upton Sinclair, Charles Boni,
publisher, 1928.

345

by Osmond K. Fraenkel.[2] Herbert B. Ehrmann of defense counsel, published a book called "The Untried Case,"[3] which makes as fascinating reading as any detective story and points conclusively to the real criminals. At the instance of Silas Bent, the "Outlook and Independent," using Jack Callahan, a reformed bank burglar, made a through inquiry into the Bridgewater hold-up, and in the issue of October 31st, 1928, published the evidence it had gathered.

The facts have come to light. They reveal the guilty parties. They prove conclusively the innocence of Sacco and Vanzetti.

I

WHAT HAPPENED AT BRIDGEWATER

IN his statement on the case, Governor Fuller emphasized the importance of Vanzetti's conviction for the attempted hold-up in Bridgewater. His criminal record weighed heavily against Vanzetti in the later case. Vanzetti himself once protested "the two trials are but parts of the same thing; I would say the reciprocals of the case."

Governor Fuller had good reason at least to suspect that Vanzetti was innocent of the Bridgewater crime. Prior to the execution, James Mede, an ex-convict,

---

[2] "The Sacco-Vanzetti Case," by Osmond K. Fraenkel, Alfred A. Knopf, publisher, 1931.

[3] "The Untried Case," by Herbert B. Ehrmann, Vanguard Press, New York, 1933; Martin Hopkins, Ltd., London, 1934.

was so troubled by his conscience that he sought the
Governor and, after urgent insistence, was given a hearing. His story, showing knowledge of the Bridgewater
affair and completely exonerating Vanzetti, was ignored. Twenty days before the execution, accompanied
by two attorneys, Max L. Glaeser and Joseph Santo-
suossi, he called on Boston's Chief of Police Bly and
offered to enlighten him as to the facts. Bly said he
had had no instructions from the Governor and ended
the conference by saying, "I refuse to take the statement because I think it is rather embarrassing and I
might be criticised."

The Governor had further reason to look into the
matter. Vanzetti's defense had been an alibi.   He
had stated that on the day of the hold-up he was selling
eels in Plymouth, and this was the testimony of many
witnesses in the case. When this was brought to the
Governor's attention, his answer was, "There isn't a
single document in this case proving that Vanzetti sold
eels.   There's only the word of his Italian friends.
Why don't you bring in some proof to show that eels
were shipped to Vanzetti?"   Search was made for the
seven-year-old express company receipt showing shipments from Boston to Vanzetti at Plymouth. At the
office of the American Express Company investigators
were told that records were not kept for so long a period.
Ehrmann set out with Felicani, the head of the defense
committee, to make the weary round of Atlantic Avenue
fishdealers. Old records were found at the office of
Corso & Gambino, 112 Atlantic Avenue; among them

was an express receipt book for 1919. An entry was discovered showing that on Saturday, December 20th, a forty-pound barrel of live eels was shipped to Vanzetti. The barrel of eels was delivered on the Monday before Christmas; Vanzetti was not at home to pay the express charges; the eels were finally delivered on Tuesday, December 23rd. The express book was turned over to Joseph Wiggin in the anteroom of the Governor's office.

With the story of James Mede and the evidence as to the shipment of eels, Governor Fuller had every reason to question the validity of the Bridgewater conviction.

The attempted hold-up at Bridgewater on December 24th, 1919, was the work of Frank Silva (alias Paul Martini), Joseph San Marco, "Doggy" Bruno, and "Guinea" Oates.

In 1916, Frank Silva was an employee of the L. Q. White Shoe Company in Bridgewater. He quit his job. In 1917 his chief hangout was Jimmy (Big Chief) Mede's taxicab, shoeshine and cigar stand on Hanover Street in the Italian quarter of Boston. One day he proposed a "job" to Jimmy and his friend Joe San Marco—the theft of the shoe factory payroll. Silva, Mede and San Marco drove to Bridgewater to look the place over. Shortly after this Mede was sent to State Prison for a term of six years. This country went to war. Joe San Marco joined the Navy and Frank Silva went into the Army.

Two years later, in 1919, Frank and Joe, through with service, broke, resurrected the idea of the payroll holdup. They gathered in a couple of "regular" fellows and notorious stick-up men—"Guinea" Oates and "Doggy" Bruno. The gang surveyed the town of Bridgewater and the surrounding territory in a Buick touring car in the possession of "Guinea" Oates.

On December 22nd a trip was made to Needham where "Guinea" Oates lived. Frank Silva wandered into a garage. From reports of Operative H. H. of the Pinkerton Dectective Agency, employed by the factory to make an investigation immediately after the crime, he talked there with a man named Hassam, who stated:

"On Monday, December 22nd, between 12:30 and 1:30 a man tried to borrow two number plates, giving as his reason that he had bought an old car and wanted to get home."

Hassam's description fitted Frank Silva. Said Hassam: "I think he was a Sicilian . . . he spoke broken English." Frank Silva was from the south of Italy and his English was poor. Hassam refused to lend the plates. Silva managed to steal them and put them underneath his coat. The plates bore the number 01173 C.

At dawn of the morning of December 24th the gang met at North End Park in Boston. "Doggy" Bruno had a sawed-off shotgun; the others carried revolvers. They started for Bridgewater, having put the stolen plates over the old ones. They arrived at about six-thirty and stopped for food at a restaurant. "Doggy" Bruno and Silva then went to the Square to watch for the Ford truck which would come to the bank to get the payroll. They parked their car on Hale Street just off Broad. It was arranged that when the Ford truck carrying the money moved up Broad Street, the Buick car would back out from Hale Street in order to block its progress. While the other three remained in the car, Silva acted as look-out, taking his position on Broad Street behind one of the trees a little way from Hale Street.

After fifteen minutes Silva gave word that the truck was coming. The Buick car started to back into Broad Street. A street car was moving down Broad Street in advance of the truck. This upset the bandits' plan. As the truck approached, San Marco and Bruno jumped out of the Buick car and shouted "Stick 'em up!" The truck proceeded on its way. The bandits, taking refuge behind trees and posts, fired. The paymaster and two guards returned the shots. The street car was more or less a screen. No one was injured. The driver of the truck dodged; someone else grabbed the wheel; the truck ran into a telephone pole.

The bandits jumped into their Buick, made for Hale Street, into Plymouth Street, followed side roads around the Square and started toward Boston. The number plates were taken off and thrown away.

In Boston the gang separated. Silva went to New York where, after nine or ten months, he was convicted of crime and sent to the Federal Prison in Atlanta. San Marco committed murder in January and was sent to jail for life. "Doggy" Bruno within a year after the Bridgewater crime was jailed in New York. "Guinea" Oates disappeared.

Such is the substance of an affidavit made by Frank Silva in August, 1928, and printed in the "Outlook and Independent." The confession was obtained by Jack Callahan, a reformed bank burglar, and was paid for. The "Outlook" naturally objected to the payment of money until Silva's story was checked. The money to be paid Silva was deposited in the Corn Exchange Bank in New York City, with the understanding that if the facts were susceptible of proof and were proved, Silva would be paid.

On the one hand, Silva's criminal record would tend to weaken the value of the confession. But obviously no confession could be expected from a Presbyterian minister, priest, rabbi or even bank president. The weight of the confession seems likewise weakened by the fact that money was paid. This is suggestive of the story of a man who, trying to cash a check at a bank, was asked for identification. The customer showed his calling card, initials on his watch, letters addressed to him. The cashier, who at one time had been a judge, refused to pay the money. Said the customer: "Judge, I've known you to hang men on less evidence than that." Replied the cashier: "That may well be, but you have to be damned careful when you're paying out money." The money payment might weaken the value of the confession, yet it would strengthen the determination of the magazine to check up the facts in every possible manner and to withhold payment until they had persuasive proof.

Silva's story was sent to Governor Fuller, with a request that he comment on it. No comment was forthcoming.

Silva was corroborated by Mede who made affidavit to the effect that he had known all four bandits for some time prior to the Bridgewater job; that the Bridgewater crime was planned in his "hang-out" in 1917 while Mede was in the Massachusetts State Prison in Charleston. He heard the story from Joe San Marco who, in 1920, was brought to Charleston Prison to serve a life sentence.

In order to check the story, a study was made of reports of Pinkerton detectives who had investigated the hold-up immediately after its occurrence, and of the testimony in the case. Frank Silva had said that after the shooting "all of a sudden I heard a noise, we heard some glass breaking." We have noted that the zigzagging truck ran into a telephone pole, which was confirmed by the testimony of Boles, an occupant of the truck and a witness at the trial. The reports of the Pinkerton detectives, as well as the statements of witnesses on the trial, were to the effect that the bandit with the shotgun had a "cropped" moustache. Alfred E. Cox, the shoe company paymaster, who was on the truck, referred to this "croppy" moustache. His description fitted "Doggy" Bruno. Vanzetti had always worn a long and flowing moustache.

The Pinkertons found Frank W. Harding, who had noted the number of the license plates on the gunmen's curtained car, "Mass. O 1173 C." We have the report of Hassam as to the endeavor of an Italian to borrow plates from him and the disappearance of the plates.

Silva could not have obtained his information from court records. He was not the kind of man to hang around a courtroom. The record of the Bridgewater trial was difficult to obtain—so much so that the "Outlook" applied to Harvard Library for its copy. In many respects the statement of Silva is somewhat different from evidence on the trial but conforms to reports of the Pinkerton detectives, which could not have been known to him.

The real check-up of the confession, however, took place when Callahan and Bent, accompanied by Silva and Mede, covered the route indicated by Silva's confession. Silva showed where the car was parked on Hale Street near Broad; he referred to the street car which had upset their plans.

"What do you mean, a street car?" asked Bent. "There are no car tracks in this street."

On inquiry, however, it appeared that there had been tracks there when the hold-up occurred; they were removed two years later. The post-office now stands on the spot where Silva said he had once played pool, during a reconnoitering visit to Bridgewater. Investigation showed that that building had been there about four years; that there had been a poolroom in the basement of the former building. Inquiry showed that a restaurant to which Silva had referred and which was no longer standing, had existed in 1919. As Bent says:

"Now, men may be mistaken in identifying another man; they may lie or be mistaken about where they were at a certain time on a certain day, but physical facts do not lie.

Car tracks do not lie. A brick post-office does not lie. A restaurant does not lie."

Silva identified the garage from which he had stolen the license plates, a fact which conformed with Hassam's testimony at the Vanzetti trial.

Only one conclusion is possible—Vanzetti had no connection with the Bridgewater crime. He was given a criminal record which played an ominous part when he was tried with Sacco for the murders at South Braintree.

II

THE SOUTH BRAINTREE CRIME

THREE Italians—Joe Morelli, his brother Frank, Tony Mancini—together with a Pole named Steve Benkosky, drove a Hudson car into Providence, Rhode Island. They picked up Celestino Madeiros at a barroom across from his boarding house. It was four o'clock in the morning of April 15th, 1920. The meeting had been arranged two or three nights before in a poolroom saloon in the vicinity.

Joe and Frank, who, with Tony, were members of the Morelli gang, at the time were under indictment for robbery in the Federal Court, charged with having stolen shoes from Rice & Hutchins, and Slater, Morrill, Inc., shoe factories at South Braintree, Massachusetts. Mancini was likewise well known in the underworld. A man of cool nerve and vicious determination, he is now serving sentence for murder in New York State.

Benkosky, known as Steve the Pole, nineteen years of age, had already earned a reputation as a highwayman. He was a member of another group of gangsters, which included Madeiros. He was later taken "for a ride" and his body, riddled with bullets, was found huddled on his doorstep. Madeiros at the time was eighteen years of age, had been a juvenile delinquent from the age of fourteen, with a record of twelve arrests and convictions, and with a reputation for acts of violence—a reputation later justified by a conviction for a murder at South Wrentham, for which he eventually paid the penalty in the electric chair.

The Morellis were desperately in need of funds for lawyers and for bail. The criminal cases against them were shortly to be tried. Their former sources of income through robbing freight cars had been blocked, but their exploits had made them familiar with the inside workings of the shoe factories at South Braintree. They knew that the payroll was delivered by express in the morning; that it was sorted in one of the two Slater, Morrill factories into payroll envelopes. Later the boxes containing the money were carried from one factory to another along a public street.

Joe Morelli carried a .32 Colt revolver; Mancini a gun of foreign make, "a Steyr"; Frank Morelli, Benkosky and Madeiros were likewise armed.

The gang drove from Providence to South Boston where they stopped at a saloon in Andrew Square to get information about the payroll money that was to be sent to South Braintree. Joe, about forty years of age, the oldest of the crowd and the leader, having some executive ability and experience in crime strategy, gave directions.

"It's a cinch; as soon as they see your guns they'll hand over the money and we'll make our getaway. Mike" (another of the gang and a brother of Joe) "has a Buick car parked in the Oak Street woods, near Randolph. We'll drive there and change into that car. Steve does the driving. The back window of the car will be out and the curtains down. You, Madeiros, sit in back and if there's a chase, you hold 'em off from behind."

The party made off for the Oak Street woods in Randolph, about three and a half miles from South Braintree, where Mike Morelli was stationed with a Buick car. That car had been stolen in Natick, Massachusetts, on November 22nd. 1919.

In the woods a change in the license numbers was made; * the bandits left the Hudson and took their appointed places in the Buick car. The car was first observed in South Braintree at about nine-thirty in the morning by Shelley Neal, an expressman who carried the payroll money into the office of the Slater, Morrill factory opposite the railroad station. Neal reported that there was another car about twenty feet away—probably the Hudson—and that as he passed between the two cars he heard the words, "All right." The cars then drove in opposite directions. The Buick car was seen elsewhere in the vicinity that morning. There is a likelihood that the party drove to Provi-

---

* At the time of the shooting the car bore number plates 49783. They were stolen in Needham from a man named Ellis in the early part of 1920.

dence and later came back to South Braintree, where they spent a little time in a speakeasy two or three miles from the place of the crime.

At any rate, in the early afternoon, the Buick took up a position near the Slater, Morrill factory to which the payroll was to be delivered. The Morellis and Tony Mancini got out of the car and wandered around. A Mrs. Kennedy and Mrs. Louis Hays Kelly, at the time working at an open window not more than ten feet away from the murder car, identified a photograph of the driver remaining in the car as Steve Benkosky. Madeiros waited in the rear. Joe and Tony walked along Pearl Street in a westerly direction until they arrived at a place perhaps one hundred feet away from the car, where they leaned against a fence and waited. Frank took up his station across the street behind a brick pile.

At about three o'clock Frederick A. Parmenter, paymaster, and Alessandro Berardelli, his guard, left the one Slater, Morrill factory and started east on Pearl Street toward the other factory. Each of them carried a steel case filled with money in pay envelopes. There was about $16,000 in all. They proceeded across the railroad tracks and there talked to a passerby for a few moments.

They continued their way. As they approached, Joe Morelli and Mancini opened fire. Berardelli, who walked slightly in advance of Parmenter, fell. The gunmen then turned on Parmenter. Shot, he dropped the money box, started to run across the street, followed by Tony Mancini who continued to fire. Joe fired into the prostrate body of Berardelli.

One of the bullets found in the body of Berardelli came from a .32 Colt, carried by Joe; the other five bullets (two from the body of Parmenter and three from the body of Berardelli) came from the Steyr gun—of 7.65 millimeter caliber, which takes .32 caliber cartridges. This revolver left upon the side of the shell an ejector or claw mark which indicated that the bullet came from some automatic pistol of foreign manufacture. It was the same type of gun as was used by Mancini in February, 1921, when he shot down Alberto Alterio on Mulberry Street, in New York.

As soon as the shooting started, the Buick, a little way down the street, crawled up to the scene. There was a slight upgrade. The engine was missing. Joe and Tony threw the money boxes into the tonneau. With Frank, they jumped into the moving car, which then picked up speed. Shots were fired from the car at people on the street.

As they neared the railroad tracks a train was coming; the gate-tender started to lower the gates. The men in the car shouted and made the crossing before the gates were lowered.

At the corner of Railroad Avenue and Pearl Street they passed Frank J. Burke, at whom Joe yelled, "Get out of the way, you son of a b . . . ."

The bandits, gathering headway, continued along Pearl Street, scattering rubber-headed tacks behind them. They turned left into Hancock Street, from there south to a railroad crossing. Instead of crossing the tracks, the car made a sharp turn and doubled back into South Braintree, thus eluding pursuit. At Granite Street a turn was made toward Randolph and the Oak Street woods.

There they found Mike with the Hudson car. The booty was transferred to the Hudson, the number plates were switched. The bandits got into that car and continued on their way.

At Orchard Street they entered the yard of a Mrs. Hewins to ask directions. They turned around, finally found the Stoughton turnpike, going due south to Brockton for three and a half miles through wild country and then for five miles through a sparsely settled district. The car was next observed at Matfield crossing, about twenty-three miles from South Braintree, where a gate-tender stopped them until a train passed. Joe Morelli shouted "What in hell are you holding us up for?" *

Eventually the gang found their way to Providence.

Mike leisurely drove away from the Oak Street woods in the Buick car. He made his way to New Bedford where between five and five-thirty in the afternoon Sergeant Jacobs saw the Buick car bearing the license number R.I. 154 E. He had seen Mike Morelli driving the car on another occasion shortly before this. Under cover of night Mike drove the Buick to the Manley woods, a densely grown area about five miles west of Matfield, with another car trailing in

* At the trial the gate-tender identified Vanzetti as the bandit who shouted at him in English without an accent. At the time Vanzetti spoke little English.

which to make his return. There Mike abandoned the
Buick and there it was found on April 17th, bearing
no number plates. The tracks of another car were
observed.

On April 24th Sergeant Jacobs again saw the
license number R.I. 154 E. This time the numbers
appeared not on a Buick but on a black Cole-8 touring car which stood at the curb in front of Joe Fiore's
restaurant at the corner of Kempton and Purchase
Streets in New Bedford. Sergeant Jacobs went inside
where he saw Frank Morelli together with three other
Italians. As the Sergeant approached the group, one
of the Italians made a movement with his hand toward his pocket. Whereupon Frank spoke up:

"What's the matter, Jake?" he said, "what do you want
with me? Why are you picking on me all the time?"

The Sergeant referred to the license number, to which
Frank answered:

"That's a dealer's plate; you see I'm in the automobile
business and we just transfer plates from one car to another."

Sergeant Jacobs said that he then suspected that
the Morellis were involved in the South Braintree
crime. Shortly after this Sacco and Vanzetti were
arrested and Jacobs, having no definite evidence,
dropped the matter.

A few weeks later, on May 1st, Madeiros was arrested for some petty crime and until December spent
most of his time in jail. Thereafter for about two
years he traveled extensively, visiting Texas, Minne-

sota and other places, with a woman.   Evidence shows
that when he started on his travels, he had $2800,
apparently his share of the booty of the South Braintree crime.   The indications are that it was paid late,
which may account for a statement once made by
Madeiros that he was "double-crossed" by the Morellis.
When Joe Morelli, in 1926, after a term of six years,
was released from the Federal Penitentiary, we find him
in Providence with a new car, chauffeur and with
enough money to rent and equip a restaurant.   For a
time he stayed clear of the law but later was again
jailed as a result of a counterfeiting enterprise.

Discovery of the facts was initiated by the note sent
to Sacco by Madeiros in the Dedham jail in November,
1925: "I hear by confess to being in the South Braintree Shoe Company crime and Sacco and Vanzetti was
not in said crime." *   Madeiros was submitted to examination and cross-examination.   He was ready to tell
what he remembered of a crime in which he had played
a part five years before, except that he would neither
name his accomplices nor make any statement which
might lead to their identification.   The story of a convicted murderer with a varied criminal career, is, of
course, entitled to little weight.   The test of truth
would depend upon corroboration and the revelation
of unknown incidents which could be checked.   He had
told of the stop at the house of Mrs. Hewins to inquire
about the road—a fact then first disclosed.   This was
confirmed by Mrs. Hewins.   The case had been tried
on the theory that there was only one car used by the

* See page 305.

bandits. Madeiros told of the change made in the Oak Street woods. This not only confirmed the testimony of some of the witnesses, but the time which must have elapsed to change license plates, shift the moneyboxes and to reconnoiter for a clear road accounted for the extraordinarily long period between the crime and the appearance of the car at the Matfield crossing —almost an hour and a quarter, which the bandits took to cover a distance of twenty-three miles. The time itself was fixed by the passage of railroad trains at both points.*

Sergeant Jacobs' notebook showing his record of license number R.I. 154 E on a Buick car driven by Mike Morelli prior to the day of the crime, his recognition of the car and number on the late afternoon of the day of the crime at New Bedford, two days before the car was found without number plates in the Matfield woods; his later discovery on April 24th of the same license number on a Cole car driven by the Morellis—all this is persuasive, independent evidence consistent only with the above narrative of the crime. Evidence derived from the bullets, the indication of the use of a gun of foreign make, traced to Mancini after his crime in New York, can hardly be regarded as fortuitous or coincidental.

Shortly after the crime Madeiros had told the story to Barney Monterio and to James F. Weeks. The latter was convicted for participation with Madeiros in

---

* James E. King made a thorough study of the time element and demonstrated that considerable delay had occurred during the escape.

the South Wrentham murder and, in 1925, was in jail. Madeiros had talked of the Morellis to Weeks and this gave the lead to further investigation.

Court records showed the connection of the Morellis with robberies of shipments from the shoe factories in South Braintree and their conviction therefor. The "spotting" of these factories explained the source of information as to how and when the payrolls were delivered.

It is fair to say that never in the annals of criminal history has an instance been found where two of a gang of five criminals are apprehended and no connection is made with the other three, nor clue nor trace leading to their identity. Yet this was the situation with Sacco and Vanzetti. This is the more inexplicable since the lives of the two Italian anarchists were an open book and their friends and associates were known and interrogated. The true story of the crime accounts not only for the five bandits observed, but also for a sixth who covered the substitution of cars.

These facts and many others, including identification of photographs by eye-witnesses, are related in detail in Osmond K. Fraenkel's book. As Fraenkel says.*

"If there were present at or near the scene of the crime a number of brothers, then the descriptions given by the various witnesses can be reconciled. It may well be that instead of these descriptions fitting one man, the witnesses saw in fact different men who resembled each other. It has never been explained how Sacco could for fifteen or

* (P. 533 of above-mentioned books.)

twenty minutes have been observed by Mrs. Andrews on Pearl Street and could during the same time have been watched by Tracy at the store in the square. . . .

"The hypothesis that the crimes were actually committed by the Morelli gang explains much otherwise inexplicable. It ties up the bandits with the factory robbed, a point important especially in view of the fact that only a short time before the crime the day for carrying the payroll had been changed, a point from which the local press deduced that the bandits had perhaps some inside source of information. This kind of information the Morellis apparently possessed, for their crimes in the Providence railroad yards were partly thefts of shipments from the two shoe factories in South Braintree. The hypothesis accounts also for the number of bandits observed by witnesses; it accounts for the two cars seen by Neal; it identifies as Steve Benkosky the pale, sickly man who was identified by so many different witnesses; it explains the confusion in the description of the fleeing automobile observed by different people at widely separate points, and particularly does it reconcile the varying descriptions of the clothing said to have been worn by the man identified as Sacco."

Ehrmann, in his book "The Untried Case," shows in detail how the facts were uncovered and confirmed. Comparing the case against Sacco and Vanzetti with that against the Morelli gang, he finds the following:

	Madeiros-Morelli	*Sacco-Vanzetti*
Character of accused	Typical gangsters and gunmen of the worst type.	One of them an industrious workman with a family and a savings bank deposit, and no

	Madeiros-Morelli	*Sacco-Vanzetti*
		previous criminal record. The other a fish peddler never before his arrest accused of crime. Both unpopular as pacifists and extreme radicals.
Motive	Desperate need of funds for lawyer and bail before trial for serious Federal offense. Source of income through robbing freight cars blocked by U.S. Marshal and R.R. Police.	Robbery for private gain alleged. No claim or evidence that either defendant ever received or had any part of the stolen money.
Opportunity to plan crime	Had been repeatedly stealing large shipments from Slater and Morrill and Rice and Hutchins of South Braintree after a member of the gang had 'spotted' them in that place.	None alleged.
Accusation by confederate	Direct testimony of participant.	None.
Identification by others	Opportunity restricted, but Joe, Mancini, and Benkosky identified from photographs by Government as well as defense witnesses. No available photographs of Mike or Frank. Undoubted resemblance of Joe Morelli to Sacco in many particulars.	Some identification of Sacco; very slight of Vanzetti, at the scene of the murder. Identifications open not only to doubt, but to the gravest suspicion owing to unprecedented manner of displaying these defendants, previous identifications of other criminals by same witnesses, changes in stories, suppression of testimony, manifestly impossible details such

	Madeiros-Morelli	*Sacco-Vanzetti*
		as the man identified as Vanzetti using 'clear and unmistakable English,' and the man identified as Sacco having an unusually large hand.
Alibi	Full of contradictions as to Morellis. None by Madeiros.	Testified to by many reputable witnesses.
Consciousness of guilt	Alleged motion to draw gun on officer—uncontradicted. Falsehoods consistent with nothing but consciousness of guilt of crime charged. Confession by Madeiros.	Alleged motion to draw gun on officer—contradicted. Falsehoods explained by terror felt by radicals and draft evaders at time of persecution of 'Reds' two days after murder or suicide of a friend [1] while in the custody of Department of Justice officials.
Bullets	One fired from pistol of type owned by Joe Morelli (Colt. 32), and five from type owned by Mancini ('Star' or 'Steyr', 7.65 mm.).	One only claimed to have been fired by weapon of Sacco, and none by Vanzetti. Sharp disagreement of experts, but if real opinion of one of the Government's experts had been known at the time of the trial he would have proved a defense witness.[2]
Other Corroborative Matter	Morellis were American-born and could have used 'clear and unmistakable' English. *Every member of the murder party accounted for.* Unwillingness of Morelli lawyer to state anything tending to im-	Testimony shows that cap claimed to be Sacco's was *not* identified by Kelly, and effort to connect Vanzetti's popular make of revolver with Berardelli's supported by most remote type of evidence, in-

[1] Salsedo   [2] Proctor

	Madeiros-Morelli	*Sacco-Vanzetti*
	plicate his former clients in the South Braintree murders.	cluding confused records of gun-shop offered by an ex-agent (unrevealed) of the Department of Justice.[3] Does not account for other members of the party.
Stolen Money	Madeiros' possession of $2,800 immediately thereafter (about his 'split' of the total sum stolen).	None. On the contrary, when arrested, Sacco and Vanzetti, supposed to be in possession of over $15,000, and ex-hypothesi, to be accomplished automobile thieves, were using street cars after an unsuccessful attempt to borrow a friend's[4] six-year-old Overland.
Attitude of Authorities	Seriously offered statements and affidavits of Morellis denying participation in crime. Declined request of defendant's counsel to interview *all witnesses* jointly to avoid vulgar contest of affidavits. Declined to investigate.	Anti-Red excitement capitalized; highly prejudicial cross-examination as to draft evasion and anarchistic opinions and associations; patriotic speeches and charge by Judge to jury; interference by Department of Justice agents who believed defendants innocent; suppression of testimony favorable to defense; intentionally misleading testimony of experts[5] on vital points.

"How horrible," says the reader, "that the truth should have been discovered after Sacco and Vanzetti

[3] Wadsworth   [4] Boda   [5] Proctor.

were executed!" Admittedly, that would have been horrible, but the truth is worse—the facts were known before the execution, were heard by Judge Thayer on a motion for a new trail, were presented to the Supreme Court of Massachusetts, were rehearsed before the Investigating Committee and Governor Fuller—all to no avail. The State had its victims.

FREEDOM OF OPINION

FREEDOM OF OPINION

"Now We Are Not A Failure" *—Repercussions of
the Sacco-Vanzetti Case—Helen Hayes—The
Case of Commonwealth of Pennsylvania *vs.*
Emerson Jennings

Ten years have passed since Sacco and Vanzetti
were executed in Massachusetts. Instead of living out
their lives "talking at street corners to scorning men"
and dying "unmarked, unknown, a failure," they have
become symbols whose lives and trials will mark history.
The extent to which the repercussions of the tragedy
have affected society, is speculative. No one can doubt
the effect on those immediately connected with the case
—or even on those millions whose emotions were
aroused for years by the appalling injustice, culmi-
nating in the awful end in the electric chair. Resentment strengthened the resolution of those inclined
toward radicalism; others were stirred by a stronger
determination to devote themselves to the fight for
justice.

Given time, money and personnel for research, the
story of the effect of the Sacco-Vanzetti case upon
individuals, upon groups, indeed upon vast cross-
sections of this and other nations, would constitute a
social study of engrossing content and inestimable

* Vanzetti to Judge Thayer. See p. 279.

value. I would like nothing better than to undertake such a project. It would be revealing. It would show how those guilty of crimes against justice defeat their own most cherished purposes, through creating a Frankenstein resentment against the entire status quo. When faith in the justice of a system is shaken, the entire superstructure is threatened.

Take, for example, Ellen Hayes,* the Wellesley professor, determined supporter of the defense, arrested for picketing the State House. She died in 1929 leaving her estate to me to use "at his (my) discretion" to "promote the ends of justice." There was litigation over the will. Ellen Hayes was eccentric. She had founded a school for working girls in West Park, New York. She left her brain to a medical school. She asked that the "Internationale" be sung over her grave. She left her estate to a stranger who, it was claimed by the contestants, might use it to overthrow the Government of the United States. (I had met Ellen Hayes only twice in my life.) Communists, atheists, radicals and other disreputable persons might benefit if the disposition were left to the sense of justice of the beneficiary. In answer I pointed out that under our system Ellen Hayes had a right to will her property as she chose; that she had denied herself and saved money dollar by dollar; that she did not want it used by her relatives for ordinary living purposes; that our opponents, arguing against a testamentary disposition, would like to confiscate this property; that they were the radicals and bolsheviks. Despite the fact that

* See pp. 142, 333.

Judge G. D. B. Hasbrouck, a dignified and learned retired Judge who represented the heirs, read (rather,
bellowed) to the New York Court of Appeals the words
of the "Internationale," The Court upheld the bequest.

Tom Mooney, the Scottsboro defendants, Angelo
Herndon and many other victims of prejudice, owe a
measure of help to Sacco and Vanzetti.

The Case of Emerson Jennings of Wilkes-Barre

Emerson Jennings, printer, of Wilkes-Barre, charged
with crime, but guilty only of opinion objectionable
to those in high places, would have been helpless had
not the tragedy of the two Italians led Ellen Hayes,
in her declining years, to brood on the injustices of
society. Jennings had no money. Thousands of dollars, for his defense, have come from the Ellen Hayes
Fund.

Emerson Jennings, in his late fifties, grey-haired,
bespectacled, with a family of children and grand-
children, has lived in Wilkes-Barre for twelve years,
conducting a small printing shop in which he and his
wife worked, taking from the till, when the business
warranted it, $30 a week. He has been a dissident in
a community long conforming to the feudal will of
coal companies, railroads, banks and parasitic politi-
cians. He has belonged to no radical political party
but has played a lone wolf role in his struggle for
human rights. Jennings is not the usual town eccentric damning courts and interests in the "pubs." His
voice and pen have been influential among an important

cross-section of the life of Luzerne County in Pennsylvania. He has talked over the radio; he has been a
constant contributor to the local press. He has organized protest groups against the utilities; he has
agitated among the unemployed. Though his words
may have been intemperate, they have made him known
beyond the confines of the printing office. Time and
again he has denounced political corruption and has
openly and loudly attacked the judiciary. District
Attorneys and Judges, and the controlling powers in
tight-held Luzerne County, have from Jennings' viewpoint, always been wrong, corrupt, arrogant and op-
pressive. Jennings has been the self-anointed Defender
of the People. When the anthracite miners went on
strike early in 1935, Jennings was their natural
champion. He protested vigorously against an injunction issued by Judge Alfred Valentine of Luzerne
County, under which a large number of miners were sent
to jail under indefinite sentences for contempt of court.

A bomb exploded in the automobile of Judge Valentine at about three-thirty o'clock on the afternoon
of March 28th, 1935. Five minutes before, Mary
Valentine, the Judge's daughter, had left the car
parked alongside the Miners' Bank Building in the
center of Wilkes-Barre. At that time, throughout the
anthracite regions, bombings were not unusual. They
were a grim feature of the industrial strife raging in
this area. That Judge Valentine was not popular
with the miners was indicated by the many threatening letters he received.

At the time of the explosion, petitions drawn up by

EMERSON P. JENNINGS

The printing press is a dangerous thing

Jennings for the impeachment of the Judge, were in circulation among the miners and their sympathizers. Grimy hands of thousands of coal-diggers scrawled signatures on the petition. The petition was not gentle in tone. It referred to the Judge as "inquisitor, judge, jury and committing magistrate." In view of the fact that questions were asked by the Judge, that he sat without a jury and committed the miners to jail, the designation isn't wholly inaccurate. When the matter came before the legislature at Harrisburg in June of 1935, Jennings, spokesman for the protesting miners, was met by a united front of judges and lawyers of Luzerne County. The proceedings came to naught. Jennings continued his attacks on Judge Valentine by speech, writing and radio. In July, 1935, a vitriolic article appeared in the "Unemployed News," with the legend "To be continued" at the end. The article wasn't continued. Before the next issue Jennings was in jail, with three others—Thomas McHale, Gerald Williams and Charles Harris.

Jennings was arrested on August 2nd in the Hotel Sterling charged with having bombed or having conspired to bomb Judge Valentine's automobile on March 28th.

A few weeks before the arrest, Thomas McHale had called on Jennings in the print shop, and suggested that he (McHale) could provide capital for the establishment of a labor paper. The "angel" was greeted with enthusiasm. The Anthracite Miners' Union, an independent organization then at war with the United Mine

Workers of America—was indebted to Jennings not only for his moral support and journalistic outpourings, but likewise in bills for printing. And Jennings was broke. Jennings thereafter met McHale on several occasions at the Hotel Sterling, sometimes visiting him in his room.

When Jennings was arrested, he demanded the charge. Assistant District Attorney Dando offered to release Jennings if he would reveal his business with McHale. Jennings said it concerned printing but would not go into details. He said his relations with a customer were as confidential as those between lawyer and client. Jennings suffers from a disease which I would call "constitutionalitis"—in fact, "ubiquitous constitutionalitis." He knew his rights. He was taken to jail without a warrant, given no food, not allowed to communicate with his wife or lawyer, but he stood firm.

The next day Jennings was held by the court in $15,000 bail on the story of Gerald Williams. Williams, who described himself as an unemployed resident of New York, said that in the early part of March he had come from New York to see Jennings at the suggestion of Al Romano, a theatrical agent; that Jennings had offered him $300 to bomb Judge Valentine's automobile; that he had refused. He stated that a few weeks later he had read in the papers that the car had been bombed; that he had returned to Wilkes-Barre; that Jennings then told him that someone else had been found to do the job. Jennings on two occasions had given him $150 to keep his mouth shut and on the night of the arrest Jennings was to give him $100 more. Williams testified he had never been in the vicinity before and had never met McHale; and that he had told his story for the first time to Thomas Lewis, District Attorney of Luzerne County, a few hours before he took the stand.

Jennings had $100 in his pocket when he was arrested.

Jennings was held. Released on bail, he went to New York to look up Romano. The theatrical agent was a stranger to Jennings but his telephone number had been given to Jennings by McHale, as a place where he could be reached. Jennings felt he should do something for his friend McHale, who had been so unjustly accused. To Jennings' astonishment, Romano had never heard of either Williams or McHale. This was really not surprising in view of subsequent developments.

In 1934, one Thomas Lynott was a bootlegger. In 1935 he was a private detective doing work for the D. L. & W. Railroad, a company with large interests in the Glen Alden Coal Mines, where the Anthracite Miners' strike occurred. Early in June, Gomer Morgan, attorney for the D. L. & W. Railroad, took Lynott to see Judge Valentine, intimating that Lynott had information about the bombing. Lynott was placed on the Luzerne County payroll to assist County Detective Leo Grohowski, who had been assigned to the case. Lynott adopted the name McHale and set to work. He had a friend in Scranton named Fred

Buchner; they had worked together on the D. L. & W. many years before. Buchner was out of work. He could pick up some easy money merely by telling a story in court which Lynott would supply. Buchner was Gerald Williams.

Obviously the arrests of "Williams" (who was Buchner) and "McHale" (who was Lynott) were merely a blind on the part of the District Attorney.

The other defendant, Harris, was arraigned before Alderman Brown, held for the Grand Jury, and later indicted. Evidence against him consisted of the testimony of Mary Valentine and a friend who said he looked like a man who had appeared to be following them on several occasions. Mary Valentine said she thought she had seen him shortly after the bombing but "I am not sure." Further, there was the testimony of a taxicab driver from New York, Jack Isler, who said that on March 4th, 1935 he had seen Jennings and Harris together in New York, where they had picked up his car in front of Romano's office.

Here, then, is the cast of characters in the case against Emerson Jennings:

Judge Valentine, grey-haired, austere in appearance. Reputedly learned in the law. Regarded by striking miners as their enemy.

Thomas Lewis, District Attorney of Luzerne County, small in stature, slight, wiry, aggressive, ferret-like. The type of prosecutor who has a ready ear for any story tending to fasten guilt upon an underprivileged accused.

Thomas Lynott, alias Thomas McHale, detective employed
by the D. L. & W. Railroad, which controls the Glen
Alden Mines where the Anthracite Miners' strike occurred. A heavily-muscled man, thick-set, arrogant in
his demeanor, sneering, loud-mouthed and venal.
Looks like a beef-slinger in the stockyards.

Leo Grohowski, County Detective, looks like a worried
hippopotamus, bulky and stupid, easy-going, who will
play any game according to the rules dictated by his
immediate superior—if he understands them.

Fred Buchner, alias Gerald Williams, former railroad
worker and one-time friend of McHale. His urge
for a steady job and the reëstablishment of his status
would overcome his natural scruples. Gullible and
of weak character. Smooth shaven, popping eyes,
drooping mouth, noticeable Adam's apple, regular
features, slender, looks taller than he is, neatly but
shabbily dressed. Quiet voice and demeanor. Comes
of good stock.

Jack Isler, New York taxicab driver, a little man "on the
make," anxious for easy money—but there's a limit.
Timid by disposition.

Charles Harris, tramp waiter, deep-set eyes, thin brown
hair, face of prison pallor, voice low, manner deliberate and dispassionate; attitude hopeless, almost
indifferent; easily influenced; friendless, a human der-
elict. Known to Lynott for many years.

The case was set for trial for September 30th. A
few days before, we of the defense were appalled to
hear that Harris had pleaded guilty of having con-

spired with Jennings to bomb Judge Valentine's automobile. We were unduly troubled, however, because after his plea Harris, with Buchner, had been taken to lunch at the Jade Inn by Grohowski. Left alone for a few hours, Harris just walked out of Luzerne County. He later stated that it was his understanding that his absence would be quite agreeable to the prosecution as the situation seemed rather "messed up." Harris was right about this. The defense had learned that not only Buchner but Harris as well had been acquainted with Lynott for years. After all, it seemed strange for a detective to find as his chief witnesses an old-time friend and a former acquaintance. One would expect a detective to do more than this to earn his money—and the County was paying Lynott $15 a day and expenses.

Jennings pressed for trial. He insisted on his constitutional guarantee of a speedy trial, but to no avail. A new district attorney, Leon Schwartz, was elected as a successor to Lewis. He moved to *nolle prosse* the indictment. The court ignored the motion.

Almost a year passed. Then in August, 1936, Harris was arrested in Hornell, New York, where he had been living peacefully and unworried. Apparently an indictment hanging over Jennings' head was all that was wanted. That would keep him quiet. But Jennings didn't keep quiet.* When Harris was told by the arresting officer that he was held for Wilkes-Barre,

---

* On one occasion, on a motion before Judge Jones of Luzerne County, the Court remarked that Jennings would have been better off if he had "let sleeping dogs lie."

he responded that that was the last place in the world
where he was wanted.

Brought back, Harris denied his guilt and repudi-
ated two confessions he had made, which on their face
were so contradictory as to show internal evidence of
manufacture. He told an amazing story of his connection with the case against Jennings.

He had known Lynott for about eight years. One
day in late June, 1935, Lynott had met him on the
street in Wilkes-Barre and "took him for a meal in the
Belmont Restaurant." In July he met Lynott again,
had a shower bath in Lynott's room at the Hotel
Sterling. Lynott had arranged for him to come to the
hotel on the evening of August 2nd, saying that he
was going to have a man there who was "queer," who
would be good for a "shakedown." Harris came, met
Jennings for the first time and was arrested. Penni-
less, friendless, lawyerless, in jail, he withstood for a
time the insistence of Lynott and Grohowski that he
tell a story implicating Jennings in the Valentine
bombing. The two detectives told Harris that many
persons brought to the jail had identified him as a
man seen in the neighborhood of the High School where
the car was parked that day, or later near the place
where the bombing occurred. They told Harris they
had "plenty" on Jennings to send him away for ten
years; that if Harris would "play ball" with them and
plead guilty, he would get a sentence of only sixty or
ninety days or else. . . . Harris sent for one lawyer,
who was not interested in the case. Another asked for

a fee of $5000. Harris sought the advice of a priest who, sent by Lynott or Grohowski, offered neither help nor advice. Finally, Harris weakened. He was brought to the office of the District Attorney. The day was Friday, the 13th of September. Harris said he was superstitious and would not plead on that day. He was then taken to the Jade Inn for lunch. For the next few days Harris was royally treated, taken to lunch, brought to a house of prostitution on occasion (this was not denied), given a trip to New York presumably to find Romano. In New York he and Grohowski went to the theatre—two shows in one evening. He was left at Bear Creek one night in a cabin with Buchner so that they might rehearse and reconcile their stories.

In the meantime Lynott helped with the confessions. There were several puzzling questions. Where and how did Harris first meet Jennings and where did Romano fit in? Confession No. 1 reads: "I first met Jennings at a lunchroom in Scranton." It then appeared that Jennings took him to New York where he met Romano. This apparently was not wholly satisfactory for Confession No. 2 reads:

"The early part of January I met Al Romano at Block's Restaurant at Scranton, Pennsylvania. I was not working at that time. I asked Romano if he could get me a job in NYC. He told me to come down and see him. I went to see him the last of Jan. or the first of Feb. While I was in Romano's office (in New York City) he introduced me to Mr. Jennings."

As this rather unimaginative crowd tried to improve upon the first draft, they became more and more befuddled.

Finally came the plea of guilt. True, Harris was asked by the Court whether he knew what he was doing and he answered "yes". On the trial, on cross-examination, he was asked why he did not tell the story to the Court, to which, in a hopeless tone of voice he responded, "Why didn't I!" Lewis asked, "Didn't you admit your guilt to me?" Harris replied, "First I told you that I didn't know whether to plead guilty or not. But you said I would have to make up my mind. Then Grohowski and Lynott came into the room. You had then left and they said to me, 'You can't talk that way to a district attorney.'" "Didn't you know," queried Lewis, "that these men couldn't promise you a light sentence, that even the district attorney would have nothing to say about it?" To which Harris answered, "I thought Tom Lewis would have a good deal to say."

So, having pleaded guilty, Harris was again taken to lunch at Jade Inn, whence he walked out of the picture.

Harris was permitted to change his plea. The case against him and Jennings was set for trial.

Leon Schwartz, the new District Attorney, sent an assistant to New York to interview Romano and Isler, the taxi driver. Romano stated that he knew none of the people involved, did not know why his name was mentioned unless someone had "picked it out of the air." Romano advertised on the radio. Jack Isler had a more interesting story. He had come to Wilkes-Barre at the request of Lynott who had picked up his taxi in New York. On the first meeting, Lynott had bought him a few glasses of beer; had told him that he had a couple of "Communists" in Wilkes-Barre whom he wished to have deported. He asked Isler to identify these men as persons he had seen together in New York. Lynott offered him $1,000 for this favor. Tempted, Isler came to Wilkes-Barre, was coached by Lynott, and received $25 for his services in addition to $5 paid by District Attorney Lewis. Later that day he read in the Wilkes-Barre papers that the case involved not the deportation of aliens but the bombing of an automobile. When Isler was later brought back to testify before the Grand jury, he refused to "play ball." Perhaps he was influenced by the fact that he didn't get the $1,000.

Having learned these facts, Schwartz refused to prosecute the case. Application was made to the Attorney General of the State, Charles Margiotti, to appoint a special prosecutor. Margiotti has a reputation for fairness and has been regarded as a "liberal." Nevertheless, and against our protestations, he appointed as special prosecutor Tom Lewis, who as District Attorney had initiated the case. Michael McDonald was his assistant. The defense of Jennings was handled by Arthur Sullivan, lawyer of Wilkes-Barre, and myself, serving at the request of the American Civil Liberties Union. Harris was represented by Ernest Herskovitz. Judge Samuel E. Shull was called from another county to preside over the trial which began on October 6th.

Personally I was surprised that the prosecution would proceed. The frame-up was too obvious. The depositions of Romano and Isler had been taken; Harris was prepared to tell his story; Chief Assistant District Attorney Dando had committed himself in writing to the effect that he had told Jennings on the night of his arrest that if he would explain his dealings with McHale (Lynott), he would let him go; Grohowski had testified in preliminary hearings that he had "nothing on Jennings" when he was arrested except that he had seen him with Lynott; and Lynott had testified, on the hearings on Harris' application to change his plea, that he had informed Grohowski each day of the evidence he had acquired. Apparently, it was admitted that there was no evidence before the arrest. This relieved us. At the time of the original arrest, word had emanated from Tom Lewis' office that conversations in Lynott's room in the Hotel Sterling had been heard on a dictograph machine and that the records were incriminating.

Tom Lewis was not easily discouraged. He apparently felt he could rely upon a Luzerne County jury where the issue was drawn between a poor printer on the one side and the courts and prosecutor's office on the other. I noted that Jennings and the lawyers of Luzerne County did not share my optimism.

In opening the case to the jury the statement was made that Williams (Buchner) would take the stand, but after three days of trial the prosecution released him from subpoena and the defense was unable to find him.

Surprisingly to us, the prosecution did have witnesses. Mr. Lewis was lucky. Many of them turned up during the trial and testified that over a year and a half before they had seen Jennings with Harris; on one occasion Jennings and Harris were with Williams; that they had seen Jennings or Harris near the High School or bank on the afternoon of the bombing. Some of the witnesses were bosom friends of Grohowski. Many of them, having seen the story in the newspapers, volunteered their bit. They were surprise witnesses—not only to me, but apparently to Lewis. There were the confessions of Harris—not binding on Jennings, it is true, but having their effect. There was a witness from the jail, Andrew Deshesky, once a cellmate of Harris', sentenced for rape by Judge Valentine. He testified that Harris had once told him he had been "paid to put the bomb in Judge Valentine's car." He was one of Luzerne County's own prisoners! Certainly no one could question his veracity! He testified not in the hope of having his sentence curtailed, but wholly out of a sense of civic duty. Then there was Lynott!

Mr. Lewis had his dictograph records, but they had been run off so often that they had become unintelligible and no longer "dicked". Mr. Lewis expressed his regret that no one in the District Attorney's office had made a transcript of the records when they were fresh. Neither Mr. Lewis, the District Attorney, nor his first Assistant, Dando, nor Grohowski, nor Lynott had ever heard the records played! Who had? What were they for?

Stenographers from the District Attorney's office had listened to the conversations over earphones. When the defense asked for the stenographers' notes, Mr. Lewis stated in open court that he had asked the stenographers who told him that "they had not transcribed their notes because they had nothing tangible and nothing coherent to place on any transcript."

Therefore, Mr. Lewis called two witnesses, Marvin and Weiss, whom he had not met until the very day they took the stand. It seemed to us that as District Attorney he had been a little careless in not having examined these witnesses before. But it really didn't make any difference. These men had supplied the dictograph machine. Thomas was once called to repair it and it just happened that in the hour he was there, he saw Jennings and Lynott go into the next room (number 60) of the Sterling Hotel. The machine wasn't working so he put the earphones to his ears and at that very moment heard Jennings say, "We want Valentine out of the way". Then, surprisingly enough, he listened no more. Mr. Weiss did even better. He heard a lot of conversation about three "grand" and Judge Valentine. The three "grand" might have been talk of $3,000 to start a labor paper and the derogatory references to Judge Valentine might have referred to his actions as Judge, or might have concerned the impeachment proceedings. But the witness did not hear this.

Some of the witnesses who claimed to have seen Jennings or Harris some time in March, 1935, at places which might connect them with the bombing, or who claimed to have seen them together, or with Williams, were apparently honest but mistaken. They were "identification" witnesses, testifying wholly from memory. At the time they had told the story to nobody. After the event, their memories were refreshed; they saw the pictures of Harris and Jennings in the papers; they read about the case.

Let us consider for a moment the philosophy of identification. Human beings have many characteristics. If one says he saw a man or a woman, that means nothing. Of all the millions of people on earth, the number is divided by two. Next, suppose the witness says that the person he saw had two arms or two legs. That would mean nothing; that is applicable to the entire human race. Suppose he says that the person had brown hair—that might divide mankind by four or five. Suppose the person were about five feet seven or eight inches in height—that would give us another opportunity for subdivision. If the person had a sharp nose or brown eyes or curious ears—again we divide the group. But if you take ten characteristics and the witness remembers seven of them but doesn't remember the other three, that doesn't prove that the person in question is the man. If that person hasn't the other three, it proves he isn't the man. And if the memory of the witness concerns characteristics that are applicable to millions of people, to wit; height, weight, color of hair, the identification means nothing at all.

Mary Valentine testified that she saw Harris imme-

diately after the bombing and that she had seen him
watching her on other occasions. At the first hearing
she had said, "He resembles the person who followed
me the day the car was dynamited, but I don't say he
is." Her friend, Martha Bellas, testified she had seen
Harris before. At the first hearing she had said, "His
face is quite familiar, I *thought* I had seen him before."

But how does the human mind work? The witness
may be doubtful at first. Then his mind fixes upon a
picture he has seen in the newspapers; then the person
in question is in the mind's eye and then the witness is
sure—oh, so sure,—that that is the person he saw on a
particular date. He may not remember anyone else
he saw on that day, he may not remember anything
else that happened that month. But a thoroughly
honest witness is unshaken in identification when once
a picture gets into his head.

There were other witnesses of the same kind. One
man, Floyd Seeley, was sure he had seen Harris in the
neighborhood of the High School two days before the
bombing, March 26th, while he was at work on Dr.
Northrup's lawn across the way. He fixes the date
because he knew it was not on a day when he was "roll-
ing" the lawn but on a date when he was "seeding" the
lawn and his notes showed he "seeded" the lawn on
March 26th.

Few of these witnesses were able to describe Harris'
clothes. Those who did credited Harris with a large
wardrobe—because most of them differed. Several of
them testified as to the hat Harris had worn. Yet
Harris swore on the stand that he had not worn a hat

for two years for the reason that a doctor had advised him that the air was a good cure for falling hair. Can there be any doubt that this statement of Harris' was true? Harris had lived in Scranton and Wilkes-Barre all of those two years. No friend or acquaintance of Harris was called to the stand to testify that he had ever seen Harris wearing a hat. Needless to say, in the hands of the zealous prosecutor, there would have been witnesses to this if Harris was not telling the truth.

We find this same kind of testimony in practically every "framed" case. Identification testimony! The record of the case of Sacco and Vanzetti, of Mooney and Billings, and others show a hodge-podge of viciously false or honest but mistaken testimony.

Then there was Lynott! Here is his story: He had called on Jennings at his office; introducing himself with a card bearing a telephone number and saying, "I'm on the lam out of New York—I'm hot and I heard you were OK." He wanted the jury to believe that he regarded Jennings and treated him as one of the underworld. From the time of the first meeting, he said, Jennings plotted with him to blow up the automobile of Judge Valentine—preferably with the Judge or some member of his family in it. There was "three grand" in it for Lynott. Jennings admitted to Lynott that he had tried once before to harm the Judge or his family, but the boy "he had hired had failed to get near the Judge." He had never talked to Jennings about a labor paper. When confused about the lies

with which he claimed he fed Jennings, Lynott explained
to us that he was "no angel."

The Jennings defense was clear. He knew nothing
of the bombing, was in his shop all day. With others,
he had heard the explosion which took place a few
blocks from his shop. His dealings with McHale
(Lynott) concerned a labor paper. The $100 in his
pocket at the time of his arrest was mostly an accumulated payroll for his shop. His books showed that
no bank deposit had been made for several days. He
had never met Harris or Williams (Buchner) before
his arrest. Jennings did not like Judge Valentine,
thought him a tyrant; had tried to have him impeached.
He and other judges of Luzerne County deserved it.
He knew nothing about dynamite (nor was any found
or even looked for on his premises). How simple!
How bare!

Mrs. Jennings, a woman of refinement, with a year of
college education, with a musical background, worked
in the shop with Jennings the day of the explosion.
She and all the men in the shop testified from the records of the work they were doing on March 28th, and
made it clear, that Jennings was not—could not—have
been absent for more than a few minutes without at-
tracting their attention. This contradicted the theory
of the prosecution that he had gone to the High School
with Harris who had there placed the bomb in the
Valentine car. There were witnesses to whom Jennings
had spoken about the labor paper and from whom he
had obtained prices for the estimates which he said he
had given to Lynott.

Evidence of the frame-up was given. Isler's deposition in which he admitted he had told a false story, at the instigation of Lynott and Grohowski, was introduced in evidence. Isler had said that he had seen Jennings with Harris in New York on March 4th and had refreshed his recollection of the date from a taxi card. Jennings had actually been in court before Judge Valentine on that date! We called for the record of the hearing where Isler had testified. It was produced. The card was there. It bore the date of March 7th (not of March 4th). The card had been in the District Attorney's office since the hearing.

We showed that Lynott was paid $1,890 for his work plus $325 for expenses, the latter amount showing no itemization. Some of the money due Lynott was paid by the County by check, payable to Leo Grohowski. Harris told his story of the confessions and the plea of guilt. The absence of Williams (Buchner) who had disappeared after three days in court as a prosecution witness, spoke volumes. Each session of the court began with the bailiff bellowing to the unresponsive corridors, "Gerald Williams—Fred Buchner." Evidence of the defense showed how the case was framed, circumstantially and in detail.

We received considerable help from the liberal rulings of the presiding Judge. It is rare that one has the opportunity to present the facts of a frame-up to the jury. Usually they come to light after the trial.

Flooded with local publicity, the trial lasted two weeks, with evening and Saturday sessions. The jury retired late Saturday night. We felt they would not be long in reaching a verdict of acquittal. After a few hours the bailiff said we would not have to wait much longer as the jury were about ready to report. Shortly, he announced, they were going to their hotel, to resume deliberations in the morning. We were not worried. The case was too clear.

Judge Shull, Tom Lewis and myself met at the hotel. Judge Shull said he would instruct District Attorney Schwartz to be in court so that he would be prepared to initiate action against those who framed Jennings, adding in a reassuring manner, "if the verdict justifies this." The suggestion left no doubt as to his thought.

We of the defense slept well that night and returned to court at nine o'clock on Sunday morning. We had not long to wait. The jury filed in. The foreman passed a paper to the Judge. His shocked expression as well as the solemn faces of the jurors was explained by the announcement—

"Guilty!"

I expected Judge Shull immediately to set aside the verdict. He didn't. He complimented the jurors. Later I asked whether this meant he had prejudged a motion for a new trial. "Not at all," said Judge Shull. "I have an open mind." He waited for hours for us to arrange bail for Jennings. This was no simple task on a Sunday. The amount fixed was $30,000, but many friends, poor people, came forward with small amounts and Jennings was freed.

Was Jennings downcast? Not a bit. He was shocked but not surprised. No longer could we blame him for saying that he couldn't get a fair trial in

Luzerne County. The verdict to him justified his cas-
tigations of the "courthouse crowd." He vociferously
demanded that we charge everybody involved with
conspiracy to frame an innocent man. The verdict
against him proved their guilt.

The calm acceptance of the verdict by Judge Shull
after his first obvious surprise, seemed quite inexplicable, but I awaited with confidence the result of a motion to set aside the verdict and for a new trial.

Francis Biddle of Philadelphia, always ready to help
in a just cause, joined us as counsel for Jennings.
Dudley Field Malone, ever champion of the unfortunate, chose to come to the assistance of Harris. He
wrote me:

" . . . This poor devil Harris never seems to have had a
decent chance in all his life. His father died when he
was a boy, and he has been kicked around the world ever
since. Harris has never criticised or tried to impeach
judges, nor fought battles against persons in high places.
He is to me just a poor, forlorn, lonely, utterly friendless
victim of fraud and fate. Harris has not even got the
consolation of that measure of public sympathy that is
given to Jennings for fighting these long years for the
underdog."

The newspapers of Pennsylvania became interested.
Paul Block, aroused by the injustice, designated a reporter from his "Post Gazette" of Pittsburgh, to investigate. David J. Stern, already engaged in a crusade to inquire into conditions in the State Courts, sent
a man from his "Philadelphia Record." The frame-up
was emblazoned on the front pages of these papers.

How could the jury have convicted Jennings? The explanation is simple: Jennings had tried to have a Judge impeached; he had attacked the courts of Luzerne County. During the trial, most of the judges had been called as witnesses. Jennings, outraged by the delay in trial, had sent a telegram to the Governor of the State, in which he spared no words of condemnation of the Luzerne County judiciary. He had even referred to them as running a "murder-mill." It is true he had crossed these words out, but he had not troubled to rewrite the telegram. The admission of this telegram into evidence enabled the defense to show Jennings' state of mind at the time. We sought to prove that District Attorney Schwartz had moved to *nolle prosse* the indictment. The Clerk's file did not contain the motion papers. The court record contained no notation of the motion. We called one judge after another to prove that the motion had been made. No one remembered. Judge Jones admitted that he had a vague memory of some such motion, but did not know the detailed facts or whether it had occurred before or after the date of the telegram—May 30th. He did not remember whether at the time the weather was warm or cold, whether it was winter or summer. Finally, a newspaper, which Jennings had read, showed that the motion was made before Judge Jones in February.

Lynott had been put on the County payroll at the request of the judges. They had approved his salary and expense account.

This array of judges and the content of the case,

made the issue clear. Jennings was a nuisance to the
"respectable" and "respected" members of the community. We had pointed out in summation that many of
the great characters in history were nuisances in their
time.

In Luzerne County jurors are named by the judges.

The jurors lived in the community. Far be it from
them to fail to show their loyalty to the men and institutions under attack! Jennings versus Valentine,
versus the Judges, versus the District Attorney, versus
the Coal Companies, the Railroads, the Water Company! And, as Lewis said, "Jennings didn't like Judge
Valentine. Who did the bombing if he didn't? Men
of Luzerne County"—and he might have said "women,"
there was one in the jury—"if you convict this man,
little children will rise up and call you blessed." Naturally, everyone on the jury wanted little children to
rise up and call him blessed.

Evidence was taken before Judge Shull on the motion
for a new trial on January 15th and 16th, 1937.

Buchner, who had returned home to Scranton after
the trial, was our first witness.

He was persuaded by his mother and brother to tell
the truth even though this might lead to a charge of
perjury. The story he had told on Jennings' original
hearing and before the Grand Jury had been concocted
by Lynott. It had been arranged that Buchner should
be present in the hotel room and submit to arrest on
August 2nd, but he had a change of heart. On the

morning of August 3rd a taxi driver had come to his
house, had given a message that his friend, Lynott,
wanted to see him at the railroad station. The call of
the driver was confirmed by Buchner's mother and by
his brother, Ralph. At the station Buchner met
Lynott and Grohowski. Lynott gave him $100. Buch-
ner went to Wilkes-Barre and testified.*

Two days later, on August 5th, Buchner went to the
Wilkes-Barre Barracks with Grohowski. For some un-
accountable reason he was then charged with complicity in the bombing. He was held at the Barracks
for a few days. The charge was dropped. Then he
was again arrested, charged (on his own story) with
having extorted money from Jennings. A cousin, Karl
Weber, went bail for him. The bond was later found
to be insufficient so he was again taken to jail. This
time Grohowski found bail for him, but only after he
had spent some time behind the bars. It began to dawn
on Buchner that he was double-crossed. Finally, released, he gave Lynott a "licking".

When the case was set for trial in October, 1936,
Buchner had been subpoenaed as a witness by the prosecution. Grohowski had called to see him. Buchner
was reluctant to testify. Then Grohowski, in the
presence of Ralph Buchner, a brother, gave Fred a
written note that if he would testify, the case against

---

* Grohowski had said that he had picked up Buchner in Wilkes-
Barre at an early hour of August 3rd. The evidence showed that
Grohowski not only did not arrest Buchner but after the hearing
drove him back to Scranton. Yet, on that first hearing he, as
well as Lynott, had heard Buchner testify that he lived in New
York; that his real name was Gerald Williams and that he had
never seen Lynott before.

him would be dropped and he would get back his job on the D. L. & W. Railroad. Buchner gave the note to his cousin, Karl Weber. On this written promise of Grohowski, Buchner had come to court. After watching the progress of the trial he decided that if he was called he would tell the truth; he communicated this to Arthur Sullivan, of defense counsel. The prosecution, learning somehow that Buchner had been in contact with Sullivan, released him from subpoena and the County Constable gave him $25 to stay out of the way. (This was undenied.) Buchner then skipped.

Ralph Buchner (Fred's brother) confirmed the written promise of Grohowski.

Karl Weber, called to the stand, refused to produce the note or to testify on the ground that he might incriminate himself. In fact, he refused to answer any questions whatever. "How do you know your answer might incriminate you before you hear the question?" I asked.

Grohowski was the next witness. He testified that he had arrested Buchner in Wilkes-Barre in the early morning of August 3rd.

"Mr. Hays: Mr. Grohowski, which jail was it?

Mr. Grohowski: I don't remember now.

Mr. Hays: We have looked up all the jail records and can find none which says Buchner was there before August 5th. What did you do with him?

Mr. Grohowski: I don't know. I'm sure I put him in jail somewhere. * * *

Mr. Hays: Grohowski, you refresh your recollection

from the jail officers and see if you can find out for us what jail you put Buchner in."

The following day.

"Mr. Hays: Mr. Grohowski, now do you know where you put Buchner when you arrested him on August 3rd?

Mr. Grohowski: Yes, sir.

Mr. Hays: What did you use to refresh your memory?

Mr. Grohowski: Well, I just thought it over.

Mr. Hays: In other words you used your memory to refresh your memory?

Mr. Grohowski: And after thinking it over I remembered it wasn't no jail. I drove him home.

Mr. Hays: Is that customary—to drive a dangerous criminal to his home after he's been arrested for dynamiting?

Mr. Grohowski: Well, I used my discretion—that's my method. I use 'molasses'."

Grohowski admitted having taken Harris and Buchner to Bear Creek to spend the night. He thought it well to earn the good will of prisoners by feeding them "molasses," and poor Harris, in jail, had asked leave to spend a night in the open air. Grohowski said he had once given Buchner's mother $50. That also was "molasses." Grohowski admitted having testified at one hearing that, when Jennings was arrested, he had "nothing" on him except that he had seen him with Lynott on a few occasions.

"Q. Was that true? A. I want to explain.

"Q. Answer my question first. Was that true? A. No.

"Q. Now explain. A. I didn't want to tell the defense all that I knew."

Poor, lumbering, stupid Grohowski! He was held by the Court for perjury. That was many months ago. Grohowski was released on bail. The case against him has not been pressed.*

There were other pleasant surprises in store for us. Despite Tom Lewis' statement at the trial that the stenographers had said that notes of the conversations in Lynott's Room 60, heard over the dictograph were "incoherent," we subpoenaed McHale** and Yeisley, the court stenographers. Their notes were most illuminating. Lynott's statements were not derived from memory but from written record:

July 24th:

Lynott (to someone in his room)—"How does Jennings look to you? Easy shakedown?"

Answer—"Yes I think so—What the hell!"

July 26th (afternoon):

Lynott—"We are going to put the case down on Mr. Jennings. * * * Here is his number, 20411, that's right, ain't it?"

After talking to Jennings over the telephone:

Lynott—"You know that is the fellow we want to get, see?"

The minutes of Monday, July 29th, and August 2nd, are fairly complete. What did these notes reveal? That someone in Room 60 (Lynott's room) at the

* Buchner was also held for perjury by the Court. After the hearing a charge of perjury was made by us against Lynott. None of these charges has been pressed by the authorities of Luzerne County.

** This, of course, is another McHale, possibly the source of Lynot's pseudonym.

Sterling Hotel spent twenty pages at least talking
about the Constitution, the rights of men, the crook-
edness of judges, the importance of a labor paper.
Lynott had said his business with Jennings concerned
only a proposal of Jennings that he get rid of Valentine; that they had never discussed a labor paper.

These minutes stamp Lynott's testimony as a pure
fabrication. They show that Jennings' statements of
his business and conversations with Lynott were true.

When this came to light Francis Biddle returned
to Lewis:

"Will you now consent to a new trial?"

"No," barked Lewis.

Yet the Pennsylvania Supreme Court said in *Commonwealth v. Nicely*, 130 Pa. 261, 270.

"The District Attorney is a quasi judicial officer. He
represents the Commonwealth and the Commonwealth demands no victims. It seeks justice only, equal and impartial practice, and it is as much the duty of the District
Attorney *to see that no innocent man suffers* as it is to see
that no guilty man escapes. Hence he should act im-
partially. He should present the Commonwealth's case
fairly, and should not press upon the jury any deductions
from the evidence that are not strictly legitimate."

One unexpected witness, disinterested and reluctant
to testify, furnished a small item of evidence which,
on analysis, should be sufficient to blast the whole case.
It concerned a relatively insignificant circumstance.
Buchner had originally testified that Al Romano of
New York had sent him to Jennings. When Lynott
had first met Jennings, he had given him Romano's

telephone number for the reason, according to Lynott, that this number (known to Jennings) would serve as a password of introduction. Jennings had testified that it was given him as a place he could reach McHale (Lynott). On the trial Lynott testified:

"Q. You learned Romano's name from Buchner? A. Yes."

Our witness, Hein, testified that a year before the bombing, Lynott, in connection with some business deal, had given him a New York telephone number with a central of "Longacre," or something like that. This identified Romano's number.

The hearings ended with the testimony of Jay Fuller and Miss Keating to the effect that they saw two young men tampering with the Valentine car just before the explosion.

The case was submitted to Judge Shull. The record was full and complete. The first to tell the truth was Isler, when inquiry was made by District Attorney Schwartz; later came his deposition. Next Harris was caught and brought back to Wilkes-Barre. For months he had been free from the influence of Grohowski and Lynott. He realized he had been double-crossed. He admitted his story was manufactured. Finally, Buchner was unable to stand the strain. After the trial, when perhaps for the first time (Jennings having been found guilty) he realized the enormity of this plot, he took the witness stand and, at great risk to himself, even in the face of warning by Judge Shull that he was convicting himself of perjury,

he followed the advice of his family and provided the
missing parts of this picture puzzle. These three men
were the tools. Having taken the first step at the instigation of Lynott, they felt themselves caught in a
net. Whether because each had a spark of decency, or
whether self-preservation indicated that truth was the
safer course, they at least deserve some consideration
for having tried to save an innocent man from going to
jail.

When one of those engaged in a conspiracy gives
way, the force of circumstances gradually undermines
one after another. Grohowski was caught in a tangle
of contradictions until finally this sodden, bulky mass
of flesh, confessed to perjury. And why did he commit this crime? Admittedly, to help the prosecution.

Finally comes Lynott. Contemptuous, brazen and
foul, he was caught by his own absurdities and the ad-
missions of his co-conspirators. Even Mr. Lewis referred to him as a "slimy worm."

We waited calmly and comfortably for the decision
on our motion for a new trial. Every once in a while
someone brings me a note of introduction from Clarence Darrow. It always reads the same: "Dear Art,
here's one of our kind." I felt this applied to our
amiable and liberal Judge. His rulings were almost
invariably in our favor. He seemed zealous to have
the truth revealed. He had held Grohowski and Buchner in bail for perjury. It is true that Jennings had
at one time publicly made statements derogatory to
him (as to practically all judges), but Judge Shull,

friendly to Jennings as to everyone else, once said to him, "Emerson, you know that doesn't make any difference to me."

I knew that some of our evidence on the motion for a new trial was not, technically speaking, "newly discovered evidence". We might have subpoenaed Buchner. But the prosecution said they intended to call him. They did not. When the defense looked for him, the witness had flown. Certainly no judge would penalize the defense because the prosecution had paid a witness to stay out of the way. Likewise, we might have subpoenaed the stenographers as witnesses at the trial, in spite of Lewis' statement in open court that they had told him they had "nothing tangible and nothing coherent to place on any transcript." * We did not call the stenographers because we were misled by Mr. Lewis. Surely no court would disregard evidence where reliance on the prosecutor was the cause of the failure to discover.

No one could gainsay that some of our evidence was newly discovered.

We felt safe with Judge Shull. His reputation, kindliness, liberality, showed that he would have no traffic with injustice.

Judge Shull denied the motion for a new trial.

Sentence—Five to ten years in the State Penitentiary.**

---

* One of the stenographers testified not only that he had not told this to Mr. Lewis, but that he had actually read to Mr. Lewis a substantial part of his notes.
** We have noted that Harris had been warned what to expect if he did not "play ball" with the prosecution.

The "Philadelphia Record" (March 20, 1937) said:

LEGAL LYNCHING IN WILKES-BARRE

If there ever was a case in which legal technicalities should not have been given undue importance, that case was the conviction of Emerson P. Jennings, of Wilkes-Barre.

Nothing but indignant amazement can greet the refusal of Judge Samuel E. Shull to grant a new trial to Jennings and his co-defendant Charles Harris.

Argument on the motion for a new trial bought into the light for the first time the extraordinary circumstances of the case. Jennings was a dissident, a "trouble-maker" in that he published attacks on the powers that be in Luzerne County. But there was absolutely nothing in his past or character that would indicate he was the man who planted a bomb in Judge W. Alfred Valentine's automobile, the crime of which he was convicted.

Nor was there evidence against him, except that which can be described as part of a palpable frame-up. The three men who did most to convict him have, in fact, been arrested for perjury.

They are County Detective Leo Grohowski, who was in charge of the investigation that led to Jennings' arrest; Thomas Lynott, an exbootlegger and "private detective" with an unsavory past, and Gerald Williams, whose story has changed too often for credence.

Judge Shull, in his refusal to grant a new trial, did not deny any part of the evidence against

Grohowski, Lynott and Williams. He did not deny that if the evidence they gave against Jennings is false, then the whole case against Jennings collapses.

His decision was based simply and solely on the ground that the story of the strange dealings of Grohowski, Lynott and Williams was not what the law calls "After discovered evidence." In other words, the frame-up may have been committed, but that should have been brought out at the first trial.

Yet it is precisely Jennings's point that his first trial was unfair. That's why a new trial is asked. Judge Shull says, in effect: "Maybe you were framed, but you should have proved it before. For that little slip you serve your 5-to-10 years' sentence.

Jennings's original "offense" seems to have been calling for the impeachment of Judge Valentine.

Is this another evidence of an unwholesome esprit de corps *among Judges?*

If Judges insist on standing together in cases like this, they needn't be surprised to find they are condemned in toto.

An appeal is pending. Samuel Untermyer has joined the defense. His first act was a letter to Attorney General Margiotti suggesting that the Bar Association of Pennsylvania be requested to investigate the acts of Thomas Lewis in this case, that he be supplanted on appeal by some disinterested lawyer, and that the State consent to a new trial for Harris and Jennings. These requests have gone unanswered, even though Daniels, a special representative of the Attorney-General who attended the hearings on the motion for a new trial, is said to have reported to his chief that the case was a palpable frame-up.

Jennings is free on bail. Harris languishes in the Pennsylvania State Penitentiary.

Some folks say: "It can't happen here."

FREEDOM IN A COLONY

FREEDOM IN A COLONY

What Happened at Ponce, Puerto Rico

PUERTO RICO is an "insular possession." The Governor is appointed by the President of the United States. The Puerto Ricans elect the legislature, consisting of two houses. The Governor has veto power, and tremendous prestige, largely because of the economic dependence of the country on the United States.

There are nearly two million Puerto Ricans, which makes this small island one of the most densely populated places on earth. The economic situation of the great bulk of these people is desperate. Work comes chiefly from the Government of the United States or from large sugar interests, controlled by American absentee-owners.

Socialists, who have become conservative, and Republicans, who have remained conservative, are in control of the legislature. The island seethes with political intrigue and activity.

Few are satisfied with the colonial status and its invidious implications. Many favor statehood. There are groups who seek independence but only on terms which would not destroy the country economically. These realize that there is such a thing as "freedom" to starve, which means slavery. They are skeptical of the enthusiasm with which the large "sugar inter-

411

ests" in the United States support the demand for independence of our sugar growing possessions.

There is one group, favoring independence, small in number, led by a former Harvard graduate, Pedro Albizu Campos.* His followers do not ask for independence. They demand it. They would sacrifice economic stability—in fact, life itself—for political freedom.

The Nationalist Party is composed to a large extent of young men inspired by a fanatical spirit, holding that to die for the freedom of Puerto Rico is a patriot's privilege. They are intemperate. They use militant fighting language; threaten to accomplish their ends by violent revolution. They form groups and committees which parallel the set-up of the present government, using official titles of municipal officers and councils, ministers of state and war. They even designate foreign plenipotentiaries. Some of the Nationalists belong to an "Army of Liberation," in connection with which they teach military technique. The "cadets" of this army wear uniform in parade, consisting of black shirt and white pants, with a small cloth cap cocked on the head in jaunty style. They carry the Puerto Rican, not the American flag, and sing "La Borinquena," not the "Star-Spangled Banner." The government authorities speak of the "Army of Liberation" as though it were a military force. They suggest that unless precaution is taken, the "Army" will use guns. But the "Army" does not use guns; it has no guns.

---

* Campos served as an officer of the U. S. Army in the World War.

It lacks the prime essentials for any kind of army, to wit, numbers and military weapons.

Five members of the Nationalist Party, in the fall of 1935, started on their way to a meeting which students at Puerto Rico University had arranged to protest against certain remarks made by Pedro Albizu Campos, the Nationalist leader.* The story is that their automobile was stopped by the police, that they shot at the police and that, as a result of the fracas, four of the five Nationalists were killed. It was said that they carried bombs and guns.

At the funeral of these men, Albizu Campos referred to them as martyrs who had died at the hands of tyrants, and named Colonel Riggs, head of the insular police, as responsible. He administered an oath to the Nationalists to avenge the death of their companions.

Colonel Riggs, a few months later, walking in a public street in San Juan, the capital, was assassinated by two young Nationalists. The assassins were seized and, while in the custody of the police, were killed within a few hours after their arrest. Colonel Riggs was popular in Puerto Rico and was himself a believer in independence. The cold-blooded murder of the two Puerto Rican "martyrs" aroused not only the Nationalists but great numbers of Puerto Ricans who opposed Nationalist methods. Continental Americans thought of the murder of Colonel Riggs; Puerto Ricans thought of the murder of the two assassins. A

---

* It is said that Campos had referred to the men students as "sissies" and to the girls as light o' loves.

huge demonstration took place at the cemetery when
the Nationalists were buried. Albizu Campos referred
to them as men who had fulfilled their oath of vengeance.

Later, Campos and other Nationalist leaders were
charged with conspiring to overthrow by force the
Government of the United States in Puerto Rico and
in August, 1936, were convicted in the Federal Court
and sentenced to six years in jail at Atlanta. Conspiracy trials in political cases almost always arouse
resentment. So often are men tried, not for what
they do, but for what they "conspire" to do—and this
is proved largely by their speeches and writings.

Governor Blanton Winship apparently felt it was
necessary to deal with the Nationalists with a heavy
hand. Permits were denied for parades and meetings,
not only to those who were militantly demanding
Puerto Rican independence, but also to those who
wished to protest against the conviction of Albizu
Campos. The Puerto Ricans take seriously their
Organic Act guaranteeing the rights of free speech
and assemblage. Resentment grew with repression.

On March 21st, 1937, the Nationalists announced
that they would hold a parade and meeting in Ponce,
Puerto Rico's second city. The Mayor granted a
permit. At the last moment it was cancelled. The insular police, commanded by Colonel Orbeta, acting
under orders of the Governor, ordered the "cadets" not
to parade. All preparations for the important event
had been made. Groups of Nationalists had come
from various towns in the vicinity, bringing along their
wives, mothers, sisters and children. Several hundred

people had gathered on the sidewalks to watch the parade. Colonel Orbeta had concentrated some two hundred heavily-armed police in Ponce. Of these, seventy or eighty were stationed on the streets and corners where the paraders gathered. Having given their orders to stop the parade, the Colonel and Chief of Police left the vicinity.

The young men cadets lined up in parade formation, three abreast. Behind them were girls—dressed as nurses—then the band. Leaders carried the Puerto Rican flag. The insular police took their stations in the front, rear and alongside of the marchers. The "national hymn" of Puerto Rico was played. The crowd cheered. A sub-chief of police warned the leader of the Nationalists. The command "Forward March" was given. The parade moved a step.

Of a sudden there was the sound of a revolver shot. Then another. Then fusillades of shots. Then desultory shooting.

Twenty people were killed. Among them were two police officers. From one hundred and fifty to two hundred were wounded. Among them were six police officers.

Governor Winship reported to Washington:

"Several days ago an announcement was made in the local press that there would be a concentration of the so-called 'Liberating Army' of the Nationalist Party in Ponce on Sunday, March 21, 1937. This announcement was in the form of a military order.

*   *   *

"At 3:30 P.M. the Nationalist band played 'La Borin-quena' at the conclusion of which the command 'Forward March!' was given by the Nationalist column commander, showing that they had determined to carry out their plan for the parade. The local chief of the police then announced in a loud tone of voice that the parade was prohibited. Immediately two shots were fired by the Nationalists, the first shot striking a policeman standing on the left of the chief and the second striking another policeman standing to the right of the chief. A general exchange of shots then took place between the Nationalists and the police, with Nationalists firing from the street, and from roofs and balconies on both sides of the street. This firing lasted for about ten minutes, until the chief of the insular police arrived on the scene and assisted in restoring order. The casualties were ten killed and fifty-eight wounded, including one policeman killed and seven policemen wounded."

The Governor refers to the preliminary efforts made to "prevail upon the leaders not to attempt to carry out their plans" and ends his message:

"From the preliminary investigation it would appear that he (Chief of the Insular Police who was not present at the time) showed great patience, consideration and understanding of the situation, as did the officers and men under him."

The Governor's message suggests a pitched battle.

The people of Ponce proposed that an investigation be made by leading citizens of San Juan. A commission was named, consisting of Emilio Belaval, president of the Athenaeum, a cultural society of San Juan, who acted as secretary; Mariano Acosta Velarde, president of the Puerto Rican Bar Association; Lorenzo Pineiro, president of the Teachers' Association; Dr. Manuel Diaz Garcia, of the Puerto Rican Medical Association; Antonio Avuso, editor of *El Imparcial;* Francisco M. Zeno, editor of the *Correspondencia;* and Davilla-Ricci, assistant editor of the *Mundo.* None of the commission was a Nationalist. Request was made to the American Civil Liberties Union to name the chairman of the commission. I was so appointed and arrived in Puerto Rico on May 13th, 1937.

Before beginning our work we called on Governor Winship, who received us at his San Juan palace with equanimity, but without enthusiasm. He suggested that our investigation await the trial of a number of Nationalists who had been charged with murder. We answered that in a murder case the question might be as to who fired the first shot, and when, and as to whether the defendant had reasonable cause at the time to believe that he was in danger of physical harm. We stated that we were not interested in finding out who fired, and when, but why shots had been fired at all. We informed the Governor that we intended to proceed with our inquiry and hoped for his cooperation. It was a vain hope. There is an old Spanish saying that "He who in a colony defends justice, offends authority."

We started from San Juan for distant Ponce, driving over a quiet countryside past towering mountains, observing on every side the material developments made during American control, but not failing to notice the miserable huts which were the homes of the mass of the people. Although our hearings were scheduled for two-thirty in the afternoon, and it was well after one o'clock, we stopped for lunch. We had about finished when another group of our committee came along. We waited while they ate a leisurely meal. No one seemed troubled by the passage of time. We arrived in Ponce about five o'clock and went to a hotel. Emerging from a shower-bath into my room I felt a certain lack of dignity in being received clad in a towel, by a committee representing some civic organization. I didn't look the part of the American chairman of the "Commission of Enquiry on Civil Rights in Puerto Rico."

We set the opening of our hearings for eight o'clock in the evening. We got under way about nine. In fact, time seemed of little importance in Puerto Rico.

There was evidence as to what had happened at Ponce not only from disinterested witnesses, but from a series of photographs which told the story in incontestable fashion. Observation in a crisis is not wholly reliable. A later memory, even of the most conscientious witness, is colored by sympathy, imagination and self-interest. But here we had only to rely upon our sense of sight.

Two photographers had taken their positions on a balcony diagonally across the way from the National-ist Club, where they had intended to take pictures of the parade. The divisions of the "Army of Liberation" consisted of about eighty young men wearing black blouses and white trousers, about twelve girls dressed in white as nurses, and a brass band of about six pieces.   The cadets carried no arms; the nurses had no first-aid kits.

A photograph showed the scene just before the shooting—about eighteen of the colonial police, armed with revolvers, shotguns and tear gas bombs, in front of the line of the cadets, about twenty policemen armed with Thompson sub-machine guns in the rear, a number of armed police on the street along the side.   A crowd of men, women and children stood across the way.

The evidence showed that there was no shooting whatever from roofs or balconies.   This was confirmed by Perez-Marchand who, as District Attorney, had made the first investigation and who later retired because, according to him, he was not given a free hand in his inquiries.   One of the photographs shows a policeman actually firing at the crowd and other policemen drawing their guns, all in menacing postures. The police who were wounded or killed seem to have been caught in a cross fire.

Jenaro Lugo, messenger of the Mayor of Ponce, a member of the conservative "Union Republican Party," saw the scene from the balcony of a convent directly across from the Nationalist Club.   To that balcony he had gone when the police ordered him off the street apparently for the reason that he was not a Nationalist.   There were two little girls on the balcony, one of them approximately thirteen years old.   This witness had a clear view of the scene.   He pointed out the photograph of the policeman who, he said, had fired the first shot.   Our witness was by no means inactive after the shooting began. He rushed down the steps of the balcony, started in one direction, then turned back. As one of the children reached the street from the balcony, he saw a policeman fire point-blank at her. Her body was riddled with gunshot. Lugo found refuge behind the walls of Dr. Pila's sanitarium, which was the next house. From there he saw the police from the rear, opening fire with the Thompsons on the defenseless crowd.

Another witness, Julio M. Conesa, proprietor of the local radio station, who had left his car at a nearby garage, stood on the balcony of a house overlooking the Thompson gun contingent behind the parade. He saw these police fire into the crowd.

Members of the Rodriguez family, father and three brothers, had come from the town of Mayaguez to Ponce to attend to some business affair. Happening to drive past Nationalist headquarters, they saw that a parade was about to start. They parked their car and walked across the street. Rafael Rodriguez, eighteen years of age, snapped a few pictures with his camera. Suddenly shots were heard. The father and two sons immediately threw themselves on the ground, face downward. There was a volley of shots. Rafael heard his brother gasp "Alas! I . . . ," whereupon the father, apparently hearing this last word, got up to throw himself over his son's body. The father was mortally wounded. Raefel, shot in the right arm, stayed where he was until he was lifted roughly by policemen and hustled into a police wagon.

Others were brought to that wagon. Among them

was a young man who was stretched out on the seat.
Blood was coming from his nose, mouth and other
parts of his body. All Rafael heard, as the man
gasped for breath, was a slow drawn sound like,
"I-am-a-National Guardsman," "I-am-a-National
Guardsman," repeated time and time again until
finally death stopped further repetition. It appeared
from the evidence that this National Guardsman had
not been at the parade but was on his way to his
home in the neighborhood. A policeman, drunk with
blood lust, shot him. He shouted, "I am not a Nationalist—I belong to the National Guard!" The
policeman continued to shoot until his victim was
prostrate.

There is another story connected with the Rodriguez
family. It should be noted that from somewhere, the
source is not hard to guess, the rumor arose that a
civilian had fired the first shot. Perez-Marchand
identified the civilian who was under suspicion. He was
a man, said Perez-Marchand, who had a son among
the Nationalists. The story was that, fearing the
police would harm his son, the father shot at the
police. Why, if he wanted to protect his son, he
should have done any such thing is beyond my comprehension, but that is the story. The identification was
said to have been corroborated by four different witnesses and pointed at Rodriguez, Senior. But
Rafael's father was dead. Said the boy on the witness stand: "I want the truth to vindicate my father.
I want the truth to go to the newspapers, not only
in Puerto Rico, but all over the United States so that

everybody will know that my father was an honored man, and a gentleman."

Other facts conclusively show that Rodriguez, Sr., met his death while engaged in what is ordinarily the innocent pastime of watching a demonstration. The photograph shows that Mr. Rodriguez was in the midst of the crowd of civilians, that a dense group separated him from the police. Yet it is said that the first shot came from this man. Rodriguez was killed but no weapon was found near him on the street; in fact, no weapon was found anywhere on any of the streets.

The Rodriguez family were not Nationalists. We asked the son whether he was a Nationalist now. He answered: "I am not registered, but I think the government has made me one. I would rather fight than be shot down like a dog!"

The father had been a commission merchant in his town. Not only was he ·killed, but another son was killed. The two sons who did not perish in the tragedy work as clerks in stores and support the widowed mother. The gentility of this boy was indicated when I asked what the police had said when they cursed him in the police wagon. The boy answered: "I don't feel I should use the words." I wanted to know exactly what was said. "But," said the boy, "there is a lady present." He afterwards went to our stenographer, "the lady," and apologized for having had to repeat the words with which the police had cursed him and the wounded and dying boy in the police car.

Other witnesses from Mayaguez had harrowing

stories. Julio de Santiago was a leader of the Nationalist Mayaguez Junta. He had brought his wife to
the parade. He was in front of the Nationalist Club
when the shooting started. The rush of the crowd,
fleeing into the club for shelter, threw him to the
ground. There was pandemonium inside, wounded people stretched all over the place. There was no linen;
there were no women to assist; the men did the best
they could. They used their shirts for bandages. A
long time elapsed before an ambulance came. The door
of the Club had been closed as the Nationalists feared
mass murder. Trying to get help for a wounded and
apparently dying woman, they opened the door and
held out a white handkerchief as a flag of truce. They
were met by a fusillade of shots. The building shows
the marks of this volley.

The leader of the girls' club from Mayaguez was
Dominga Cruz Becerril. She told her story in a quiet
but determined manner. I shall never forget her, her
sturdiness and composure at the hearing, her dark,
immobile face, her simplicity—as though the story she
was telling were an every-day occurrence. When the
police in the rear opened fire with the submachine
guns, the girls started to flee. One of them was
wounded. Dominga immediately went to her assistance.
A young cadet came up. Dominga then noticed that
the flag-bearer of the girls' group had fallen. She
went to the middle of the street and raised the flag.
We asked her why. She replied simply: "My master
says we must keep the flag raised." The "master"
was Albizu Campos. Dominga then made her way

into the home of Mr. Mario Mercado, to help the
wounded. Some were in bad shape. There was linen
in a basket. Dominga bandaged wounds. No nurses
of this force, designated as dangerous in reports to
the United States Government, had had "first-aid"
training.

One of the wounded was a girl who still lies in
a hospital in Ponce. She had another story of hero-
ism. This girl, who was in a position of safety, rushed
to the front of the line to help a fallen cadet. Her
abdomen was riddled with small bullets from a shotgun.
She fell back, her legs outstretched, screaming for
mercy. Shotgun bullets are now imbedded in all parts
of both legs. When we saw her, the girl still required
morphine to numb her pain. She cried softly. We
asked her if she had had a gun. She said, "No, but
I wish now I had. I would be in the cemetery, but
I would have killed that policeman."

Think of the self-immolation of the dying boy who,
without using initial or name, wrote in blood on the
wall: "Viva La Republica! Down With The Assassins!"

In front of the convent, opposite the Nationalist
headquarters, a woman was clubbed to death. Her
husband ran over, took her in his arms. Whereupon a
volley of shots was poured into him. He lived for
some days but eventually realized his wish—to die with
his wife. Life had no further hope for him.

In houses down the street panic-stricken men,
women and children had taken refuge. About seventy-
five yards away from the Nationalist Club was the

mutilated body of a man who had smeared the wall with blood. His dying effort was to trace the word "valiente." He succeeded only in writing the letters "v-a-l." Even further away people were wounded. A fruit vendor had his stand on the corner of the Square. When the police passed him, several blocks from the Nationalist Club, one of them opened his skull with a club. The mere fact that people were wounded or clubbed far away from the immediate vicinity shows that the police ran amok.

The people of Ponce have given a properly descriptive title to the tragedy. It is the Ponce massacre.

No one of the eye-witnesses saw anyone on any roof-top or balcony. There were only two houses in the vicinity that had terraced roofs. The homes in the neighborhood are occupied by people of high repute.

It was said by the police they later found weapons in the Nationalist Club. The evidence shows there were no weapons there.

Reports, apparently inspired, stated that scientific tests had proved that at least twenty Nationalists had fired guns. Inquiries showed that reference was made to the much publicized paraffin test. In order to find out whether such a test was reliable, we sought the aid of the head of Puerto Rico's Criminal Investigation Department as an expert. He received instructions not to testify. We explained our predicament to the audience composed, to a large extent, of university teachers. We asked if any of them, chemists or engineers, could give us information about the paraffin tests. Several men arose. One of them, Hector Cruz

Monclova, said if we would give him an hour and a half to look up some references, he could tell us all that was known. He left the hall, later returned. He is an engineer of high distinction, with degrees from American and European universities. Monclova proved a well-informed witness. The paraffin test, at best, merely shows that there are nitrates or nitrites in the skin. This may come from soil, tobacco and a variety of other substances, as well as from gunpowder. Anyone who had been in close proximity to gunpowder might show a positive reaction in such a test. There is no question that many of the wounded were immersed in clouds of gunpowder. Lawyers for the Nationalists were present at some of the tests. Their observations were quite different from those of the official investigators who, incidentally, smoked cigarettes continually during their work, which alone might affect the result. Some of the tests were taken several days after the event, from wounded victims in the hospitals. The paraffin test may show, where the reaction is negative, that one has not fired a gun. Even under the best of circumstances and the most rigid controls, it rarely proves that one did fire a gun.

It was reported to the press that the caliber of bullets were not all of a size used in police guns. The doctors who took the bullets from the bodies of wounded, testified that the bullets were of one of the two calibers used by the police.

The Nationalists admit that they were ordered not to parade, but insisted that they intended to march, relying on their constitutional rights as American citizens.

It has been said that the Nationalists were provocative in attempting to parade. A well known defender of civil liberties once said, "It is the business of radicals to be provocative; it is the business of the police not to be provoked."

To me, the views of the Nationalists are wrong. I do not think anyone gains by violence. In my view the Nationalists believe so firmly and fanatically in their cause, that they will become, even if they are not now, dogmatic and intolerant, so that by force— if they have it—and by intimidation—if they haven't —they will try to make other people conform.

Clarence Darrow once said that if you believe a thing strongly enough and think it important enough, you will send others to the stake to make them conform to your views. The Nationalists instil the virtues of the warrior who is ready to die for his country.* Movements of this kind have the germ of Fascism, whether the leaders intend it or not. They know the way to salvation—there is only one way—their way.

If I were a Nationalist leader and had been notified a few days in advance that a parade was prohibited, I would have called it off. No one without a martyr complex would cause a group of defenseless people to face machine-guns. But if I had arranged a parade and there was an attempt to stop it at the last moment,

* The Nationalists claimed that the R.O.T.C. had the same purpose.

my self-respect would compel me to go through with it. It may be just as irrational, but that's the way we human beings behave. When the issue is drawn we insist upon our rights. If I had led that procession I would have said, "Forward March!"—or, at least, I hope I would.

Albizu Campos is in jail. The Campos type is often put away. It's dangerous to have such men around. Governments will never learn that the most effective place from which to carry on propaganda is a prison cell. Governments are not wise or very practical. Perhaps they think they can deny the prisoner visitors, or keep him from writing to others. But that in itself would make propaganda. Perhaps they think the situation would be helped by sending him to remote exile. Absurd! Every effort to silence a man makes his voice louder. "The blood of the martyr is the seed of the church."

Our opponents call people of "our kind" idealists. They mean we are not practical. Their method is to suppress, to try to stamp out something they do not like. Ponce massacres throughout history have been the result. That method does not work. Even "hard-boiled" realists should understand that the best way to maintain order is to let people alone, unless they break the law by committing an overt act. The realists hate to be called idealistic, but in truth they are. Their ideal is not "order through liberty," but "order through acquiescence." Their ideal is not practical except among slaves.

I shall never forget the photograph of those cadets,

whom the newspapers have described as agitators, ruf-
fians and gangsters, standing quietly with their hands
at their sides, defenseless, but not one of them running away.

Many Nationalists have been indicted for murder.
We examined them in a court room in Ponce adjoining
the jail. They range in age from eighteen to thirty-
five. Some are married, with families; others live
under the parental roof. With two exceptions, they
reside in Ponce. One of the exceptions is a colored boy
of nineteen who said he did not know why he was there,
that he was not a member of the Nationalist Party,
but that he went to Ponce with friends. Neither these
cases, nor those of two policemen, likewise indicted,
have as yet been tried.

The problem of the Nationalists in Puerto Rico cannot be solved by intimidation or repression.

It has been suggested that the Puerto Ricans, of
Spanish origin, are more volatile than other Americans
and that one's views on liberty should be adapted in
such a way as to be "suitable to the climate." The
Ponce massacre is said to be an illustration of Latin
hot-headedness. Here is an editorial from the New
York *Evening Post* of Tuesday, July 13th, 1937.

"LIBERTY IN CHICAGO

"Chicago police killed ten strikers and wounded almost
one hundred more outside one of Girdler's Republic Steel
plants.

"They then arrested forty of the strikers and announced that warrants would be sworn out for the strikers on charges of conspiracy to commit murder.

"Showing of the famous Paramount film of the police attack on the strikers was forbidden in Chicago.

"Twenty policemen last week raided a hall in which the pictures were secretly being shown, arrested those in charge and confiscated the film.

"Yes, we said Chicago, not Milan or Duesseldorf."

And we might add, not Ponce.

Recently I sent a thousand dollars from the Ellen Hayes Fund to start the Puerto Rican Civil Liberties Association. Thousands of miles of ocean separate Boston from San Juan, yet the fight for liberty in Puerto Rico will be promoted indirectly by the "good shoemaker" and the "poor fish peddler."

FREEDOM OF SPEECH, BUT—

FREEDOM OF SPEECH, BUT—

Repressions in Puerto Rico—Jersey City and Labor Under the Frank Hague Regime—The Deportation Case of John Strachey—The Mary Ware Dennett Case and The Sex Side of Life —Teachers' Oaths: Saluting the Flag— Rosika Schwimmer and Other Pacifists—The C.I.O.: Changing Fashions in Repression

Killings and frame-ups are dramatic expressions of the tyranny of majorities. They show the lengths to which authority will on occasion go. They are the tragic consequences of a course of action which denies citizens their rights or which intimidates them, so they do not attempt to exercise their rights.

Rights of free speech and assemblage, and the right to petition, include large gatherings as well as small, and apply in times of stress as well as in normal times. The only important question involves policing and administration. In Puerto Rico, following Spanish custom, an assemblage is usually preceded by a parade or parades, the crowd falling into line and coming from various quarters. The same principles apply here. From time immemorial public streets have been used for parades.

In Puerto Rico meetings of protest at the conviction of Albizu Campos and his associates, or agitational gatherings for independence—meetings not only of Nationalists but of others—were prohibited. The government felt that such meetings might stir up passion. Apparently, it never occurred to the authorities that a denial of rights might arouse more public excitement and indignation than could possibly be aroused by any demonstration.

Many Puerto Ricans felt that if the Nationalist Party leaders had incited the assassination of Colonel Riggs, they should have been charged directly with this crime and tried in the insular courts; that a charge of sedition—with trial in the Federal courts—was both unjustified and inappropriate in a colony to which the administration has virtually offered independence if the people so desire.

A united attempt of various groups in San Juan to obtain an injunction to prevent interference with public meetings was unsuccessful. There was a huge concentration of troops in the town. Even on April 16th, an official holiday in Puerto Rico, known as De Diego's birthday, when the people ordinarily go to church to attend mass and then to the cemetery to pay tribute to De Diego's memory, meetings were prohibited in San Juan. The Cathedral was closed. Insular police were stationed at the cemetery. People were allowed to go to the grave, stop for a moment and then pass on. To the people of Puerto Rico permission to enter a cemetery and, one by one, to lay flowers on the grave of a national hero, does not seem to accord full constitutional right.

The same situation with regard to repression could

be duplicated throughout Puerto Rico, with the exception of one city—Caguas—a town of about fifty thousand people, about twenty-five miles from San Juan.

In spite of repeated efforts of the police, the Mayor of Caguas, Julio Aldrich, insisted upon granting permits for meetings to Nationalists and others. He said: "I know my people. I trust my people."

A letter written by the police officer in charge of the district pointed out that a permit should be denied because it was contemplated that the meeting would "let the public know about the so-called Ponce massacre, for which a permit was denied in Ponce." Other reasons given were that there might be a clash with the police and that the granting of the permit might set a bad precedent since "all Mayors throughout the Island have cancelled all permits given to political organizations which express themselves against the regime by criticizing the Government."

In spite of this pressure, Mayor Aldrich was adamant. The Mayor is a quiet, unassuming man. He showed the Commission his enlistment card in the American Army in the World War. The card bore the number "1," indicating that he was the first volunteer from Caguas. The Mayor believes in Puerto Rican independence, but, said he: "I will defend the Constitution and the American flag as long as we are citizens of the United States."

The proposed meeting was held in Caguas. There was no disorder.

It has been recognized, ever since democracy was established, that free speech and assemblage are a safety valve. Dissenters express their grievances and emotions in this way; they carry on their agitation openly; they rely upon methods of persuasion to further their cause. The autocratic method is to prevent the spread of ideas through suppression. The result has been disorder. Protest has been driven underground. Underground movements explode; then comes violence.

Evidence before the Commission of Inquiry was concluded on May 20th, as dawn was graying outside the long windows of the Teachers' Hall in San Juan. I had asked the spectators at this hearing whether they wished to have our report made at a private indoor meeting or at a public meeting on the Square. With considerable enthusiasm, but some skepticism, they elected a public meeting. I requested the Committee in charge to apply to the Mayor for a permit.

On Thursday afternoon I was busily engaged preparing the report of our Commission, with the assistance of a charming Puerto Rican girl, Miss Lolita Masson, one of the executives of *El Imparcial*, a newspaper of Puerto Rico. She acted as my secretary, guard (to avoid numerous telephone messages and callers), nurse (my eyes were out of condition after an all-night session), general manager of the Commission, and discoverer of mislaid papers, minutes and exhibits. In a startled manner she announced to me that Ernest Gruening, Chief of the United States Bureau of Insular Possessions, was on the telephone.

I have known Gruening for many years and have always regarded him as a genuine liberal quick to resent

The peaceful town of Ponce, Puerto Rico

violations of civil liberties. He had been with us in
the Sacco-Vanzetti fight; he was at one time editor of
The Nation; he had fought the public utilities in
Maine; he had shown his sympathy with the aspira-
tions of oppressed peoples in Mexico and South
America. He said he wanted to see me. I told him
I was working on our report. He expressed astonishment that we could already have reached a conclusion.
I told him that it did not take long for us to decide
that the Ponce affair was properly designated a "massacre" of civilians by the police. He said that he was
shocked. He protested my statement that the right of
public assemblage was denied in Puerto Rico.

On the following morning it appeared that our Committee had not received a permit to hold a meeting on
the Square. Thereupon I wrote Gruening as follows:

"The Condado Hotel
San Juan, Puerto Rico
May 21st, 1937.

Dr. Ernest Gruening,
P.R.R.A.,
San Juan, Puerto Rico.
My dear Dr. Gruening:

I told you over the telephone yesterday that the constitutional right of public assemblage was denied in Puerto
Rico. You said that was not your view. I told you that
the citizens of Ponce intended to apply for a permit to
hold a meeting in the public square of San Juan, at which
the report of our commission, formed to investigate civil
rights in Puerto Rico, and dealing with the Ponce affair,
would be rendered. I said to you:

"Do you think officials here will be stupid enough to deny such a permit?"

Your answer was: "Of course not."

I know of nothing that could prove to you more definitely the denial of civil rights in Puerto Rico than merely to tell you that such a permit was applied for, for a meeting on Friday night, and was not obtained. It may have been because of misunderstanding, in that the Mayor indicated that he was not certain that a permit was necessary, and he would not take responsibility of granting it. Yet I understand that application for a permit is more or less a custom. The Municipal Authorities would seem to have some authority in the matter, limited, however to the time and place of meeting and the proper control of the streets and parks.

I personally am applying for a permit today to hold such a meeting on Saturday night at 8:30 in the public square. If I receive no answer to such an application, I shall announce the holding of a public meeting in the public square, and we shall proceed with our meeting. If the authorities wish to prohibit the meeting, they will have to say so directly. In the absence of any prohibition, we shall hold the meeting.

If the authorities do prohibit the meeting, we shall not proceed, as obviously peaceful and defenseless citizens cannot meet the force of arms, rifles, carbines, machine guns, tear gas bombs and other paraphernalia which I had always supposed were intended for use in the protection of citizens and not for use against citizens, and I say this because of my knowledge of the Ponce affair.

If the authorities feel that such a meeting may lead to disorder, we ask that they provide such police protection as necessary to avoid disorder. I am not fearful that there will be any disorder among the people. Our investigation has shown that plain-clothes men are employed by the department, and one can never be sure that some *agent provocateur* may not cause trouble.

If our meeting is held, we shall therefore ask for sufficient police protection to prevent any one causing disorder.

In ending this letter let me suggest this to you. When you told me over the telephone that 'of course' such a meeting would be permitted, we then began to consider quite reasonably, whether we wanted to hold the meeting at the public square or whether it would be more convenient to hold an indoor meeting. Now, however, since a permit was not granted for an outdoor meeting, you leave us as citizens having some self-respect, no recourse except to insist upon our rights. In other words, the matter is no longer one of rational consideration as to the most convenient way of holding the meeting, but has become one of our asserting our civil rights. This may be regarded by the authorities as provocation. It is so intended. We have a right to be provocative, when our rights are denied.

But I suggest to you that if men of our age, experience and standing, find our emotions so aroused at a denial of our rights, that you give some consideration to the effect of such denials upon young men of militant spirit and sense of self-sacrifice who belong to the Nationalist party, when their rights are denied. It may bring you to a realization that the handling of these problems by attempted suppression stirs up such psychological feeling, that men of spirit are ready, if necessary, even to sacrifice their lives to maintain their rights.

With personal regards, I remain

Sincerely yours,

(signed) Arthur Garfield Hays"

I sent a copy of this to the Attorney-General and applied to the Mayor for a permit. At five-thirty in the afternoon, the Mayor courteously informed me that he would be delighted to comply with our wishes.

On Saturday night the report was made to the citizens of Puerto Rico. An intense crowd of thousands gathered in the Square. Through amplifiers and radio we told the truth to the people of Puerto Rico.

I left the island the following day. Since then there have been occasional disturbances. No violation of law occurs—in fact, there is hardly a crime committed in Puerto Rico—that is not attributed to the Report of the Commission of Inquiry on Civil Rights.

When General Miles, leading the American troops, landed in Puerto Rico in 1898, he made the following proclamation:

"We * * * bring you protection not only to yourselves but to your property; to promote your prosperity and bestow upon you the immunities and blessings of the liberal institutions of our Government."

Governor Winship, in a statement to Congress "with reference to the investigation of the Ponce affair by Mr. Hays," said:

"Ever since the American occupation there has been free speech and free press in Puerto Rico. The rights of peaceful assemblage and of orderly political discussion have always been enjoyed in the fullest and freest manner, and are now. They have never been curtailed or diminished in the slightest degree."

An an indication of freedom, the Governor pointed out that many political meetings have been held during his regime. The answer is that the test of repression is not whether meetings have been held, but whether they have been prohibited.

I have heretofore referred to the excuse that the Latin-American temperament must be considered, that in spite of the guarantees contained in the Organic Act of Puerto Rico there are delicate questions of administration which have to be left to the determination of the authorities. The Latin-American temperament has nothing to do with the matter.

The same view of "Freedom of Speech, But—" is widely held in the United States. Hear the story of Jersey City under the regime of Mayor Frank Hague.

During the seamen's strike, in the winter of 1937, maritime trade unions endeavored to picket steamships in various seaports of the United States, including the docks of the Dollar Steamship Line in Jersey City. The strikers were informed by the Chief of Police that no picketing, however peaceful, would be allowed. Seamen were barred from Jersey City, the officials stopping them at the city line. If seamen happened to get by, they were hunted up and run across the city line. In Germany they throw dissenters into concentration camps; in Jersey City they throw them into Hoboken.

On occasion the seamen were faced by police officers armed with machine-guns and tear gas bombs. Complaints at police heaquarters were ignored. Proprietors of hotels in Jersey City were ordered by the police to "get rid of the seamen." Taverns and restaurants patronized by them were illegally closed by the authorities.

However, the strikers managed to form a picket line on Provost Street which, while in a lonely neighborhood, was the nearest point of access to the docks of the Dollar Steamship Line. Their placards and union buttons were torn from them. They were assaulted and thrown into Hoboken. One of the observers of the American Civil Liberties Union, Reverend J. T. Wright, had his head cut open by a blow, while the police were "around the corner." An injunction was sought by a committee of the maritime workers. On their behalf, together with A. J. Isserman and Sol D. Kapelson, Newark attorneys, I appeared in the Federal Court in Newark before Judge William Clark.

Chief of Police Walsh, Daniel Casey, Commissioner of Public Safety, and Joseph Glavin of the Corporation Counsel's office, represented Jersey City. Judge Clark invited us into his chambers for a conference. When the situation was outlined to him, he expressed his amazement. After considerable discussion, we arranged for a picket line of four men to walk up and down Provost Street in Jersey City, bearing placards indicating that the seamen were on strike.

The next day, a Saturday, in the afternoon I was busily engaged in my office when word came to me that the police had assaulted the men on the picket line, had maintained "order" in Jersey City by evicting the

offenders. I telephoned Judge Clark and suggested that
it might be a good plan for me to go to Jersey City,
inform the police of his disposition of the matter and
to lead a picket line. Judge Clark intimated that he
would like to go with me.

I drove through the Hudson Tunnel, made my way
to a little saloon at a corner near Provost Street. Accompanied by another lawyer and two seamen, I started
to approach Provost Street carrying a large sign hung
by a cord around my neck, bearing the words "Seamen
Are On Strike." A host of policemen barred my passage. One grabbed at my sign. I demanded that he
arrest me if I was breaking the law. He started to
shove me around. I told him that while he shoved,
I'd move, but that when he let go I would come back.
When I said that I was a lawyer, my policeman was
reasonably gentle, but my companions were roughly
handled. Finally, I made my way toward Provost
Street, still bearing my placard. I started to picket,
walking up and down the lonely highway, a storage
plant on one side and the docks about a mile away. At
each corner two or three officers were stationed. At
the entrance to Provost Street there was a platoon of
police. Every once in a while my companions, by
devious byways, managed to join me, but they were
quickly hustled away.

The ground was snowy, the night was cold. At each
end of the street, when I approached the police, they
wanted to know how long I intended "to keep this up."
They were rather discouraged when I told them that
I expected to stay all night. So was I. Finally the

sergeant decided that he might be more effective if
he barked at me and showed just a little force. In the
ensuing struggle I lost my banner but ·continued to
walk, or rather, to limp. I found, however, that without a placard there seemed to be far less point in
my undertaking, so I made my way back to the saloon
and there obtained an American flag. I started out
again with three others toward Provost Street. I
unfurled the flag. Met by a gang of police I again
inquired what law we were violating. "Break up the
parade. You can't parade without a permit." My
companions were rushed into Hoboken. Again I
marched up and down Provost Street. After some
hours I felt that we had obtained sufficient evidence,
so I went home.

We applied for an injunction. On the day of the
hearing, Judge Clark again laid down the law to Mr..
Glavin. I remarked that the Court's words seemed to
be of no great importance in Jersey City; that I was
sure the orders of the police would be unchanged. I
stated that with others I would again go to Jersey
City and try our luck on Provost Street. I assured
the Court that I wasn't fond of Provost Street but I
had formed the habit of walking there and it was the
one place in Jersey City that attracted me.

Few police were on the corner near Provost Street
when we arrived from Judge Clark's court. We started
walking up and down. Soon patrol wagons arrived.
The police didn't arrest anybody, but again used the
tactics of assault and eviction. For a while the sergeant let me alone, but soon his ardor got the better

of him. He told me he didn't want to shove me because I had a lame leg. I told him I would go along with him only if he placed me under arrest. This he refused to do. Finally he muscled me out of Provost Street. I didn't wait until I got to Hoboken, but immediately went back to the court to see Judge Clark. There the Corporation Counsel made the statement that I had reached Jersey City before his orders had penetrated to, into and through the police force.

The seamen's strike was then over, so our fight for freedom of speech and assemblage was in vain. We arranged, however, to test the right to picket in other instances.

The Uneeda Slipper Company, a New York concern, had trouble with the Boot and Shoe Workers' Union. They then incorporated in New Jersey, moved to Jersey City and lowered wages. They engaged quarters within the Harbor Terminal, a place that looks like a huge fortress, in which "happy and contented" families of workers are employed by those industrial benefactors who provide work and taxes for Jersey City.

There was a furniture factory in Jersey City, the stock of which was owned partly by the workers. A strike broke out. The police prevented picketing, claiming that there was no labor dispute. The employees were not "workers"—they were "stockholders."

David Clendennin of the Workers' Defense League, Harry Poth and Charles E. Clift, Jr., of the American Civil Liberties Union, went to Jersey City to confront the guardians of the peace and to test the right to picket. The Harbor Terminal is at the mouth of the

Hudson Tunnels. They were, therefore, not thrown into Hoboken but back into the tunnel toward New York. When they attempted to picket the furniture factory they were likewise escorted to the tunnel.

Once again appeal was made to Judge Clark on an application to enjoin these actions of the police. Commissioner of Public Safety Casey, and Assistant Corporation Counsel Glavin, threw a new light upon American rights. It appeared that Jersey City is kindly to labor and objects not at all either to labor unions or to picketing when there is a strike, and when those who take part in the strike are not Communists or undesirables. All Communists are "undesirables" and all "undesirables" are Communists.

We called Commissioner Casey to the witness stand. Here is part of the record:

"A. * * * With the seamen's we didn't allow them to picket.

Q. Why not? A. It wasn't a bona fide union, it wasn't a bona fide strike."

(Information as to whether or not there is a strike is obtained by the police from the employers.)

"Q. But you decide whether or not there is a strike, don't you? A. I decide, yes.

* * * *

Q. Have you ever heard of a place being picketed in order that workers may be persuaded to unionize and join the union? A. I had never known it before until I heard it here in court.

Q. Would you permit picketing? A. I would not, not if there is no trouble in that factory.

* * * *

Q. * * * You decide, or the Police Department decide whether or not there is a strike and picketing is denied or allowed depending upon your conclusion, isn't that correct? A. Yes, sir.

Q. You also decide, do you not, whether or not the union is a bona fide union? A. I certainly do.

Q. And you also decide whether or not the strike is a bona fide strike? A. A bona fide strike. By that I mean a legitimate strike.

Q. So if you decide that there is a strike but it is not a legitimate strike you likewise prevent picketing, don't you? A. Why, certainly.

Q. Can you refer me to any authority that the Police Department in Jersey City has a right to make decisions on these subjects, any law book that says so or any law that you know of?

Mr. Glavin: He is not a lawyer, your Honor.

A. I am not a lawyer, as I told you before, Mr. Hays. All I believe in using is good, sound judgment."

I next inquired of the Commissioner whether the police had any right to do anything other than arrest a man if he was breaking a law. I wondered upon what theory citizens were assaulted. Our constitutional rights go by the board if we cannot first get ourselves arrested. There is no such thing as indictment, trial by jury, trial before an impartial court or any other civil right that is worth anything, if the citizen cannot get a court decision. Otherwise, a policeman acts as an arresting officer, judge and jury and is likewise the man to carry out the sentence. If he commits an assault he is arresting officer, judge, jury and assaulter. If he evicts, he is arresting office, judge, jury and evicter. If he kills, he is an arresting officer, judge, jury and executioner. We no longer have judicial determination. This is fascism, not democracy.

Mr. Casey was questioned on this subject:

"Q. If a policeman sees a man committing a disorderly act what are his duties, to arrest him? A. Well, at times; it is according to what it is. Trifling violations, that I would consider trifling violations, I don't think a man should be arrested for.

Q. What should be done? A. A warning.

* * * *

Q. So we have warning and arrest? A. Certainly.

Q. What else has he a right to do, if a man does not obey him? A. If he does not obey him he has a right to arrest him.

Q. Has he a right to do anything other than arrest him? A. Well, as I just told you before, Mr. Hays, it is according to what the case is.

* * * *

Q. Now, listen, you mentioned two things an officer has a right to do. Has he a right to do anything else than either warn a man or arrest him? A. That is according to what the crime is, what the man has done.

Q. What else can he do in any crime other than warn and arrest him? A. That's all he can do.

Q. That is what I am getting at. Has an officer a right

to shove a man around?   A. It is according to how he shoves the man around.

* * * *

Q. I mean any way, has an officer a right to shove men around any way?   A. They have a right to escort them out if they are doing anything wrong; if the case don't warrant an arrest they have a perfect right to do it.

The Court: They haven't a right—you don't want to be quoted as saying they have a right to expel them from Jersey City.

The Witness: Well, I wouldn't say expel them; they don't belong there, your Honor.

* * * *

Q. * * * Do you say that you instruct your policemen that they have a right to escort people out of Jersey City, have they that right?   A. If they have no right there, yes.

* * * *

Q. Commissioner, let us get back to this point. You say that the police under certain circumstances have been given instructions that they have a right to put people out of Jersey City, is that it?   A. If they are undesirable.

Q. Who is to make up his mind or the policeman's mind whether a person is undesirable?   A. That is the man in charge, if it is a detail.

Q. And the man he should ask is his superior if he is undesirable?   A. If there is a man in charge.

Q. That is usually what the police captain or sergeant is for?   A. The sergeant, captain or the lieutenant.

Q. So that your instructions are if the sergeant of the police or the captain or lieutenant deems a person undesirable that a policeman can put him out of Jersey City;

are those the instructions?   A. Well, that's the instructions, yes.

*   *   *   *

Well, a policeman does at times use good, sound judgment; if a person is undesirable or not, instead of locking him up he orders him out of town; the court orders men out of town not to come back again.

The Court: No, they don't, Commissioner.

The Witness: Well, we have it done, your Honor. I have had judges where prisoners were locked up, order them out of town and to stay out of town.

Q. That was in Jersey City?   A. No, Jersey City is not the place that you are trying to paint it, Mr. Hays. There are law-abiding citizens in Jersey City."

In view of what happened in these strikes, and the testimony of the Commissioner, it can hardly be said that the police of Jersey City are among these law-abiding citizens.   I was intrigued by the question as to who decided whether people were undesirable.

"Q. Commissioner Casey, who decides whether people are undesirable in your city, does the Mayor decide that? A. The Mayor does not.

Q. Does the Commissioner of Public Safety?   A. At times, yes.   If we decide we can get along better with him out of the community and he is going to cause trouble for us we keep him out if he don't belong there.

*   *   *   *

Q. Now, does anyone else decide on undesirables in Jersey City?   I understand Mayor Hague stays out of it.

A. I don't know why you are always talking about Mayor Hague.

Q. Well, we will leave him out. A. If he was here he could defend himself."

We ought not to judge Commissioner Casey too harshly. He is a good American. He has no interest other than to maintain order in Jersey City, and to him this means keeping out "undesirables." Not only that, but he was guided by the advice of the Corporation Counsel's office, with Mr. Joseph Glavin, an assistant, in charge. I put Mr. Glavin on the stand.

"Q. Well, let me ask you as Corporation Counsel of Jersey City, under the law has a policeman a right to evict anybody from Jersey City? A. To evict somebody from Jersey City?

Q. Take somebody from Jersey City, evict them from Jersey City? A. If the circumstances necessitated it I should say they had.

Q. Will you tell me under what law they are given that right, do you know of any case? A. I don't know of any case but the law of necessity. * * *

Q. Has a policeman a right to shove a man around in Jersey City?

* * * *

A. Well, I don't know that he has any fundamental right to go up and shove a man or push him, no.

* * * *

Q. Who is to determine whether a man is to be evicted, the police officer or his sergeant or his captain? A. Well, that, of course, I don't know. That is a matter of routine, I suppose, in the Police Department."

I was interested to find out where Mr. Glavin got his ideas of the law.

"Q. Have you ever looked up these questions? A. What questions?

Q. The questions I have put to you about the rights of the police. A. Yes, I have looked them up.

Q. Then I understand after you looked them up you came to the conclusions that you have presented, is that right? A. The answers I gave, yes.

Q. That was after looking up the law? Now can you refer me to any case in the law in New Jersey that gives the police a right to evict a man from a city? A. Well, I haven't looked that question up."

When a citizen has his skull opened by a club, when he is thrown out of a community, he has a right to feel that the question involved is sufficiently important to warrant some study by the Corporation Counsel. The explanation may be that Frank Hague is Mayor of Jersey City and that Hague has given orders. In Jersey City, as in Ponce, the authorities feel that the obligation to maintain order warrants disorder and violation of law on their part.

I remarked to Judge Clark that under the law all citizens were equal, that I could not understand why I alone should have been permitted to picket on Provost Street. Mr. Glavin responded:

"Hays wrapped himself in an American flag."

I answered:

"That's true. It's necessary for a man to do this to walk the street of Jersey City."

Judge Clark granted an injunction against the police. That was many months ago. On application of the Corporation Counsel of Jersey City the Circuit Court of Appeals stayed the operation of the injunction pending an appeal. That was likewise many months ago.

Jersey City believes in American rights, in freedom of speech, but— So does Pineville, Kentucky, but—.

Boston believes in freedom of speech, but—. California believes in freedom of speech, but—. Chicago, Detroit, Tampa, Passaic, Camden, Terre Haute—all places, at all times where the emotions of people are involved and where the situation appears to the authorities to be tense—all of them believe in freedom of speech, but—.

The Federal Government likewise believes in freedom of speech, but—.

John Strachey, eminent English writer and lecturer, once a Labor Party M.P., spent some months in this country in the year 1935. He had often been here on lecture tours, was well known to American audiences. With him was his wife and baby. They planned to return to England on March 29th.

Some researching member of the Department of Immigration—certainly someone with considerable ingenuity and detective training—discovered an ominous fact which Strachey had been proclaiming for years in books and lectures, to wit: that Strachey was a Communist. This was appalling. Imagine our having a Communist, and particularly an English Communist, in our midst! The authorities felt we had enough Communists of our own. In order to protect us from indoctrination, the Immigration Act provides for the elimination of those who believe in the "overthrow of the United States by force and violence," or who are affiliated with an organization "believing, advocating and teaching the overthrow by force and violence of the Government of the United States." Strachey was arrested and held for deportation.

Strachey insisted that he was not interested in overthrowing the Government of the United States. He was merely interested in the income-producing business of telling us about Communism.

On principle, the case involved not so much the right of an alien to speak, as the right of Americans to hear. Most of us will take the chance of contamination for ourselves but most of us in turn believe it is a good idea to keep some one else from being contaminated, particularly by Communists, and more particularly by foreign Communists.

The Government put Strachey in a position where he would have to remain in the United States for a protracted period in order to find out whether he could stay. Strachey wanted to go home. The Government wanted him to go home. It was estimated that the court proceedings would take anywhere from six months to a year. The situation was quite distressing both to Strachey and the Government.

Nevertheless, the law must be served. So out goes Strachey to Chicago to attend a hearing before an inspector of immigration. The inspector:

"I read into the record the following excerpt * * * "
(The reference was from an article entitled "Notes from
the Road,' written by Strachey.)

"The experiences of a Communist drummer—for that
is what I am at the moment, peddling Marxism instead
of pink pills—have their humorous side.

Q. Have you anything to say?
Strachey said that they did have their humorous
side.
Inspector to alien:

"I read into the record the following excerpt from the
same article: 'But it is the special quality of Americans
that they are willing to experiment; and to experiment in-
tellectually as well as practically. Their minds are
genuinely open, they do genuinely desire to hear and discuss unfamiliar theories and views. And it is this willing-
ness to experiment which may enable them to find sooner
than the British people, the one solution to their difficulties; that is, the abolition of the profit or capitalist system.'
Have you anything to say?"

Mr. Strachey:

"This passage together with its context does accurately
express my position which is that the abolition of the
profit or capitalist system is one solution of our difficulties."

Inspector to Alien:

"I read into the record the following excerpt from this
same article: 'Communists believe that that degree of dislocation and violence, which class history teaches us has
hitherto always accompanied the breakdown of one form

of society and the building up of another, is very greatly
attributable to the fact that the mass of the population
has always hitherto been denied effective access to the
true facts of the situation.' Have you anything to say?"

Mr. Strachey:

"This passage seems to me particularly relevant to these
proceedings. As you notice I make it a point that any
dislocation and violence, which occurred in the past, has
been very greatly attributable to just such attempts as
you, as a representative of the United States Government,
are now engaged in, to deny to the population effective
access to the facts and discussion of the facts of the
existing situation."

The Inspector referred to a statement by Strachey:

" 'I'm not a member of the Communist Party * * *
but I do believe in the principles of that Party.' Were
you correctly quoted?"

Mr. Strachey:

"Yes, I cannot recollect whether this report was accurate or not, but as I have already stated in this hearing
I do believe in general in communistic principles. May
I read on in the report 'When I was in school I used
to read about the Government of the United States and
how it was based on a constitution which permitted changes
at the will of the people and also provided a guarantee
of free speech. I'm beginning to wonder about those
things now.' "

The Inspector presented "The Communist Manifesto" of 1848 to Strachey and asked him what he

had to say about that. Strachey reminded the Inspector that he had not written The Communist Manifesto. Strachey did take occasion to point out that
several principles of the Manifesto have by this
time been adopted by almost all civilized nations, to
wit: a public school system; graded income tax and
graded inheritance tax. In fact, said Strachey, that
is an indication of how the democratic system works.
Ideas which at one time are regarded as radical, gradually become part of the system.

Strachey was asked if he advocated the overthrow
of government by force. His answer was:

"If I might use a simile, I might say that when sitting
on the seashore, I might take the view that the tide would
come up and wet my clothes but this would not mean that
I should favor or advocate the coming up of the tide."

Strachey pointed out that the "weather man" may
prophesy that it will rain tomorrow. He doesn't advocate rain—he might be violently opposed to it. He
might want to go fishing.

In fact, said Strachey, his reading of history had
brought him to the conclusion that when, if ever, the
time arose when the capitalist system was actually
threatened, that then those in control, the "propertied
classes," would forget democratic principles, would
suppress free speech, free press and free assemblage,
and would use force and violence. The result would
be that those in opposition would be forced to use
violence.

Strachey said he didn't advocate this; he prophesied it. He expressed the hope that democratic America would come through great changes in its economic system without this becoming necessary. He said that the attempt to deport him made his hopes seem a little vain because, even now when the system could hardly be said to be threatened, there was an attempt to prevent the spreading of ideas that were regarded as dangerous.

We pointed out to the Inspector that Henry A. Wallace, the Secretary of Agriculture; Harold L. Ickes, Secretary of the Interior, and even President Roosevelt had ventured upon dangerous prophecies of social change in America.

Finally Mr. Strachey was given an opportunity to set forth his views on the question of force and violence.

"I would like to summarize my position. I am not a member of the Communist Party and therefore I have no right to speak for that party, but to the best of my belief the Communist Party itself does not favor force and violence. I can speak, however, for myself and I declare again that I do not believe in or favor force or violence. What is true is that I cannot conceal from myself the fact that force and violence have been used and is now being used by the capitalist class all over the world. I believe that this use of force and violence has happened and I admit that I believe that it may happen again, but that does not mean that I am in favor of it happening again or that I advocate it in any conceivable way.

"On the contrary, I believe that the undeniable fact that an ever growing use of force and violence hangs over the world today is a nightmare to me and to all decent people. As we sit at this hearing today the continent of Europe is on the brink of an outbreak of force and violence between the capitalist governments of that continent. First Europe and then the whole world is in the opinion of every expert observer about to be plunged, if not this year then in some future year, into the inferno of international capitalist war and I cannot conceal from you, Mr. Inspector, that I consider that for any capitalist government today to accuse me of advocating force and violence is an insolent presumption.

"Every capitalist government today is preparing to use force and violence on an unparalleled scale. They are not merely advocating it, they are using it already and preparing to use it a hundred times more. How can they accuse others of advocating something which they themselves are so busily engaged in doing or preparing to do?

"Finally, I should like to repeat that here in America I advocate nothing; I do not advocate force and violence because I do not advocate any political action in America. As I have stated in this record repeatedly, I do not consider that this is the job for which I came to America and I would consider it inappropriate for me to engage in this activity in America. Thus, I would like to place it upon record that if I am deported it will be because the discussion of our vital, modern, political and economic problems is now forbidden in the United States of America."

The editor of the Santa Barbara Press wrote a letter to the United States Commissioner of Immigration:

"March 23, 1935.

COLONEL DANIEL W. MacCORMACK,
U. S. Commissioner of Immigration,
Department of Labor,
Washington, D. C.

Dear Colonel:

I have just read the terrible news in an Associated Press dispatch.

Good gracious!

To think your department was clever enough to find out that John Strachey is a—ss-ss-sh—Communist!

Of course everyone else in the world who can read the English language has known that for, lo, these many years. But for your department to ferret out the fact shows an unexpected intelligence.

We note with satisfaction that in your indictment of him you make the following statement:

"In one of these publications he uses the term 'we Communists' and in another refers to himself as a 'Communist drummer' in these words: '. . . a Communist drummer, for that is what I am at the moment, peddling Marxism instead of pink pills.'"

That's pinning it right on him, Colonel, old boy. Let's see, isn't it the U. S. Immigration Bureau that the movies always have something about 'they always get their man'?

Well, sir, Colonel, you wouldn't believe it but—ss-ss-sh—just between you and me—John Strachey was right here in Santa Barbara last month. Yes, sir!

And, not only that, Colonel, but he gave a lecture at Rockwood, under the auspices of the Santa Barbara

Woman's Club (they ought to be ashamed!) on the perils of Fascism.

Worse still, Colonel, instead of wearing long whiskers, boots and a fur coat, so we would know he was a Communist, he was clean-shaven, his hair was neatly brushed and he wore well-fitting dinner clothes.

The hall was jammed. We don't believe there were more than a dozen Communists there. A careful assay of the crowd would probably show the following:

Republicans, 78 percent, Democrats 12 percent, Socialists 2 percent, Fascists 1 percent, Utopians, Anarchists, Technocrats, Buddhists, Platinum Blondes, Single Taxers, Communists, EPICers, Dirt Farmers and Tenors, a trace.

Most of the women were in party gowns and many of the men wore formal dress. What is more, they all seemed to like the lecture.

A prominent banker said, as he was leaving:

'His logic was unanswerable.'

A widow whose fortune is well over a million said:

'What a delightful sense of humor!'

A hard-boiled businessman who always has, and always will, vote the straight Republican ticket, said:

'I don't imagine Strachey made a single convert. But he gave us all something to think about; and what all of us need is to learn the other fellow's ideas first-hand.'

But you haven't heard anything yet, Colonel.

After the lecture about 30 or 40 men and women gathered at a well-known home (Republican) in Montecito and there actually conversed and argued with this former member of the British Parliament.

And while he was here he was guest in another prominent Montecito home (Republican).

Of course, Colonel, there is only one thing for the U. S. Immigration Bureau to do.

You must quarantine both Santa Barbara and Montecito at once! (We understand Communism is 'catching.') And you must see that every one who came within a block of John Strachey is promptly inoculated with an anti-Communist virus. (I was vaccinated years ago, but I don't suppose that counts.)

As for Strachey's book you mentioned, 'The Nature of Capitalist Crisis,' we never even heard of it. But now that you've mentioned it, I—in common with tens of thousands of other Americans—will promptly buy it and read it. (advt.)

Congratulations, Colonel, old top. You and your Bureau deserve the thanks of every true American. We must keep this country safe—for the Huey Longs, the Upton Sinclairs, the Theodore Bilbos, and the rest of the hundred-percenters.

Excitedly,
THE EDITOR.

P.S. Have you ever given any serious thought to naming Gracie Allen as assistant Immigration Commissioner?"

Confronted with the absurd situation of keeping Strachey here for the purpose of getting him out, the Department dropped the proceedings on the day Mr. Strachey was due to sail. Certainly, Strachey was right when he said the experiences of a Communist drummer have their humorous side.

For centuries the physical sciences have been free from governmental control and social prejudice. The human mind, unhampered, has soared into realms and brought results originally inconceivable of accomplishment. We see with a million eyes, hear with a million ears, walk with a million legs—even fly with a million wings.

The social sciences, on the other hand, have been hampered and repressed by fear and prejudice. We endeavor to maintain the status quo in politics, economics and social forms. There are "respectable" ways of thinking, talking and writing on politics, economics, marriage, sex and a variety of subjects.

One instance will suffice. For ten years Mrs. Mary Ware Dennett distributed a pamphlet called the "Sex Side of Life" which she had written for her sons when they were of the ages of eleven and fourteen. She had examined all available material on the subject and had concluded that nothing had been written that was simple and adequate.

In the introduction she said:

"From a careful observation of youthful curiosity and a very vivid recollection of my own childhood I have tried to explain frankly the points about which there is the greatest inquiry."

The approved American method has been to leave adolescence in a state of "inevitable curiosity satisfied only by the casual gossip of ignorant playmates," or by barndoor and back-house tidbits.

The pamphlet contained many statements which

might be called "theological heresies." Boys have been trained to be continent by the threat of incurable venereal disease, and girls by the danger of pregnancy. Mrs. Dennett pointed out first, that venereal disease was not always the result of a sexual episode, even though that took place outside of marriage; secondly, that venereal disease can be cured; thirdly, that there were effective methods of contraception. Her greatest heresy, however, was to suggest that the climax of sex emotion is an unsurpassed joy. That, of course, should never be told to young people. It should be indicated that sex emotion is a thing to be ashamed of; that yielding to it is an indulgence; that all thought of it should be rigorously postponed—at any rate, until after marriage.

In spite of the fact that the pamphlet was distributed by various youth groups, including Y.M.C.A.s, there was no trouble until it was received by Mrs. C. A. Miles, of Grottoes, Virginia, who, it is said, is a member of the D.A.R. Mrs. Miles was shocked.

The postoffice department had ruled in 1922 that the little book was obscene and had prohibited its distribution by mail. Of course, this did not prevent transportation by express or by hand, but Mrs. Miles, naturally, felt that if one was not entitled to be contaminated through the mails, he was likewise not entitled to be infected by any other method of transportation.

In order to get complete evidence in a case where the facts were not only admitted but proudly proclaimed, the Department rigged up a decoy to order a pamphlet from Mrs. Dennett. It invented a fictitious woman, had stationery printed with her name, and sent for the pamphlet.

An indictment was sought and secured in December, 1928, in the Federal District Court, which sits in Brooklyn. The case came on for hearing before Federal Judge Moskowitz in January, 1929, on a motion to quash the indictment. The Judge was troubled. He was unwilling to decide himself whether the pamphlet was obscene and resorted to an extraordinary proceeding. He called in to sit with him on the Bench three clergymen—a Catholic priest, a rabbi and a Protestant minister—so that they might "aid the conscience of the court on the matter." The courtroom was crowded with doctors, teachers and clergymen, many of them ready to testify to the merits of the pamphlet. The professional vice crusaders were likewise there.

We have no information to the effect of the pamphlet on the reverend gentlemen advising with the Judge, but apparently, without benefit of clergy, Judge Moskowitz declined to quash the indictment.

The case was tried before a jury in April, 1929, with Judge Warren B. Burrows sitting. Mrs. Dennett was defended by Morris L. Ernst of the American Civil Liberties Union. His efforts to introduce testimony showing the motive in writing the pamphlet, its wide endorsement by educators and doctors, and its similarity to publications in the United States Public Health Service, were blocked by the Judge. Only the pamphlet itself was put before the jury. In forty minutes the twelve good men and true decided that young people were endangered by the libidinous thought which the truth might arouse, and found Mrs. Dennett guilty. She was sentenced to pay a fine of $300 or to spend three hundred days in jail. The case went to the United States Circuit Court of Appeals, which sits in New York City. Judge Augustus N. Hand wrote an opinion which reversed the conviction.* He stated:

"It also may reasonably be thought that accurate information rather than mystery and curiosity is better in the long run and is less likely to occasion lascivious thoughts than ignorance and anxiety."

Decisions such as this, as well as the decision of Judge Woolsey in overruling the ban on the importation of "Ulysses" by James Joyce, have raised some question as to the morality and judgment of the Federal Judges sitting in New York City. A law has recently been proposed under which indictment may be found at the place where "obscene" material is received as well as the place from which it is mailed. Provincial judges may well try to keep us all in a state of moral and blissful ignorance.

After the conviction of Mrs. Dennett I read in the newspapers that Canon William Sheafe Chase intended to write a pamphlet on the "Sex Side of Life" which, so he stated, would spike some of Mrs. Dennett's "lies." Canon Chase, of Brooklyn, is an estimable and amiable gentlemen who has reached the years of discretion. He

---

* *United States v. Dennett*, 39 Fed. Rep. (2d Series) 564.

has been a crusader against the dissemination of information which might be harmful to the human race.

I wrote him asking just to what "lies" he referred. He answered to the effect that Mrs. Dennett had said that the climax of sex was the greatest human physical pleasures. Said Canon Chase: "That is a lie. The greatest of these pleasures is that of a mother nursing her baby." I answered Canon Chase: "That may be so, but how do you know?" I was not surprised at his reply: "My wife told me so."

The American Freeman was prohibited the use of the mails because it carried an article during the depression which, incidentally, was reprinted in many other papers, asking: "Why Don't the Workers Raise Hell?" Material has been barred from the mails where a sticker on the envelope contained the words: "I don't read Hearst." If one seeks to enjoin prohibition by the Postoffice Department he finds that the present rulings require that he shall bring suit in Washington, D. C.

Trends in recent repressive legislation run toward bills providing that teachers must take oaths of loyalty. Some people take that sort of thing seriously. They are not wholly logical or oaths would be required, not once, but every week, every day, at the opening of every school exercise. We ought to make teachers "Heil Hitler" all over the place. That would make them loyal, or hypocritical, or at any rate, sufficiently timid and properly orthodox. Such an oath would have made it unnecessary for Yale University, in failing to renew the appointment of Associate Professor Jerome Davis of the Divinity School after twelve years on the faculty, to refer to a "lack of scholarship and teaching ability." The president of the University had described him as a "nuisance." He might have been called "disloyal." He has often been in Moscow.

Issues of religious liberty have for years involved the prohibition of the teaching of evolution, compulsory Bible-reading in the schools, the rights of non-believers to testify in court and the refusal on conscientious grounds to perform military service in state institutions where it is compulsory. To these questions have recently been added conspicuously the cases of scores of children, members of the religious sect known as "Jehovah's Witnesses," expelled from school for refusal to salute the flag. They have been taught not to worship an idol or symbol. Members of this sect are stiff-necked people. They are haled into court for refusing to send the children to school. But they don't believe in courts and they abominate lawyers. They insist that God's will be done and thus take the consequences.

The views of people; that is, honest people, often stand in the way of their welfare, even at times of their desires. Stubbornly, they call these "views" principles or convictions!

Rozika Schwimmer, a woman well on in years, known internationally as a pacifist, applied for citizenship, but she would not take the oath to support by force of arms the Government of the United States. Under

no circumstances would she kill another human being.
The court inquired as to what she would do if she
were a nurse in time of war and saw an enemy soldier
approaching her charge. She would not kill, said
Madame Schwimmer, she would throw herself in the
way of an enemy bullet to protect her patient. Citizenship was denied. The Appellate Court reversed
the ruling, holding that it was no duty of an American
citizen to be able to guess conundrums. The Supreme
Court of the United States held otherwise.

Dr. Douglas Clyde MacIntosh, of Yale, having
fought with the Canadian forces all through the World
War, sought citizenship. He would defend the government with arms in any war which he believed just,
saying that he felt his duty to his God was greater
than his duty to his country. The court disagreed.
Miss Marie Bland, a Quaker, then took up the battle
and refused to take the oath on the ground of religious
conviction, but with no greater success. In Chicago,
a Mennonite clergyman from Kansas has recently
raised the question again. The five-to-four decisions
which penalize views of pacifism, may be reversed by a
more liberal Supreme Court.

The changing scene means changing fashions in repression. The cases in this book are important, not
so much because of the tragedy, injustice or absurdity
involved, as because of their significance as illustrative
of an intolerant spirit. This spirit manifests itself on
every issue in every city, community and hamlet in the

United States which might upset the ordinary calm, comfort and established order of the community.

During the war, the hue and cry was directed against so-called "Pacifists" and "pro-Germans," terms applied to any one who tried to keep a level head, who refused to swallow avidly all stories of German atrocities, or who had the treasonable idea that commercial and banking interests, the capitalist system or imperialism were in any way responsible for the mass murder.

Socialists were heretics. They still are in many places.

Following this, and for years, our fears have been directed against Communists. Some day they will overthrow the government by force and violence!

Today, in the fear of Fascism, the Communists have joined in a united front with liberals and independents of all kinds. They would pass laws to suppress propaganda of Fascism. New Jersey passed a statute which, in order to prevent anti-Semitic propaganda, made it a crime to say anything that would stir up racial antagonism. The first case that arose was against a member of "Jehovah's Witnesses" for distributing a pamphlet which attacked the Catholic church.

Negroes continually have been the subject of repression. The sharecropper system in the South is virtual peonage.

Depending upon the militance of the movement, Labor has been the subject of sporadic attack. The present concerted drive against the Committee for Industrial Organization (C.I.O.) has resulted in a denial of civil rights, wherever freedom of speech and assemblage may, in the judgment of those in control, tend to upset order. Powers Hapgood and other leaders of the C.I.O. were sentenced in the spring of 1937 to six months in jail, in Maine, for speaking at a meeting of strikers in violation of an injunction. Among them was Sidney Grant, lawyer of Boston, who had said at a public meeting that in his opinion the court had no power to grant an injunction which would prevent workers from striking.

We read in the papers of the violence of the C.I.O. The Republic Steel massacre in Chicago was first designated as a riot in which the police protected themselves from the workers. The Paramount motion picture revealed the facts—showed the police mercilessly shooting down and clubbing defenseless people.

The LaFollette Civil Liberties Committee of the United States Senate said:

"It is being developed that employer and agency have two separate vested interests in violence. The agency's interest in violence, and by the same token that of the strikebreaker's, is that it will prolong and embitter the fight so that a stronger guard will be called out and more money expended through the agency. The employer's interest in violence is that it shall, by being attributed to the workers, bring discredit to them, thus alienating public sympathy for their cause."

The LaFollette report showed the general situation of provocation by industrialists with illuminating documents. One letter from the Railway Audit and Inspection Company, a notorious strike-breaking agency, read:

"A former police commissioner of the city of New York * * * came south during the last textile strike with about 300 guards * * * recruited from the gutter and dregs of New York, Chicago and Detroit. They were gunmen of the first water and, believe you me, they used every kind of roughneck method known to them to quell the disturbances."

The report refers to: "A colossal daily drive in every part of the country to frustrate enunciated labor policy and to neutralize American labor laws." It refers to "vigilante and violence groups," "private espionage and strike-breaking forces maintained by the industry itself," "individual and communal violations of free speech and assembly by various authorities and organizations."

The report continues:

"Both industrial espionage and strike-breaking thrive on industrial strife * * *

Although, as the investigations reveal, the employer directs his spy forces against any kind of union activity, he cloaks his hostility under the pretext that he is defending himself and the country against communism."

Those rights which are regarded as elemental among Anglo-Saxons, originating in Magna Charta, reinforced by the Bills of Settlement Acts in 1789, guaranteed by the Federal and every State Constitution, must be reëstablished in almost every labor dispute. We believe in freedom of speech, but———.

Scottsboro, Angelo Herndon, the Tampa killings, the Ponce and Chicago massacres, the Mooney and Billings case and the Jennings frame-up—innumerable instances of the kind—almost lead one to despair of justice and of democratic and judicial methods in the United States.

A few months in Germany, Italy or Russia, however, dissipate pessimism. In 1933, coming from Europe, after a few months in Germany at the Reichstag trial, I met Litvinoff, Russian Secretary of Foreign Affairs. Said he:

"Which do you now prefer, Mr. Hays, Fascism or Communism?"

My answer was:

"Thank heaven there are other systems under which human beings can live."

Democracy was then at a low ebb. We were in the midst of the depression. Even Wall Street bankers prophesied the end of our present system. Since then there has, fortunately, been a recrudescence of faith in democracy. Hitler's blood-purge in 1934; the Russian executions of dissenters (traitors) in 1935, 1936 and 1937, have made clear that systems of dictatorship and tyranny, however pretentious their claims and alluring their theories, do not promote progress or happiness. One returns from these countries to the United States with a realization that, after all, we have a fair measure of liberty. Everyone does lip service, at least, to the principles of freedom. In civil liberties cases one sometimes wins but he never loses. Whatever the legal result, the exposure of injustice has value. Repression is always resented by public opinion.

Freedom is an ideal. It is not merely a means to an end, but an end in itself, almost as necessary to a satisfactory existence as the food we eat or the air we breathe. In Fascist or Communist societies, people may be physically comfortable but they are always apprehensive.

A letter to me from the late Supreme Court Justice, Oliver Wendell Holmes, helps to maintain a sense of proportion:

"SUPREME COURT OF THE UNITED STATES

WASHINGTON, D. C.

April 20, 1928.

My dear sir:

The duties of my occupation make it impossible for me to do more than glance through your book * but the kind inscription and the spirit that moves you lead me to venture a line or two. I cannot but suspect that you are a little overwrought upon your theme. I can remember the time before the Civil War when I was deeply moved by the abolition cause—so deeply that a negro minstrel show shocked me and the morality of Pickwick seemed to me painfully blunt. I have no right to an opinion as to public conditions for I am a recluse and don't even read the papers. Moreover, at times I have felt as you do. Nevertheless, I rather more than hope that there is more intelligent and high-minded thinking on public matters than ever before. One has to remember that when one's interest is keenly excited evidence gathers from all sides around the magnetic point,

* First Edition of "Let Freedom Ring."

and that one must mistrust the suggested conclusion. Just after the Civil War there appeared on the fences and everywhere S T 1560 X. I believe it was an advertisement, perhaps of bitters, which then had a *locus standi*. I said and proved to myself that if one should accept that as a revelation of the secret of the universe one would be astonished by the corroboration that a fortnight would furnish. I think that a type of the way our minds act. I venture this word of caution from the experience of an old man.

Very sincerely yours,

O. W. HOLMES"

The rights of self-expression won by Anglo-Saxons are worth preserving. Whatever may seem to be the immediate consequence, we should be so regardful of the principles underlying our Bills of Rights, that we must attack violation in whatever form it may appear.

In the memorial address to the Great Assembly of the Commonwealth of Virginia, James Madison said:

"It is proper to take alarm at the first experiment upon our liberties. We hold this prudent jealousy to be the first duty of citizens and one of the noblest characteristics of the late Revolution. The freemen of America did not wait until usurped power had strengthened itself by exercise and entangled the question in precedents. They saw all the consequences in the principle and they avoided the consequences by denying the principle. We revere this lesson too much, soon to forget it."

Protest at the slightest infringement, a capacity for indignation, courage, faith in democratic processes, vigilance, are necessary if we are to maintain liberty.